Dear Reader:

The book you are about to read is the latest bestseller from the St. Martin's True Crime Library, the imprint *The New York Times* calls "the leader in true crime!" The True Crime Library offers you fascinating accounts of the latest, most sensational crimes that have captured the national attention. St. Martin's is the publisher of John Glatt's riveting and horrifying SECRETS IN THE CELLAR, which shines a light on the man who shocked the world when it was revealed that he had kept his daughter locked in his hidden basement for 24 years. In the Edgar-nominated WRITTEN IN BLOOD, Diane Fanning looks at Michael Petersen, a Marine-turned-novelist found guilty of beating his wife to death and pushing her down the stairs of their home—only to reveal another similar death from his past. In the book you now hold, ONE LAST KISS, Michael W. Cuneo examines the details of a horrific family tragedy.

St. Martin's True Crime Library gives you the stories behind the headlines. Our authors take you right to the scene of the crime and into the minds of the most notorious murderers to show you what really makes them tick. St. Martin's True Crime Library paperbacks are better than the most terrifying thriller, because it's all true! The next time you want a crackling good read, make sure it's got the St. Martin's True Crime Library logo on the spine—you'll be up all night!

Charles E. Spicer, Jr.
Executive Editor, St. Martin's True Crime Library

Also by
Michael W. Cuneo

Almost Midnight

A Need to Kill: Confessions of a Teen Killer

from the True Crime Library
of St. Martin's Paperbacks

ONE LAST KISS

MICHAEL W. CUNEO

St. Martin's Paperbacks

ONE LAST KISS

For information address St. Martin's Press, 175 Fifth Avenue, New York, NY 10010.

ISBN: 978-0-312-53972-6

Printed in the United States of America

St. Martin's Paperbacks edition / August 2012

St. Martin's Paperbacks are published by St. Martin's Press, 175 Fifth Avenue, New York, NY 10010.

10 9 8 7 6 5 4 3 2 1

To
Brenda Michelle Cuneo

A convicted defendant is entitled under American law to appeal his conviction, in an effort to overturn the jury's finding of guilt. As of going to press, an appeal of Chris Coleman's conviction in federal court is planned.

PROLOGUE

May 5, 2009
6:43 a.m.

Justin Barlow was sound asleep when his cell phone rang. He reached over and grabbed it on the third ring. As one of only two full-time detectives with the Columbia, Illinois, Police Department, he'd grown accustomed to getting calls at odd hours.

It was a neighbor on the other end—a guy named Chris Coleman who lived catty-corner to Barlow's house in the Columbia Lakes subdivision of town. Coleman said that he was just then crossing the Jefferson Barracks Bridge into Illinois, returning home from an early morning workout at a gym in south St. Louis County. He said that he was concerned about his family. His wife, Sheri, should have been up by then with their two boys, eleven-year-old Garett and nine-year-old Gavin, but no one had answered when he'd tried phoning home. He asked Barlow if he'd mind going over and checking up on them.

Barlow said sure, no problem, he'd go over right away. He could certainly appreciate why the guy might feel concerned. Chris Coleman was head of security for the world-famous Joyce Meyer Ministries, and in recent months he'd received some disturbing messages in connection with his job. First there was a series of e-mails sent to his company laptop on November 14 and November 15. And then there were two typewritten letters that he retrieved from the mailbox at the front of his driveway, the first of them on January 2, and the second on April 27. All of the messages threatened terrible harm to Coleman and his family unless he stopped working for Joyce Meyer and publicly renounced her ministry.

Coleman had reported the messages to the police, who in turn had provided increased patrols in the neighborhood. After the second typewritten letter was retrieved from the mailbox, Barlow had taken it a step further. With the help of a colleague from the Illinois State Police, he'd installed a video surveillance camera in the window of his three-year-old son's second-floor bedroom. The camera was trained directly on the Coleman house, which meant that anyone leaving an untoward letter in the mailbox was certain to be videotaped.

Barlow slipped out of bed and got dressed, taking care not to awaken his wife and two sons. He put on a pair of cargo pants, a light jacket, his off-duty gun and holster, and his signature Chicago Bears cap. Then he grabbed a portable police radio and contacted the station. He informed the dispatcher where he was going and requested uniformed backup.

He went outside and crossed over to the Coleman residence, which was a white two-story affair located at the end of a winding street called Robert Drive. With its black shutters, brown shingle roof, and attached two-car garage, it looked scarcely different from most other houses in the subdivision. Barlow went to the front door and rang the bell. He waited several seconds and rang again but no one answered. It was a bright, sunny morning, and he could see light filtering into the living room through the shaded window. He looked down the street and saw a squad car approaching.

Barlow was surprised that Chris Coleman still hadn't arrived. When Coleman had called, he'd said that he was crossing the Jefferson Barracks Bridge, which was no more than a seven-minute drive away.

* * *

Sergeant Jason Donjon was sitting in the patrol room checking his e-mail when the dispatcher called to him from the dispatch center at the front of the Columbia police station.

"Hey, Jason," he said. "Come on up here."

Donjon shut down his computer and went up front, where the dispatcher filled him in on the relevant details. Chris Coleman—the same guy who'd reported receiving those threatening messages—had phoned Detective Justin Barlow just moments before. Coleman had told Barlow that he was on his way home from a gym in south St. Louis County and was worried about his family, since he hadn't been able to get through to them on his cell phone. Detective Barlow had then contacted the station and requested uniformed backup, saying he was going over to the Coleman residence on Robert Drive to check on the family's welfare.

Donjon went out the rear door of the station and got into his squad car. He turned right onto North Main Street and drove over to the Columbia Lakes subdivision. He made a left onto Robert Drive and parked at the curb outside the Coleman residence. It was now 6:53, ten minutes since Chris Coleman had phoned Justin Barlow.

"No answer?" Donjon asked, joining Barlow on the front porch.

"I rang twice," Barlow said. "Maybe they're in the shower."

Donjon left Barlow on the porch and went to the rear of the house. A basement window was open, its screen leaning against a lawn chair. The grass in the backyard was lush and dewy. There was no indication of anyone other than Donjon himself having walked across it that morning: no footprints, no telltale depressions. Still, the open window was a concern. Perhaps an intruder had somehow managed to get through it without leaving a trail on the lawn. Donjon radioed Barlow, who hurried around to the back of the house.

Barlow looked at the open window, and then he and Donjon exchanged glances. Both men stood there wordlessly for the briefest of seconds. Barlow was the older of the two by several years, a strikingly handsome guy in his early thirties with blue eyes and dark hair. Donjon was soft-spoken and earnest, with a sweet smile and an athletic build. Barlow shined a flashlight through the window. The basement floor seemed clean and dry. There was no broken glass, no grass clippings, no residue of any kind. Donjon radioed dispatch for backup.

They took their department-issue Glock .40-caliber pistols from their holsters and climbed through the window. Barlow's tennis shoes made a squeaking sound on the floor. Donjon called out, "Columbia PD!" Nobody answered. He called out several more times. The house was quiet. Donjon and Barlow searched quickly through the basement, making sure that it was clear.

Barlow led the way up the stairs to the main floor. Upon reaching the doorway leading into the kitchen, he was hit with the pungent smell of fresh paint. Then he took a step inside and paused for a count of three. Donjon could tell that something was terribly wrong from the way Barlow was breathing during this short pause. It was the sort of tactical breathing that they were taught in the police academy. *Inhale through the nose and then exhale deeply through the mouth as a way of calming the heart rate during situations of intense stress.*

Donjon stepped into the kitchen and immediately understood why Barlow had deployed the tactical breathing. On the wall next to the doorway, there were a dozen framed photographs of the Coleman family, most of them featuring young Garett and Gavin in smiling poses. Somebody had scrawled a message in red spray paint across the wall and in the process smeared paint on some of the photographs.

FUCK YOU
I AM ALWAYS
WATCHING

On the adjoining wall, there was a second message. This one, too, was scrawled in red spray paint:

I SAW
YOU
LEAVE

Donjon followed Barlow into the living room. On the beige-colored wall adjacent the hallway, there was another spray-painted message:

FUCK YOU
BITCH
PUNISHED

They then noticed yet a fourth message, on the wall of the stairway leading up to the second floor:

U HAVE
PAID

Donjon was a devout Catholic, with a healthy respect for the possibility of both supernatural good *and* evil. Standing in that house right then, he knew that the situation was far worse than he could have imagined while driving over from the police station. He feared that something terrible had happened—that the mother and the two boys had been murdered or kidnapped. He feared that he and Barlow had entered the house too late to save them.

Standing there right then, he also felt the chill of evil. It filled the air with its acrid stench. It clung to the walls in bloodred obscenities. It was an evil that defied rational explanation.

He felt that Satan was in the house, laughing at Barlow and him.

Officer Steve Patton had been on duty for almost an hour. He knew that Jason Donjon had gone over to the Coleman residence in Columbia Lakes to assist Justin Barlow on a basic welfare check. Now, since not much else was happening, he decided that he'd also go over and see if everything was okay.

He left the station and drove the first mile or so at the speed limit. There seemed no cause for alarm—at least, not yet. Chances were that Chris Coleman's wife, Sheri, was simply in the shower, which was why Coleman hadn't been able to get through to her. Patton had actually met the couple several months earlier. He'd gone to their house on January 2, after Coleman had contacted the police about the first threatening letter that he'd retrieved from his mailbox. He'd found it curious that they had two sons named Garett and Gavin. Patton also had a son named Garett, and he and his wife had talked about naming their second child Gavin if it turned out to be a boy.

Patton was halfway to the Coleman home when he heard Donjon over the radio, saying something about an open window at the rear of the house. He hit his emergency lights and hammered it the rest of the way. An open window definitely put a different complexion on the situation.

He arrived just as Chris Coleman was pulling into the driveway in his green Ford Explorer. He radioed dispatch, saying, "Five-oh on scene too." The time was now 6:56. Thirteen minutes had elapsed since Coleman had telephoned Justin Barlow.

Coleman opened the garage door with the automatic opener on his visor. He then stepped out into the driveway and started to walk toward the interior garage door that led into the kitchen. Patton ran over and intercepted him.

"Don't go inside the house, Chris," he said. "Police officers are inside. Stay out here with me."

"What's going on?" Coleman asked. He sounded nonplussed.

Justin Barlow and Jason Donjon were standing at the foot of the stairs leading to the second floor when they heard the garage door opening. Barlow raced through the kitchen and stuck his head out the side door.

"Stay there!" he shouted to Coleman. "Stay there!"

Coleman nodded. "Okay," he said.

Barlow gave Patton an urgent look.

"We need you inside, Steve," he said.

Patton started toward the door. Just before going inside, he turned and made eye contact with Chris Coleman.

"Stay right here in the driveway," he said.

Coleman nodded again.

Steve Patton was a big, handsome guy with brown hair and blue eyes. He was also sharp-witted and brave, precisely the sort of guy you'd want in your corner in a tough situation. Going inside that house, however, proved almost more than he could bear. He saw the lurid spray-painted message on the kitchen wall, with some of the paint oversprayed onto the photographs of young Garett and Gavin. He walked from the kitchen through the small dining area and saw the spray-painted message in the living room. And then he saw the message on the stairway wall.

Patton had never been more frightened in his entire life. He thought that the family might've been kidnapped or, more likely, murdered. He thought that the killer or killers might still be in the house.

The three men made a quick search of the main floor. They checked behind the living room furniture and looked into a closet and a bathroom. They then started up the stairs toward the second floor.

They went up single-file with their handguns drawn, past the spray-painted message that read U HAVE PAID. Jason Donjon led the way, followed by Justin Barlow and then Steve Patton. Patton felt fear in the pit of his stomach. He knew that ascending the stairs placed them in a highly vulnerable position. Somebody could stick his head around the corner and easily blow all three of them away with a shotgun. They had shotguns themselves in the trunks of their squad cars, which really didn't matter at this point. They didn't have time to go out to their squad cars.

They reached the top of the stairs, which gave way to a small hallway. Eleven-year-old Garett's room was almost directly across from them, and through the open doorway they could see Garett curled up in bed—with red spray paint on his blanket.

The three men split up now, each taking responsibility

for a separate bedroom. Justin Barlow went into Garett's room. The boy was lying on his left side, the blanket covering his lower body. His lips were bluish in color, his skin a ghastly gray. There were ligature marks on his neck, which suggested that he'd been strangled. Barlow leaned over and touched the neck with his fingertips. It was cold and stiff.

Rather than spelling out a message, the paint on his blanket was merely a blotch. Barlow wasn't certain what to make of this. Had the perpetrator run out of spray paint? Or had he simply exhausted his fund of obscenities?

Barlow looked into the closet and beneath the bed. Then he got down on one knee and called for an ambulance.

Steve Patton went along the banister at the top of the staircase and into nine-year-old Gavin's room. The first thing that he saw was a message in red spray paint. It was scrawled on the sheets, with overspray on the wooden bed frame:

FUCK
YOU

Gavin was sprawled facedown on the bed, lying absolutely still. His bare right foot poked out from underneath the tangled sheets. The sheets came up to his upper back. His arms and shoulders were uncovered, and there were ligature marks on his neck too. He was wearing Spider-Man pajamas. A baseball glove lay on the floor beneath the window.

Patton went up to him and touched his arm.

"Hey, buddy," he said.

He gently shook the boy's shoulder.

"Hey, buddy," he said again.

Gavin's arm and shoulder were cold to the touch. His skin was purplish, especially around the eye sockets and the lips. There were broken blood vessels behind his left ear.

"Hey, buddy," Patton repeated, though he knew it was no use.

Jason Donjon went to the master bedroom down the hallway and saw Sheri Coleman, the mom, lying facedown on a circular bed. She was completely naked, her hair draped over her face. She seemed tiny, scarcely bigger than a child. Donjon paused at the doorway and called out, "Columbia Police Department."

There was no response from Sheri, not the slightest movement.

Donjon went into the room, gun still drawn, and checked inside the bathroom and the walk-in closet. Then he holstered his gun and walked over to the bed. He tried to pull Sheri's hair away from her face in order to see her eyes, but the hair was a tangled mess. So instead he put the palm of his hand under her shoulder and tried to lift her up. When he did so, her arms and neck and head—everything—moved as if locked into place. It was then that Donjon noticed that the front part of Sheri's body, which had been lying upon the bed, was a purplish red. The skin on the rest of her body seemed slightly jaundiced but otherwise normal.

Time froze for Donjon. He felt a sense of calm that defied the awful horror of the moment. He felt that God was somehow present and helping him make sense of what he was observing. He knew from his training that the rigidity of the body meant that rigor mortis had already set in. And that the purplish red discoloration of the skin on the front part of Sheri's body indicated livor mortis, which was a pooling or a settling of the blood. He put two fingers on her neck. There was no pulse, and the skin felt thick and tough. It reminded Donjon of the dinosaur exhibit at the Saint Louis Science Center. It seemed clear to him that Sheri had been dead for quite some time.

Donjon then heard Steve Patton calling out.

"The boy in here's dead," Patton said.

"The mom's dead, too," Donjon replied.

The three men met in the hallway. There was panic, fear, and disbelief in their voices.

"Oh, my God," they kept saying, "Oh, my God."

PART ONE

Sheri, Chris, and the Boys

CHAPTER ONE

Angela DeCicco and Don Weiss started dating in high school. Angela was a sophomore and Don a senior. She was pretty and petite. He was lean, handsome, and quietly reflective.

They lived in Berwyn, Illinois, which was located just west of Chicago. It was a nice suburban community, with busy shopping districts and neighborhoods of old brick bungalows. It was made up mostly of white ethnics: Italian, Polish, and Bohemian.

Angela was the youngest of eight children. Her family was of Italian origin, one side from Naples, the other from Calabria. Her father, Dominick, grew up in Chicago during the Prohibition era. As a young man, he ran with a tough crowd and reputedly had connections with organized crime. Upon meeting Angela's mom, Josephine, he learned that her father had been abusing her. Dominick threatened the guy, saying he'd kill him if he ever touched her again. The threat apparently proved effective.

When Dominick proposed to Josephine, she said that she'd marry him only if he stopped hanging out with gangsters and got a steady job. He promised her that he'd go straight, and he made good on the promise. Shortly after getting married, he found a job as a printer for the Physicians' Record Company in Berwyn, where he ended up working for fifty years.

Don was the youngest of three boys. His paternal grandfather was Jewish German, and his mother's side of the family, the Rutherfords, hailed from northeast Arkansas. His father, Maurice, was a blue-collar guy with a lively mind and boundless curiosity. He had worked for the same trucking company in the Chicago area for more than twenty-five years. His mother, Dortha, was a sweet and wholesome woman who always tried to see the positive in people.

Angela got pregnant before the school year was finished. Don graduated and landed a union job as an order picker at a paint warehouse. It paid $4.75 per hour, which was decent money at the time. They told their respective families about the pregnancy and got married at the courthouse in downtown Chicago on September 7, 1974.

Angela gave birth to a boy on February 11, 1975, when she was still just seventeen. She and Don named him Mario. They didn't want Mario to be an only child, and so they were thrilled when Angela got pregnant once again. This time they had a girl, whom they named Sheri. She was born on July 3, 1977.

The family bounced around over the next several years, switching apartments almost annually. They finally settled into a nice place in Cicero, an old town located only seven miles west of the Chicago Loop. Mario and Sheri loved it there. They had Mexican friends, Italian friends, and Polish friends. They'd play stickball in the street and spend hours exploring the network of alleyways in their neighborhood.

Though scarcely older than a kid herself, Angela adapted well to motherhood. She'd read to Mario and Sheri, take them on outings, and involve them with projects at home. She enrolled them at Woodrow Wilson Elementary School in Cicero, where she soon became a familiar face. She created a PTA chapter at the school and started weekend fund-raisers in the gymnasium. She organized the student vote whereby the school's sports teams became known as the Wilson Dragons.

Angela also made certain that the kids didn't have much idle time on their hands. She signed them up for floor hockey and other sports. She put Sheri in the Girl Scouts and Mario in the Boy Scouts, where he became a fixture on the roller derby team. She encouraged them to join the school band and saw to it that they put in the requisite hours of practice. Mario played the trumpet, and Sheri the drums.

The two children mostly got along together, though they were dissimilar in temperament. Mario was smart and articulate, with a brooding quality about him. He seemed like a kid with things on his mind. Sheri was almost preternaturally upbeat. She was a crowd-pleaser, the life of the party. She was the sort of kid who seemed genuinely happy only when everybody around her was also happy.

There's an old family photograph of Mario and Sheri in which they're standing side by side in a doorway and wearing Chicago White Sox T-shirts. He's about nine years old, and she's seven. They both have dark hair, and they're as skinny as waifs. Mario is smiling, but the smile seems somehow cautious, tentative. Sheri's gap-toothed smile is as bright as a summer morning.

As the older brother, Mario was always protective of Sheri. Occasionally he was protective to a fault. One day Sheri ran home and told him that a neighborhood boy had made her cry. Mario went looking for the kid, marched him into an alleyway, and beat the dickens out of him. Years later he finally got around to asking Sheri what the kid had done to make her cry. She said that he'd kissed her.

Don Weiss left the paint warehouse after Sheri was born and tried his hand at various technical service jobs. He worked as a typewriter repairman for IBM in downtown Chicago for several years, and in a similar capacity for a smaller company for several more years. He then took a job at the Chicago branch office of a data communications hardware company that was based out of Largo, Florida. He eventually accepted an offer to work for the company in Florida, which meant uprooting the entire family.

They moved to Largo on New Year's Day, 1978. Mario was twelve years old, and Sheri ten. It was a new and different world for them. Located in the Tampa Bay area, Largo was a prototypical bedroom community, with none of the urban charm to which they'd grown accustomed in Cicero. The neighborhood where they now lived didn't even have sidewalks.

The transition was especially difficult for Mario, who was rather a loner and didn't make friends easily. He missed the old gang in Cicero, the kids with whom he'd grown up and played stickball in the street. He missed his beloved White Sox and the occasional trips to Comiskey Park for a ballgame.

It got a bit easier for Mario once he started high school. He and a classmate became good buddies, and the two of them would go bike riding all over town. One day they rode to a restaurant where Mario was hopeful of landing a job. He lied about his age and the guy who ran the place hired him on the spot as a busboy. It proved the first of many jobs that Mario would have as a teenager.

Sheri adapted without much fuss to the new life in Florida. She was more sociable than her older brother and so vivacious that other kids sought her out for friendship. She positively flourished throughout her mid- to late teens. She was a cheerleader for the Largo High School Packers football team. She played shortstop and second base for the school's varsity softball team. She threw right and batted left, and was perhaps the team's fastest player.

She thought that she might want to become a model, and her mom and dad paid for her to attend the Barbizon school of modeling in Tampa. She was certainly no less attractive than any of the other girls in the school, but her tiny stature proved an obstacle that even her zest and resolve couldn't overcome. She stood barely five feet tall.

Sheri was a huge fan of the Chicago Bulls basketball team and absolutely adored the team's superstar, Michael Jordan. Her closet was full of Chicago Bulls jerseys, most of them bearing Jordan's signature number 23. In 1994, Jordan decided that he'd also give baseball a shot. He signed with the minor league Birmingham Barons, who were holding spring training in Sarasota, Florida. Sheri made the three-hour drive to Sarasota for a preseason game, hopeful of meeting her hero in person. Prior to the game, she purchased a bouquet of flowers and asked a clubhouse attendant to give them to Jordan. The attendant must have pointed her out to him, because afterward Jordan stopped his Corvette at the gate where she was standing and rolled down his window. "Thank you for the flowers," he said. Sheri melted.

She had lots of friends, most of whom she'd met at school. Her best friend was Tara Lintz, a beautiful young woman with thick brown hair and an infectious laugh. Tara was in the drama club with Sheri. Some people thought that she showed real promise as an actress.

Tara had moved to Florida from Palisades Park, New Jersey, when she was four or five years old. Sheri thought the world of her, but Mario and Angela were less sure about her. She struck them as aloof and superficial, and obsessed with material success. She also struck them as being jealous of Sheri and her more stable family situation. They wondered if she was somebody whom Sheri could really trust.

Sheri got a job as a waitress at a Thai restaurant on Clearwater Beach during the summer between her junior and senior years at high school. When she wasn't working, she'd hang out on the beach with Tara Lintz and check out the guys. Apart from maybe catching a Chicago Bulls game on television, there was nothing that she enjoyed doing more. Mario had graduated high school by this time and was driving a 1992 Camaro RS with a T-top. He got so tired of Sheri borrowing it that he bought her a car of her own: a 1982 Chrysler K-car for $850.

Sheri was seventeen now, and she'd blossomed into a real beauty. She was petite and athletic, with lustrous dark hair and fine features. She radiated joy and confidence. Ever the protective older brother, Mario would half jokingly warn his buddies against trying to make time with her. "You touch her and I'll crack your head open," he'd say.

During her senior year at high school, Sheri's happiness was put to a severe test. Her parents' marriage was falling apart. The family home, once a place of peace and stability, was now fraught with bitterness and animosity. Don and Angela, once so happy together, were now at loggerheads. They argued constantly, and bitterly. It seemed only a matter of time before the marriage disintegrated completely.

Mario and Sheri blamed their dad. It was he who wanted out of the marriage. It was he who was responsible for making all of their lives miserable. There was a certain truth to this. Don did indeed want out. It wasn't another woman. It wasn't any one thing in particular. After twenty years, he simply thought that his marriage to Angela had run its course. Time was passing him by and he wanted to set his life on a fresh path.

Sheri graduated Largo High School in 1995 with a 3.35 GPA, and at roughly the same time Don and Angela formally separated. Don moved out of the house and got his own apartment, and divorce proceedings were set in motion. The actual divorce wouldn't be finalized for another year and a half, but the entire process proved grueling for everyone. Mario and Sheri thought that their dad had betrayed them. They thought that he'd also betrayed their mom, who'd dedicated her life to the marriage and the family. They weren't certain that they could ever forgive him.

Sheri worked as a waitress for a year or so after graduating high school. Then, out of the blue, she announced that she'd decided to join the Air Force. She said that she was looking for adventure, and that she also wanted to escape the turmoil at home. She seemed to think that the Air Force might be just the ticket for her. Mario tried to talk her out of it. He seriously doubted that his little sister was cut out for the highly regimented life of the military. He knew that he himself wasn't.

Sheri wasn't about to be dissuaded, however, and in September 1996 she went to Lackland Air Force Base, on the outskirts of San Antonio. Her mom and Mario visited her there in November of the same year and saw her graduate from basic training. Her dad tried to visit her also but she refused to see him. Don realized that this marked a decided deterioration in their relationship. The communication lines between them were now shut down almost completely.

After basic training, Sheri was stationed at the Marine Corps base in Quantico, Virginia. There she was assigned to the military police's K-9 unit, which meant that she was responsible for handling a military working dog. She functioned essentially as a police officer at Quantico, patrolling the vast base with her German shepherd. She seemed to enjoy the job, and in February 1997 she fell in love with a young Marine who was also assigned to the K-9 unit.

The young Marine was Chris Coleman, a strapping twenty-year-old who'd joined the Corps practically right out of high school. In early September 1997, upon discovering that Sheri had gotten pregnant, the couple decided that they'd leave Quantico and start a new life together elsewhere. Elsewhere was Randolph County in southwestern Illinois, which was where Chris's family lived.

CHAPTER TWO

Percy is a dreary little town strung out along Route 150 in southwestern Illinois. It's located on the eastern edge of Randolph County, which is hardscrabble farming and coal-mining country.

The town was once a going concern, when coal mining in the region was at its peak. Now, however, it's in a state of prolonged decline. Quite a few of its businesses are shut down. Others are hanging on by a thread. Where once there were four grocery stores, now there are none. The population has hovered around the one thousand mark for decades now.

Chris Coleman's family had deep roots in Percy. His paternal great-grandparents were Griff and Pearl Coleman. Griff was a coal miner, and he also grew beans and corn on a small farm just outside of town. His paternal grandparents, Gene and Doris, were two of the town's most prominent citizens. Gene worked as a strip-mine pit boss before running successfully for town mayor. No one was surprised when he was reelected for a second term, mostly because Gene was the kind of mayor who got things done. He'd personally see to it that water leaks and potholes were repaired. He and Doris had a swimming pool in their backyard, which was the only pool in town. On hot summer days they'd make it available to anybody wanting to use it. The only provision was that kids required adult supervision.

Gene resigned as mayor in the mid-1970s, and he and Doris went to Nicaragua for a spell. Gene worked in heavy construction while there, and Doris did volunteer work at several hospitals and schools.

Chris Coleman's father, Ron, was the third of Gene and Doris's six children. Ron went to Trico Senior High School, which was a consolidated three-county school located just a few miles down the road from Percy, in the village of Campbell Hill. His aunt, Linda Coleman, was a teacher there at the time. Ron ran cross-country on the varsity team, and he was also an accomplished swimmer.

During his senior year at Trico, Ron began to date a pretty girl named Connie Tope, who was several years younger than he was. Connie lived in the nearby town of Ava, where her parents ran a restaurant. Old-timers remember it as a friendly place with hearty food. Connie and her siblings would help out after school and on weekends, serving tables and working the cash register.

Ron graduated in 1968, as part of a senior class that numbered almost two hundred. He put in a year at Southern Illinois University in Carbondale, making the hour-long commute several times weekly from his home in Percy. He then decided that higher education wasn't exactly his cup of tea and went to work in the mines.

Connie graduated high school in 1972. She and Ron had been dating all along, and eventually they got married and started a family. Chris was born on March 20, 1977, and two more sons, Brad and Keith, followed over the next several years.

Ron toiled in the mines for roughly a decade, and seemed naturally suited to the work. As the years passed, however, his thoughts inclined more and more toward religion. He and Connie became involved with a Methodist church in Belleville, Illinois, which was a good ninety-minute drive from their home in Percy. They then began to attend a prayer meeting that would fundamentally alter their lives.

The prayer meeting had sprung out of the First Baptist Church in Chester, Illinois. Some leading members of the congregation had grown dissatisfied with the worship services at the church, finding them staid and uninspired. They'd wanted a livelier, more charismatic form of worship, and toward this end they'd started to meet on their own in the basement of a local physician's home.

The physician was Dr. James Krieg, who'd served as a U.S. Navy doctor for a couple of years before moving to Chester in 1980. He and his wife, Betty, lived in a big, historic house on the outskirts of town, just past the covered bridge on Illinois Route 150. They were gracious hosts, and the weekly meetings at their home proved highly successful. The meetings featured spontaneity of prayer and speaking in tongues. They featured a heightened, more impassioned spirituality. As word spread, an increasing number of people from the surrounding area started to attend, including Ron and Connie Coleman.

The prayer meetings soon outgrew the Krieg family basement, and the group cast about for a larger space. They settled on the old Nite Hawk Tavern, which was located on Illinois Route 3 heading south out of Chester. They rented the ramshackle building and did their best to make it resemble more a house of worship than a drinking establishment. Once they'd finished renovating the place, they opened it up for worship and christened it Grace Bible Church.

Ron Coleman had thought for quite some time now that he might want to give up coal mining and try his hand at preaching instead. The folks at Grace Bible Church gave him his chance in the mid-1980s, installing him as a part-time pastor. By some accounts, he wasn't terribly effective at first. He was hardly the most verbally fluent of men, and his preaching was tentative and dull. He plodded rather than soared. He worked hard at the craft, however, and took inspiration from whomever he could.

The person from whom he took the most inspiration was Joyce Meyer, an up-and-coming preacher based in the St. Louis area. In the mid- to late 1980s Meyer was just beginning to win a reputation as one of the brightest new stars on the evangelical scene. Ron and Connie would drive up to see her whenever they could, sometimes bringing their three boys with them. They loved her blunt, plainspoken style. They loved the way that she spoke to people on their own terms. If ever there was a preacher worth emulating, they thought, it was surely Joyce Meyer.

Grace Bible Church flourished in the old Nite Hawk Tavern—so much so that the congregation built a brand-new building on a piece of property that had previously been home to the Camp Town Trailer Park. The building opened for worship in April 1994, and shortly thereafter Ron Coleman was offered a promotion from part- to full-time pastor. He accepted the offer, which meant that he was able to give up coal mining for good. He was now leader of the flock.

Ron had improved somewhat, but he still wasn't the most dynamic of preachers. The church elders would sometimes encourage him to become more animated in the pulpit. Furthermore, unlike his wife, Ron was not especially warm or vibrant in his personal interactions. Whereas Connie would greet people with a big smile and a hug, Ron was stiff and diffident. He had little patience for small talk, and he was just about the last person to give somebody a hug.

Still, there's little question that Ron possessed a certain quality that seemed to inspire allegiance. He had a way of commanding the loyalty of those who crossed his threshold. People who joined the church would invariably find themselves drawn to him. They'd want to curry his favor. They'd want to please him, even if it meant sacrificing their own best interests.

There's also little question that church membership continued to grow under Ron's stewardship. People would drive to the new church from towns throughout Randolph County. They'd drive across the Mississippi River from Missouri. The parking lot would be jammed for Sunday and Wednesday services. The place was booming.

Ron and Connie and the boys were living in Chester by now, having moved from Percy several years prior to the new church opening. Their oldest boy, Chris, finished his elementary school education at St. John Lutheran and went on to

Chester High. By all accounts he was a good kid. Everybody seemed to like him. Everybody found him to be humble, respectful, and sweet natured.

Chris didn't cuss or drink or fight. He disliked killing small animals, and so he rarely went hunting with his dad. He played baseball and football and was a favorite among his teammates. He went to church and shouted and sang and spoke in tongues whenever the Holy Spirit so moved him. He very rarely caused his parents trouble. He seemed uninterested in drawing attention to himself.

His younger brothers, Brad and Keith, were a different story. They seemed far more aggressive than Chris. They carried themselves with an air of arrogance. Several ex–church members describe them as having been rude and foulmouthed. One woman says that when Keith was about sixteen, he was caught in a compromising position with a neighborhood girl in the church parking lot prior to Wednesday evening services. Brad and Keith seemed intent on drawing attention to themselves.

All three boys resembled their dad far more than they did their mom. They had the same sandy hair, the same sallow complexion, and the same loose-legged gait. Like their dad, they were about five nine, with lean builds. But it was always Chris who seemed the closest to his dad and the most eager to please him. It was Chris who seemed most clearly to be under Ron Coleman's spell.

Chris breezed through high school. He performed decently in the classroom and on the athletic fields. He did nothing to raise any eyebrows.

A recruiter from the Marines visited his senior class one day, and Chris loved the guy's confidence and sense of bravado. He enlisted almost immediately upon graduating and was stationed at Quantico, Virginia. He was assigned to the K-9 unit and worked on several presidential security details. While at Quantico he met Sheri Coleman, who was also assigned to the K-9 unit. She was a pretty, petite girl from Chicago via Florida. She had a gorgeous smile and a hearty laugh.

When Sheri got pregnant, the young couple decided to leave the military. They decided that they'd get married and make a life together. Chris was twenty-two years old and Sheri a year younger.

CHAPTER THREE

The couple left Quantico in September 1997. Sheri wanted to introduce Chris to her mom, Angela, and her brother, Mario, both of whom had returned to the Chicago area from Florida not long before. She had no interest whatsoever in introducing him to her dad, Don Weiss, who was still living in Florida. She hadn't yet forgiven him for divorcing her mom, nor was she certain that she ever would.

On their way to Chicago, they stopped by Chester to see Chris's parents. Chris had called them in advance to say that he was coming. He apparently hadn't mentioned anything about Sheri.

Ron Coleman was looking out his front window when Chris's car pulled over at the curb.

"Connie," he called to his wife. "He's got somebody with him."

Ron and Connie's initial impression of Sheri was hardly favorable. They seemed dismayed that their firstborn son was even in her company. Chris must've sensed their disapproval, because he said nothing about his and Sheri's plans to get married. Instead he simply introduced her as a good friend who lived in Chicago and said that he was in the process of driving her home.

Then he and Sheri left and drove to Chicago.

"We didn't pick up anything," Ron Coleman would recount years later. "Except she was a worldly little girl, little short shorts, tattoo on her leg, not the person we thought he'd be with."

If Sheri wasn't an instant hit with Chris's parents, neither was Chris with Mario. Upon being introduced later that same day, Mario found the guy distant, quiet, and aloof, and almost entirely devoid of personality. Having grown up just outside of Chicago, Mario was accustomed to a certain verbal repartee, to an exchange of friendly insults. Chris seemed to him incapable of friendly banter. He seemed rather a dullard.

There was also the rural twang in Chris's voice, which was a reflection of his small-town roots in southwestern Illinois. Mario thought that the guy sounded like a hillbilly. He couldn't understand what his sister saw in him. He was convinced that she could do much better for herself.

On the second day of the visit, Mario had an opportunity to speak privately with Sheri in the basement of their aunt Marion's house, where Mario was living at the time. He asked her why she was so intent on getting married.

"I mean, what's the big hurry?" he said.

Sheri shifted uneasily in her chair. She said that she and Chris were in love, and so, of course, they wanted to get married.

"It's good that you're in love," Mario persisted, "but why not try living together first? That way you get to know Chris better. Marriage is a big step. You might as well be sure."

Sheri merely shrugged.

"Okay," Mario said. "But let me ask you one more thing, and please don't take it the wrong way. Are you pregnant?"

No, Sheri lied. She wasn't pregnant.

The visit lasted four days. On the third day Sheri and Chris went to the Richard J. Daley Center in downtown Chicago and got married. They went by themselves. They didn't even mention anything about it to Angela or Mario until afterward.

Chris called home outside the Daley Center and got his father on the line. "Dad, you'll never believe what we did," he said. "We got married!"

Ron Coleman was deathly quiet on the other end.

"Dad, you don't seem excited," Chris said.

"Give me a few minutes," Ron said.

The next day Sheri told her mom that she and Chris planned on having a wedding reception the following July. They planned on having it in Chester, which was where they'd be making their new home.

Sheri and Chris drove from Chicago to Chester later the same day. Sheri would wait another month before telling her mom that she was indeed pregnant.

Though it's only a five- or six-hour drive away, Chester could scarcely be more different from Chicago. Going there for the first time, Sheri must have felt as if she'd entered some strange and exotic new continent.

The town is located on the bluffs of the Mississippi River about sixty-five miles south of St. Louis. Its population is almost entirely white and has wavered around the 8,500 mark for decades now. There's a decidedly insular quality to the place. Outsiders are mistrusted, and anyone moving to town from elsewhere might never succeed in attaining full acceptance.

Chester also has a particular claim to fame: It's the birthplace of Elzie Crisler Segar, creator of the *Popeye* comic strip. The town hosts the annual Popeye Picnic and parade, and statues of the strip's colorful cast of characters—from Wimpy to Olive Oyl to Popeye himself—adorn the downtown area.

The town is home to two landmark institutions. The first of these is Menard Correctional Center, which once housed Illinois's death row. Opened in 1878, Menard is the second oldest prison in Illinois and the largest maximum-security facility. With its ancient stone walls and razor-wire fences, it looms above the Mississippi like a haunted fortress. Adjacent to the prison is Chester Mental Health Center, which received its first patients in 1901, making it the state's oldest hospital for the criminally insane.

Chester and environs is also a bastion of evangelical Christianity. It's an area where people read their Bibles and take going to church with utmost seriousness. Where speaking in tongues is commonplace, and heaven and hell are regarded not as mere metaphors but rather as real destinations.

Driving west along Illinois Route 150, the first thing that one notices upon entering town is a sign on the highway shoulder. "Welcome to Chester," it reads. "Home of Popeye." There's a big picture of Popeye on the sign, signature corncob pipe in his mouth and a bag of spinach in hand.

A bit farther along, there's a white billboard with a picture of a pink butterfly in the upper right-hand corner. The billboard is an advertisement for Ron Coleman's church. "Jesus changes you!" the message on it proclaims.

The church itself—now known simply as Grace Church—is a mile farther along, on the south side of the road. It's a large brick-fronted, aluminum-sided structure with a vast parking lot and a manicured lawn. An electronic sign out front flashes various inspirational messages, such as "Get Exercise—Walk with the Lord."

Sheri's first several months in town must have been a period of considerable adjustment. She was pregnant and newly married, and living in an environment quite unlike anything that she'd ever experienced. And her new in-laws might not have been thrilled with the idea of welcoming her into their family.

According to some reports, Ron and Connie didn't much care for Sheri. They didn't much care for her ethnic background or her big-city roots. They didn't care for her willfulness, her determination to do exactly what she was intent on doing. They thought that she'd trapped Chris—their oldest son, their golden boy—into getting married. But what seems to have galled them most was that she didn't share their faith. She wasn't born-again. They were dismayed that Chris had gotten involved with this "worldly little girl." He'd made a big mistake, and they were quite certain that he himself soon realized as much. He realized that the marriage hadn't been "godly."

"My gosh, he was raised in church," Ron recounted years later. "He was repentant and broken over it."

"He said, 'Oh, I just got caught up in the moment,' " Connie added. "We said, 'Well, it's a lifetime.' "

"But we found out later that she was pregnant," Ron said.

Connie apparently decided that she'd try to make the best of a bad situation. She decided that she'd try to convert her worldly daughter-in-law.

As Sheri would later confide to friends, Connie would invite her to church and then afterward take her aside and pray over her. She'd read the Bible to her and talk about sin and salvation. She seemed to have made Sheri her own personal project.

Sheri was naïve about religious matters. She'd scarcely given religion a second thought. She and Mario had been raised in a household that was nominally Catholic at best. They'd received First Communion and Confirmation but otherwise had very rarely gone to church. Their mom wasn't especially religious, and their dad was anything but. The only person who'd take them to Mass when they were kids—which wasn't often—was their maternal grandmother, Josephine DeCicco. Never before had anyone taken the trouble to pray with her, as Connie was now doing.

Connie's efforts weren't in vain. In the fall of 1997, not long after moving to Chester, Sheri converted to evangelical Christianity. She was, so to speak, born again. The conversion seems to have been heartfelt and lasting. Henceforward, Sheri would be no less ardently religious than her in-laws. Her Catholicism, nominal as it was, now seemed a thing of the distant past.

In early April 1998, Ron and Connie drove to the Chicago area and visited Sheri's mom at her home in suburban La Grange Park. Angela invited them into her living room and offered them coffee. They made small talk for a while, and then Connie reportedly shifted the conversation to the subject of religion.

"So I understand you're Catholic," Connie said.

"You understand correctly," Angela said.

"But don't you realize?" Connie went on. "Catholicism goes against the teachings of the Bible."

"Oh?" Angela said. "That's very interesting."

She gritted her teeth and carried on with the rest of the visit. When he found out about it later, Mario wished that his mom had thrown them out. He couldn't believe that Ron and Connie had had the audacity to insult her in her own home.

Sheri seemed to be enjoying married life in Chester. She and Chris had rented a nice house on East State Street, almost directly across from Grace Church. Chris had gotten a job at Chester Mental Health Center as a security therapy aid. The couple was getting along together just fine. Perhaps Mario had been wrong. Perhaps they hadn't needed to live together prior to getting married to find out if they were compatible.

Sheri was baptized and began to speak in tongues in early 1998. Now she was fully a member of her newly adopted evangelical community.

On April 30, 1998, Sheri gave birth to a healthy baby boy. She and Chris named him Garett Dominick. The middle name was in honor of Sheri's maternal grandfather, Dominick DeCicco.

Garett looked just like his dad, sweet-faced and blond, with fair skin. Most people thought that he was Chris's spitting image.

CHAPTER FOUR

Later the same year, Ron and Connie spoke with Joyce Meyer at a prayer conference. Meyer told them that she was looking for somebody to train a guard dog. Ron and Connie put her in touch with Chris, who had plenty of experience in this regard from his stint in the Marine Corps. Chris trained the dog, and soon after also landed a full-time job in the security department of Joyce Meyer's ministry, which was based out of Fenton, Missouri.

The new job seemed a nice opportunity for Chris. Joyce Meyer was an established star on the evangelical scene by this point, with a robust following and a burgeoning television ministry. Long gone were the days when she would hold early-morning Bible classes with just a handful of people in attendance.

Fenton, Missouri, was quite a distance from Chester, so Chris and Sheri packed up and moved to the inner-ring St. Louis suburb of Affton. There they rented a furnished three-bedroom house that belonged to Meyer's ministry.

Affton was an old, somewhat scruffy community with a distinctly urban feel to it. Sheri didn't mind this in the least. Having spent the earlier part of her childhood in Cicero, she was perfectly at home in an urban environment. She loved taking young Garett to the park or to the local library. Or, when the weather turned chilly, bundling him up for a stroll along Gravois Road, which was the main shopping strip.

Sheri soon became pregnant again, and on January 25, 2000, she delivered another healthy baby boy. This one they named Gavin Christopher. He, too, strikingly resembled his dad.

Chris apparently decided that two kids was enough, or perhaps he and Sheri made the decision in tandem. Not long after Gavin's birth, he got a vasectomy.

Chris was flourishing in his new job. Joyce Meyer certainly seemed to like him, as did her husband and children, and theirs were the only votes that really mattered. He felt more confident than ever before, and in late 2000 he applied for a position as head of security for the entire ministry.

On the application form for the position, Chris wrote that he'd been "attached to the United States Secret Service" while a member of the Marine Corps and had worked quite a few presidential security details. In the "spiritual criteria" section, he wrote that both he and his wife were born-again and that he began to speak in tongues in 1986 and she in 1997. He added that he didn't drink, smoke, or use drugs, nor did he have any other "habits or bondages." He wrote that he first learned of Joyce Meyer and her ministry through his mother, "who used to attend meetings when there was [*sic*] 14 or 15 women attending them."

Chris got the position, and he was quick to leave his mark. He tore down the old security system, which he considered antiquated, and built a new system from scratch. He hired his own staff, favoring former police and military people who carried themselves with a certain swagger. With the help of an ex-cop named Dan Ward, he wrote a new procedural manual for the security department. He seemed intent on turning the department into his personal fiefdom.

Sheri was also working at Joyce Meyer's ministry by this point. She'd shift around quite a bit, subbing in various departments, but the bulk of her time was spent in World

Outreach. Here she was part of a team that traveled with Meyer on missionary trips throughout the world. She went to India on one such trip, and the experience left a deep impression on her. She encountered sick and suffering people at almost every turn, and she only wished that she could've done more to help them in a practical vein. Upon returning home, she decided that she'd someday undertake training to become an emergency medical technician, so that on future mission trips she'd be able to minister not only to people's spirits but also their bodies.

Sheri also had her hands full with child care. By almost all accounts, she was an attentive and loving mother who loved nothing more than playing with her two boys and engaging their imaginations. The boys were old enough now that their personalities were starting to come to the fore. Garett was more like his dad. He was shy and reserved, with a penchant for sitting back and observing. It wasn't easy to tell exactly what he was thinking. Gavin, on the other hand, was a real crowd-pleaser. He'd come into a room wearing a big smile and pull off a somersault or some other stunt, then gauge everybody else's reaction. He was just like his mom.

Chris wasn't as emotionally involved with the boys as Sheri was, or nearly as indulgent. Whereas Sheri was inclined to let them have the run of the house, Chris was a stickler for order and obedience. He'd demand that toys be properly put away and that voices be kept down. He seems to have subscribed to the old dictum that "children are best seen and not heard." If the boys needed to be disciplined, it was Chris who took care of it.

Don Weiss was still living in Florida, and feeling hopelessly cut off from his daughter. He'd hear from Mario occasionally but never from Sheri. And Mario seemed reluctant to tell him much about her.

But then one day Mario phoned and confided that Sheri was not only married but also had two sons. He said that she was living in the St. Louis area, and that both she and her husband were involved with Joyce Meyer's ministry.

Don was grateful for the update, yet he also felt regret and sadness. He realized that Mario and Sheri felt betrayed over the divorce, and he understood why. But it was a terrible thing for a father to be so isolated from his children, to have no idea what was going on in their lives. He'd had no idea that Sheri was married, let alone the mother of two little boys. He'd never even heard of Joyce Meyer.

He wondered if there was the slightest chance of ever salvaging some sort of meaningful relationship with Sheri.

Not long afterward, Sheri surprised Don with an e-mail. Her tone was cordial if not exactly warm. It was a start, though, which was all that Don had hoped for. He wrote back, and over the next several months they corresponded fairly regularly. Don saw it as a fragile communication—superficial, faltering—but also very sweet. He was thrilled simply to be in contact once again with his long-estranged daughter.

At the time, Don was engaged to get married again. He eventually worked up the nerve to ask Sheri if he and his fiancée, Deborah, could come to the St. Louis area for a visit. Sheri agreed, and Don and Deborah flew up on the first weekend of August in 2002.

They met Sheri, Chris, and the boys at a restaurant for lunch, which went as well as anybody could've expected. Sheri seemed to like Deborah, and the two women did most of the talking. This suited Don just fine. He was content simply to sit back and listen. Afterward they went to the Science Center in downtown St. Louis, and Don gave each of the boys a wrist walkie-talkie in the parking lot before going inside.

They spent a couple of hours at the Science Center, then went to Chris and Sheri's house, where the boys played almost nonstop with their new walkie-talkies until bedtime. Gavin would deliberately talk gibberish into his, which so annoyed Garett that he finally gave up and laid his aside. Don took over and responded to Gavin's gibberish with some of his own. The little boy loved it.

Sheri said that she, Chris, and the boys were planning on

going to church the next day, and she invited her dad and his fiancée to join them. Don and Deborah declined, but everybody met after church for a late lunch at a barbecue restaurant in Fenton. Don took some photographs so that the memory of the occasion would be forever preserved.

On the plane trip back to Florida, Don felt pleased with how the weekend had gone. He and the boys had gotten along great, and Sheri had seemed happy to see him, though he hadn't succeeding in getting a good read on her husband. Chris had seemed a shy, quiet guy. Conversation with him had proven difficult. Perhaps he was simply the sort of person who preferred hanging in the background.

Don mildly regretted not having sat down for a heart-to-heart with Sheri. But the weekend had been going so well that he hadn't wanted to risk spoiling it by saying the wrong words. The heart-to-heart could come later. Right then it was more than enough that his daughter seemed open to the idea of letting him back into her life.

Later that same month, Mario and a couple of cousins drove down from Chicago for a visit. They ended up taking Sheri, Chris, and Garett to a Cardinals–Cubs game at the old Busch Stadium, while Gavin stayed home with a babysitter. Mario wore a White Sox cap to the game (he almost always wore a White Sox cap), and Garett also wore one, which Mario had given him some time before.

Some of the fans in attendance apparently found this worthy of some good-natured ribbing.

"Hey, what's with the White Sox caps? You guys even know what game you're at?"

"What's up with you guys? You take the wrong exit off Interstate 55 or something?"

Mario found this immensely amusing. It made him feel that much closer to Garett.

The game didn't turn out very well for Sheri, who was now an ardent Cubs fan after having been raised in the White Sox camp. The Cubs surrendered a big lead in the late innings and wound up losing ten to nine.

But young Gavin certainly seemed pleased with the outcome. Though not yet two years old, he'd already declared himself a Cards fan and had been home watching the game on TV.

"The Cards won!" he exclaimed as soon as they walked through the door. "The Cards won!"

Mario found this amusing too. Talk about divided allegiance! He and Garett were White Sox fans, Sheri a Cub fan, and Gavin a Card fan. He wasn't yet certain where Chris stood.

The months seemed to pass quickly, as they often do with young families. Chris kept busy with work, and Sheri with work, the kids, and the house. They'd drive down to Chester most weekends for church and a visit with Ron and Connie. Occasionally Sheri would take the kids to Chicago for a visit with her side of the family.

Most people who saw Sheri and Chris during these days thought that they made a great couple. Most people thought that they were very much in love.

Chris's job performance at Joyce Meyer's ministry continued to draw rave reviews. He seemed disciplined, dedicated, and resourceful. He seemed in total control. Not a single vehicle would arrive at the ministry's complex in Fenton without him knowing about it. Not a single person, employee or otherwise, would get close to Meyer without his approval.

Whenever Meyer was scheduled to appear at an out-of-town conference, he'd travel to the location ahead of time and do reconnaissance work. He'd meet with the local police and map out escape routes in the event that anything should go amiss. He'd plan for every possible contingency, leaving nothing to chance. The ministry seemed to have made an excellent choice in promoting him to head of security. The guy was thorough, meticulous. He seemed absolutely top-notch.

However, not everybody at the ministry was quite so certain about Chris Coleman. Several people who worked there at the time found him smug and remote, and sometimes downright rude. They say that he'd routinely ignore people who tried saying hi to him. That he'd brush past people in the hallway as if they didn't exist. They couldn't help but wonder if his freshly minted power had gone to his head.

George Wise is a big, affable man who worked in the communications department at the ministry for a couple of years. His office was a scant thirty feet from Chris's, and the two men saw one another on a regular basis. George remembers Chris as an aloof, arrogant guy who'd rarely give his coworkers the time of day.

"He was staunch and erect in his bearing, very spiffy and military-like," George said. "He definitely didn't have a friendly demeanor. He was also a perfectionist, and very tightly wrapped. He struck me as being potentially explosive, the kind of guy who was always struggling to keep his temper under control. He'd get upset over seemingly minor things, like somebody being on a computer when they weren't supposed to be."

It didn't seem to matter to Chris what his coworkers might think. None of them would dare challenge or criticize him—certainly not to his face. He had too much power, too much influence. He was the architect of the well-oiled security system that was protecting their boss and safeguarding their jobs.

For a small-town boy from the Bible Belt of southwestern Illinois, this must have been intoxicating stuff indeed. In scarcely no time at all, he'd become an indispensable aide to one of the most celebrated preachers in the land.

Chris Coleman was riding high. He was Joyce Meyer's right-hand man.

PART TWO

Joyce Meyer Ministries

CHAPTER FIVE

If not the best-known preacher on the evangelical scene today, Joyce Meyer certainly ranks among the top three or four. For the past decade or so, she's been almost impossible to ignore.

Meyer came to preacherly fame along a hard road. She was raised in a tough working-class section of south St. Louis and reportedly suffered sexual abuse at the hands of her father while a young girl. She married a car salesman after graduating high school, but the marriage was marred by accusations of his sexual infidelity and lasted only five years. She hung out at local bars after the divorce, occasionally going home with stray men, before marrying an engineering draftsman named Dave Meyer in January 1967.

While praying in her car one morning in 1976, she thought that she heard God calling her name. Later the same day, upon returning home from the beauty parlor, she underwent a religious conversion. After years of living without purpose, as she would later recount, she suddenly felt "full of liquid love" and "drunk with the Spirit of God." She subsequently became active in a local charismatic church, the Life Christian Center, where she presided over an early-morning Bible class. The class proved so popular that she started a daily Bible-study program on a St. Louis radio station, and she was also named associate pastor of her church.

She resigned her pastorship at the Life Christian Center in 1985 and founded her own ministry, which she christened Life in the Word. Her daily radio program flourished over the next several years, expanding to six stations throughout the Midwest. In 1993, at the urging of her husband, she also launched a television program that initially aired on Black Entertainment Television and Chicago-based WGN-TV. This, too, proved immensely popular, and in 2003 she changed the name of her ministry to Joyce Meyer Ministries and began calling both her radio and television programs *Enjoying Everyday Life*.

Since then she hasn't shown the least sign of slowing down. She's published a number of best-selling inspirational books. She's expanded her television ministry to the point where *Enjoying Everyday Life* now enjoys a vast international audience. She's preached to overflow crowds at some of the biggest venues in the land. She's increased the annual revenue of her overall ministry to upwards of $100 million. And she's made *Time* magazine's list of the most influential evangelicals in America.

Joyce Meyer credits God for this remarkable run of success. This would seem only fair, but there's no denying that Meyer herself is a talented woman. Onstage she's smart and funny, with a wonderfully expressive face. She'll crack jokes in her working-class St. Louis accent. She'll punctuate a point with an exaggerated frown or her thousand-watt smile. She has a personable, plainspoken style that dissolves distance. She's not so much a celebrity on TV as some favorite aunt, wise in her ways, joining you for a cup of tea in the kitchen. When Joyce Meyer speaks from the podium or over the airwaves, she's speaking directly to *you*.

All the more so, it would seem, if you're a woman. While Meyer's appeal cuts across sex lines, it's women who seem especially drawn to her. A big reason for this is that she'll talk frankly onstage about her own life as a woman. She'll talk about her failed first marriage and her subsequent experiences picking up men at bars. She'll talk about her insecurities and anxieties. She'll talk about things with which ordinary women can identify, and in so doing she establishes a vital sense of kinship. If Joyce Meyer can overcome obstacles and put her life in order, then so, too, can the women in her audience. If she can emerge from hard times strong and unscathed, there's no good reason why they can't also.

Meyer has legions of followers, people who'll spare no effort to attend her conferences or watch her on TV. They love her practical emphasis, the way she'll relate the Bible to concrete problems of everyday life. They love her blunt, no-nonsense approach, the way she'll insist that audience members take responsibility for their own lives rather than making excuses or wallowing in self-pity. Many of her followers claim that she's empowered them to change their lives for the better. That she's helped make them better parents, better spouses, and better Christians.

But Meyer also has her detractors, some of whom claim that she's merely a scam artist hiding behind a Bible. That she steals from the poor, the naïve, and the vulnerable. And that she preaches a false Gospel, the so-called prosperity Gospel, which is a travesty of authentic Christianity.

The prosperity Gospel is a relatively new development on the American religious scene, although its roots run deeper than is sometimes imagined. The message of those who advocate it—the prosperity preachers—is disarmingly simple. If you're a born-again Christian, they say, you're entitled to worldly wealth. You're entitled to the fruits of the earth. God wants you to prosper. He wants you to amass material riches. All that you have to do is make a positive confession of faith, and God will take care of the rest.

And how should you go about making this positive confession? It's simple, the preachers say. Just send them money. Make a donation to their ministries. They call this "sowing a seed of faith." Send them money and in due time you'll reap a harvest of financial plenitude. You'll get back tenfold what you send, perhaps a hundredfold. Who can tell? The sky's the limit.

But make sure you don't skimp. You can send just ten

dollars, but what kind of faith would this show? You can send a hundred dollars, but wouldn't a thousand be so much better? And don't think that you can't afford it. So what if you're strapped for cash? So what if you're a pensioner barely meeting monthly expenses? All the more reason to dig deep and send whatever you possibly can! Otherwise you betray a lack of faith in God's power and promise. Remember. God will bless you with riches beyond your wildest imagining, providing you only do your part. Send in the money!

The prosperity preachers will typically load their sermons with personal testimonial. They'll talk about how they themselves were once strapped for cash. Mortgages were due. Furnaces were broken. Wolves were howling at the door. But did they despair? No. They sowed a seed of faith. They went into some nearby church and gave their last few remaining dollars to the preacher, confident that God would thereby reward them with material blessings. And not long afterward, sometimes that very same day, they received a financial windfall seemingly out of nowhere. Such is the power of faith.

In support of their position, the prosperity preachers turn to their Bibles. They're especially fond of quoting several passages from the New Testament.

"Therefore I tell you, whatever you ask for in prayer, believe that you have received it, and it will be yours." (Mark 11:24)

"I have come that they may have life, and have it the full." (John 10:10)

"You may ask me for anything in my name, and I will do it." (John 14:14)

However, there are other New Testament passages that would seem to run directly counter to the prosperity Gospel. These the preachers conveniently ignore.

"Do not store up for yourselves treasures on earth, where moths and vermin destroy, and where thieves break in and steal." (Matthew 6:19)

"When Jesus heard this, he said to him, 'You still lack one thing. Sell everything you have and give to the poor, and you will have treasure in heaven . . . How hard it is for the rich to enter the kingdom of God!' " (Luke 18:22–24)

To be fair, not all prosperity preachers come across as high-pressure salesmen. Some—the Houston-based pastor Joel Osteen, for example—prefer a more nuanced, laid-back approach. They'll preach prosperity without hitting their audience over the head with it. But quite a few others operate as if there's sinfulness in subtlety. They're shrill and aggressive, and not always above trying to make poor people feel guilty about being poor. After all, isn't poverty a consequence of lack of faith, a matter of not fully trusting in God's promise? It's among preachers of this sort that financial success seems almost to have taken over for the cross as the defining symbol of Christianity.

Joyce Meyer defines herself first and foremost as a practical Bible teacher. There's no question, however, that she's also a prosperity preacher. During her public appearances, she's not in the least shy about proclaiming the material benefits of faith. Nor is she shy about invoking her own good fortune as a shining example of such. God has made her rich, she says, and there's no reason to think that he won't make you rich also. "If you stay in your faith, you are going to get paid," she once told an audience in Detroit. "I'm living now in my reward."

Meyer made this comment in 2003, several years after her ministry had exploded in popularity. At the time, her reward for staying in the faith included a $10 million corporate jet, a $2 million house for her and her husband, Dave, and houses worth an additional $2 million for their four children. It also included a $500,000 vacation home on Lake of the Ozarks, a $105,000 Crownline boat, and Dave's $107,000 silver-gray Mercedes sedan. And this wasn't even the half of it.

In November 2003 the *St. Louis Post-Dispatch* ran a story about Joyce Meyer's corporate headquarters in Fenton, Missouri, which was built two years previously for a cool $20 million. From the outside, the gleaming glass-and-brick office complex with manicured grounds might almost have passed for a hotel in some swanky resort. Its interior was no less impressive.

Through a Jefferson County assessor's report, the *Post-Dispatch* learned that Meyer's ministry had spent nearly $5.7 million outfitting the complex. No one, of course, could fault the ministry for spending money on computers and basic office furnishings. But what about the $49,000 for a conference table and matching chairs, or the $44,000 in woodwork for Joyce's office and her husband Dave's? Or the $11,000 for a French clock, the $19,000 for a pair of Dresden vases, and the $18,500 for six crystal vases?

The assessor's report listed quite a few other expenditures of this sort. There was the $30,000 for a malachite round table, for example, and the $14,000 for a custom office book-case. There was also a fleet of vehicles worth an estimated $440,000, including Joyce Meyer's Lexus SC sports car with a retractable roof. And for sheer ostentation—sheer vainglory—perhaps nothing beat the $23,000 that the ministry spent on a marble-topped antique commode for Meyer's private office suite.

In an interview with the *Post-Dispatch*, Meyer was unapologetic about such extravagance. "You can be a businessman here in St. Louis, and people think the more you have, the more wonderful it is," she said. "But if you're a preacher, then all of a sudden it becomes a problem. The Bible says, 'Give and it shall be given unto you.' "

Meyer certainly isn't averse to asking her followers to give. The *Post-Dispatch* attended several of her conferences in 2003, where the appeal for money was loud and insistent. "Make your checks payable to Joyce Meyer Ministries/Life in the Word," she urged an audience in Buffalo, adding that, "And million is spelled M-I-L-L-I-O-N." Earlier the same year in St. Louis, she went so far as to ask for a $7 million check. "That would really bless me," she said.

Meyer doesn't seriously expect conference-goers to bless her quite so lavishly. However, she does expect them to fork over as much money as possible for ministry merchandise.

When it comes to hawking merchandise, a Joyce Meyer conference is something to behold.

At the conferences attended by the *Post-Dispatch*, there were calendars and coffee mugs for sale. There were books and CDs and audiotapes. Large video displays on either side of the stage flashed advertisements. "Buy $500 worth of product and get $100 free." "The music now playing is from our *Free at Last* CD and is available at the product table." Joyce Meyer's daughter, Laura, took the stage several minutes ahead of her mom and urged those in the audience who hadn't yet done so to load up on books and other merchandise. She assured them that the lines at the product tables would move quickly, since there were fifteen Life in the Word employees working the cash registers.

The selling didn't slacken even when Meyer herself came onstage. She sang and she preached. She quoted scripture and cracked jokes. She mugged for the audience. And through it all, she rarely missed an opportunity to appeal for money.

"Sowing and reaping is a law," she informed the Buffalo audience. "If you sow, you will reap. I believe stingy people are very unhappy people. I want you to give your best offering. I believe one person could write one check to cover all of the expenses of this one conference."

It would be wrong to say that a Joyce Meyer conference is strictly about money. But money is certainly a big part of it. And conference-goers seem not to mind this in the least. They seem not to mind that Meyer leads the life of a pasha. That she wears designer outfits and expensive jewelry, and stays only at the most luxurious of hotels on her tour stops. Insofar as they're concerned, Joyce Meyer can do no wrong.

And give Meyer her due. For all of her excesses, she's by no means the most egregious or heavy-handed of prosperity preachers in the land. She'll routinely warn her followers against placing too great an emphasis on monetary blessings, saying this could result in a distorted faith. She'll encourage them to strive for balance in spiritual and practical matters alike. She'll funnel significant monies from her ministry into worthy charitable projects. And to a greater extent than many of her rivals on the evangelical scene, she'll aim for transparency and accountability with her ministry's bookkeeping.

Still, she has her detractors: people who resent her sumptuous lifestyle, and who believe that the prosperity Gospel is mere gimmickry intent on exploiting the poor and subverting authentic Christianity. One can well appreciate why Joyce Meyer would be concerned with security. Who could tell, after all, what her detractors might be capable of? Who could guarantee that one or more of them might not resort to violence?

It was Chris Coleman's job to make certain that nothing of the sort ever happened. It was his job to keep Joyce Meyer safe.

PART THREE

Columbia Lakes

CHAPTER SIX

In early 2004, Chris Coleman was awarded a hefty pay hike. He was now making $76,000 per year, which meant that he and Sheri were finally in a position to move out of the Joyce Meyer rental home and purchase a home of their own. The only question was where. They scouted around and decided on the small city of Columbia, which is located on the bluffs of the Mississippi River in Monroe County, Illinois. By just about any criteria, it seemed a sensible decision.

With only about thirty thousand people, Monroe County is easily the most sparsely populated county in the metropolitan St. Louis area. A majority of its residents are descended from Germans who came to the region during the mid-nineteenth century and turned their talents to farming. The county remains largely agricultural even today, with wheat, corn, and soybeans the principal crops.

There are just two cities of any note in Monroe County, both with populations of roughly ten thousand. One of these is Waterloo, which is the county seat. The other is Columbia, which is in the northern part of the county and a scant twenty-minute drive from downtown St. Louis across the Jefferson Barracks Bridge.

Columbia actually consists of two rather distinct communities. There are the longtime residents, the locals, most of whom live in the older section of town. The locals are overwhelmingly white, staunchly Republican, and culturally conservative. Many of them work for either Walmart or the school district, which are the two biggest employers in town.

Then there are the newcomers, a growing population of upwardly mobile people who have moved to Columbia from elsewhere in recent years for the easy lifestyle, the excellent school system, and the low crime rate. The newcomers are mostly white also, though somewhat more diverse politically than the locals tend to be. They're commuters for the most part, driving daily across the river to white-collar jobs in either south St. Louis County or St. Louis proper.

With few exceptions, the newcomers live not in the older section of town but rather in a relatively new subdivision known as Columbia Lakes. Some of them scarcely venture into the older section, preferring instead to make the short drive across the Jefferson Barracks Bridge into Missouri for shopping and recreation. Columbia Lakes might lie within Columbia's municipal boundaries, but in practical terms it's almost an entity unto itself.

Construction for the subdivision got under way in the early 1980s when a developer purchased a couple hundred acres of farmland that included several artificial lakes. The previous owner of the land had created the lakes years before and rented them out for fishing. Apartments went up during the first phase of construction, and then spacious, single-family homes on faux-bucolic streets during subsequent phases.

Sheri, Chris, and the boys moved into Columbia Lakes in the spring of 2004. Their new house, which had been built about five years earlier, was at the very end of a winding street called Robert Drive. The house was a white two-story affair with black trim and an attached garage. It seemed the perfect place for raising a family.

Sheri was thrilled.

Vanessa Riegerix lived around the corner from Sheri and Chris's new house on Robert Drive. Vanessa was in her late twenties and slim, pretty, and blond. She had a son, Brandon, who was five years old at the time.

The day after the Colemans moved in, Brandon came racing home in a state of obvious excitement.

"Mom," he said. "I want you to meet these new kids."

Vanessa was aware that a young family had just moved into the big white house around the corner, and she'd been intending to drop over and say hi.

"I want to meet them too," she said. "But I also want to meet their parents."

Vanessa walked to the house on Robert Drive and rang the bell. When no one answered, she went around to the backyard. Two boys were bouncing gleefully on a trampoline. A young woman was bouncing with them, only she was so small that Vanessa at first assumed her to be no more than twelve or thirteen.

The young woman, of course, was Sheri.

"Where's the mom?" Vanessa said.

"I'm the mom!" Sheri cried out, still bouncing on the trampoline with her arms akimbo.

The two women soon became fast friends, and over the next several years they'd see one another almost daily. They'd meet for lunch and then do some gardening or perhaps work on some other household project. As often as not, they'd drive over to south St. Louis County and go shopping.

Vanessa enjoyed shopping for clothes. Sheri positively loved it. She'd always be on the lookout for some new dress or blouse or accessory. She'd especially get a kick out of finding some new bathing suit that flattered her slim figure.

"But do you really need it?" Vanessa would ask. "You already own just about every bathing suit in the store."

"I know," Sheri would say. "But it's so nice."

Sheri would often seem oddly self-conscious about her figure.

"I'm fat," she'd tell Vanessa.

"Really?" Vanessa would say. "Where exactly?"

Vanessa had never before met anyone as innately cheerful as Sheri, or as eager to help out when it was tough going.

One time Vanessa ran into some health problems that landed her in the hospital for several days. Sheri visited her twice daily and saw to it that Vanessa's son and fiancé were properly fed. And on Vanessa's first evening back home, she came over with a big Crock-Pot of lasagna.

Vanessa was impressed. Girlfriends whom she'd known ten years or longer hadn't bothered to make so much as a token appearance during her hour of need.

Chris's job took him away from home for a week or two at a stretch, but Vanessa still saw quite a bit of him. Her impressions were mostly favorable. He'd take her son, Brandon, to the movies with Garett and Gavin. He'd drive all three boys to school whenever he could and then pick them up and bring them home. He'd help Vanessa and her fiancé hang up their outdoor Christmas lights.

"During those early years," she said recently, "I thought he was an absolutely awesome husband and father and friend."

Meegan Turnbeaugh first met Sheri in the late spring of 2004, not long after the Colemans had moved into their new house in Columbia Lakes. Meegan was blond and petite, with green eyes and a winning smile. She was also a veritable dynamo, with enough energy to sustain any four or five ordinary mortals.

Meegan was working on a multimillion-dollar computer project for Joyce Meyer Ministries at the time, and she needed an assistant. She interviewed Sheri for the position and hired her on the spot, and before long the two women were as close as sisters. They'd eat lunch together a couple of times weekly at the St. Louis Bread Company in Fenton. They'd take dance classes together, give one another makeovers, and, of course, go clothes shopping.

Meegan was amazed at how bubbly and loquacious Sheri was. She'd never before heard anyone laugh so much—or talk so much. Sheri would talk endlessly, as if she were racing against time to say everything that needed to be said. If she weren't otherwise so sweet, the constant chatter might almost have become annoying.

But there was far more to Sheri than mere talk. Meegan's older sister, Shauna, was fighting lung cancer at the time, and Sheri played a pivotal role in organizing a benefit to help out with medical expenses. The one-day affair was held in August 2004 at the Eagle's Club in Arnold, Missouri. Anheuser-Busch and several other corporations donated money toward the cause. Kurt Warner, Marshall Faulk, Chris Carpenter, and other local sports heroes donated signed memorabilia. After all was said and done, about $20,000 was raised.

Shauna died the following year, when the cancer metastasized into her brain, but Meegan would never forget the efforts that Sheri had made on her behalf.

Sheri's conversion to evangelical Christianity hadn't been a passing phase. She seemed to be growing more devout by the month. She'd pray daily and attend church as often as she could. She'd talk about God with Meegan and leave inspirational scriptures on her desk. And she'd sometimes send Joyce Meyer–authored books to family members in Chicago.

The conversion seemed to have distanced Sheri from some of those very same family members. Her newfound faith was of utmost importance to her, and yet it wasn't easy to share it with them. They seemed stuck in their old ways, nominal Catholics who rarely read scripture and knew nothing about speaking in tongues. They seemed to inhabit a different universe.

Meegan's husband, Lonnie, was an intelligent, soft-spoken man who also worked for Joyce Meyer Ministries. He and Meegan lived in a beautiful house in a secluded corner of south St. Louis County, and they'd occasionally invite Sheri, Chris, and the boys over for dinner. Sometimes they'd arrange to spend an afternoon or an evening with just Sheri and Chris. They might go to the movies, or perhaps pistol shooting at the Wil-Nor hunt club in Dittmer, Missouri. There weren't many things that Sheri and Chris seemed to enjoy more than shooting pistols at a gun range.

Meegan and Lonnie had the advantage of knowing Chris not only socially but also professionally, by virtue of working with him at the ministry. Meegan liked and respected him, and considered him a friend. She believed him to be smart and confident, if not especially articulate. She'd never heard a single person at work suggest that he was anything other than a top-flight security man.

Lonnie liked him also, though he thought that Chris could sometimes come across as arrogant in the workplace. He'd heard reports of him snubbing people and behaving as if he were a cut above everybody else.

Meegan and Lonnie both thought that Garett and Gavin were terrific kids.

"They were real boys," Lonnie said recently. "They loved playing sports, anything rough-and-tumble. They had so much vim and vigor, they could tear up a ball bearing."

"But they were also pretty disciplined for kids their age," Meegan added. "If they were getting a bit rambunctious, all Chris had to do was give them a look and they'd straighten up right away. If Chris wasn't around and they started to act up, Sheri would say, 'I'm going to call your dad,' and sometimes she would call him. This would definitely get their attention."

Neither Meegan nor Lonnie ever saw Chris lay a hand on the boys. Doling out physical punishment seemed to run against his grain.

Significant perks came with being the head of security for Joyce Meyer Ministries. Not the least of these was having the chance to participate in quarterback Kurt Warner's annual flag football game.

Kurt Warner was a celebrated figure in the St. Louis area, admired not only for leading the NFL Rams to victory in Super Bowl XXXIV but also for the charitable work that he performed under the auspices of his First Things First foundation. Every year the foundation would host a flag football game at the Rams practice facility in Earth City, Missouri. Warner was a good friend of Joyce Meyer, and he'd usually quarterback her ministry's team at the event. Quite a few other sports heroes would also participate, including Warren Moon, Donovan McNabb, and Phil Simms.

Lonnie Turnbeaugh played for the Joyce Meyer Ministries team, and so, too, did Chris Coleman. Chris played five straight years. He loved cavorting with the stars and catching touchdown passes from Kurt Warner.

He must've thought that he was practically a star himself.

CHAPTER SEVEN

When Chris was preoccupied with Joyce Meyer–related business, Sheri would sometimes pack up the boys and drive to Chicago for a couple of days. She'd visit her mom and Mario, of course, and she'd also make a special point of visiting her godfather, Joe Miglio, his wife, and their two kids.

Joe Miglio was a tall, handsome man with a talent for living life the right way. He'd rarely speak ill of anyone. He'd give everyone he met the benefit of the doubt. He'd treat people with utmost respect unless they proved themselves undeserving of it. Joe Miglio was a study in class.

Joe was more than twenty years older than Mario and Sheri, and so people would sometimes assume that he was their uncle. But this wasn't the case. His mother, Marion, was Mario and Sheri's mom's older sister, which made him their first cousin. Joe Miglio spent quite a bit of time with Mario and Sheri when they were kids in Cicero. He'd visit their house and take them to White Sox games at the old Comiskey Park. Once he took Mario on a deep-sea fishing trip to Florida.

Eventually Joe got married and had two kids of his own: Joseph, who was born in 1986, and Jenna, three years later. Sheri would baby sit them when she was just twelve years old. It was a great job for her. She thought the world of Joseph and Jenna, and their dad was certain to pay her well.

After their parents got divorced, Mario and Sheri grew even closer to Joe Miglio, whom they came to regard as a surrogate father of sorts. They also grew closer to Joseph and Jenna, whom they now counted as not merely second cousins but also as best friends.

So Sheri was certain to visit the Miglio household in Palos Park whenever she happened to be in the Chicago area with her boys. And where once Sheri babysat Joseph and Jenna, now it was Jenna who was mostly given the job of babysitting Garett and Gavin.

Jenna bore a striking resemblance to Sheri—so much so that she might almost have been mistaken for her. She, too, was pretty and petite, with fine features and lustrous hair. She, too, was ebullient and never at a loss for words. And both young women possessed a certain impulsive streak. They tended to say whatever came to their minds, rarely bothering to tally up the potential consequences.

Jenna would take the boys into the family basement while everybody else talked upstairs. The basement was equipped with a slot machine, an arcade game, and an Xbox, so there was little chance of the boys ever getting bored. They could easily while away an hour or so just on the Xbox, playing baseball and other sports games.

Jenna found Garett to be much the calmer and quieter of the two. He was perfectly happy keeping to himself, assembling Transformers, reading comic books, or creating his own fantasy games with action figures.

Gavin, on the other hand, was very much the extrovert. When he was just six years old, Sheri enrolled him in a hip-hop dance class at a studio in Columbia, and he loved to show off his latest moves. Jenna was a dancer herself, and they'd have dance contests in the basement. One day he told her that he'd learned how to spin on his head and then proceeded to give her a demonstration. Jenna was impressed. This was something that even she couldn't do. She filmed the demonstration on her cell phone, and afterward showed it to her friends.

"Can you believe this kid?" she said. "He's utterly fearless."

In early April 2005, Jenna, Joseph, and their dad spent a couple of days at Sheri and Chris's house in Columbia Lakes. Jenna played on the trampoline in the backyard with Garett and Gavin, who got a kick out of showing her the flips that they'd been perfecting over the previous year. There was also a new pond in the yard, which the boys treated as their own personal adventure land. They'd skip stones across the water or fashion boats out of various household objects and set them afloat.

It was the final weekend of the NCAA March Madness tournament, and Joseph and his dad had tickets for the championship game between Illinois and North Carolina at the Edward Jones Dome in downtown St. Louis. On the evening of the game, Jenna and Sheri went to a free outdoor concert in St. Louis starring Kelly Clarkson, who'd risen to fame after winning the inaugural season of the *American Idol* television series. Jenna and Sheri were huge fans of *American Idol*, and they loved Kelly Clarkson.

For the first several numbers they were stuck at the back of the crowd, unable to see the stage, since they were both so short. Sheri grabbed Jenna's arm and led her, bobbing and weaving, right up to the very front row. Nobody complained about their stealing their way to the front. How could anybody complain? They were both so tiny and sweet. They looked like a couple of teenyboppers.

Jenna and Sheri had a blast at the concert. They swayed to the music and sang along to their favorite tunes. They took lots of pictures on their cell phones.

Jenna wasn't especially close to Chris. She saw him only once or twice a year, largely because he was on the road so much with Joyce Meyer. On the basis of their limited contact, however, she was favorably impressed. Chris struck her as an attentive father and a good husband. Not once did she pick up any negative vibes from him. If pressed on the matter, she'd have said that she liked him.

In late 2006, Sheri visited the Miglio household in Palos Park with her two boys. She told Jenna that Chris was away on ministry-related business and that she really missed him. Jenna thought that this was sweet. Sheri and Chris had been married for quite a few years by then, and yet, they still seemed very much in love. Their romance hadn't faded.

Jenna was envious of this. It was something that she wanted for herself.

Don Weiss was still in contact with Sheri, though their relationship hadn't deepened as he'd hoped it would. Not long after the weekend visit to Affton in August 2002, he'd invited her to attend his and his fiancée Deborah's wedding in Florida. Sheri had agreed to come but then hadn't shown up. Nor had she bothered to explain why.

Don had continued to correspond with Sheri via e-mail and also to chat occasionally over the phone. But their communications had remained frustratingly fragile. It was almost as if they were casual acquaintances rather than father and daughter.

Don's frustration finally boiled over in early 2007. He'd always sign off his e-mails to Sheri with some expression of affection. "I love you," he'd write. "I miss you." But Sheri would never reciprocate, preferring instead to maintain a tone of bland cordiality. Don sent her an angry e-mail taking her to task for this. Sheri responded with several angry e-mails of her own, and then she severed communications altogether. Once again she refused to have anything to do with him. The promise of that wonderful August weekend in 2002 seemed to have come to naught.

Don would talk with his mother and his two brothers about the situation. "Give her time," they'd tell him.

But Don doubted that he could afford to give her much more time. He worried that time was passing them by.

CHAPTER EIGHT

Sheri was blessed with wonderful friendships during the years that she lived in Columbia Lakes. There was her neighbor Vanessa, who would happily take care of Garett and Gavin for a week at a time when Sheri was away on a mission trip. There was Meegan, who was fiercely loyal and a bundle of energy in her own right. And there was also Kathy LaPlante.

Kathy was an attractive, thoughtful woman who worked for a number of years at Joyce Meyer Ministries, which was where she first met Sheri. The two women would chat now and again at the complex in Fenton, but their friendship didn't really blossom until the fund-raiser for Meegan's sister in 2004, when they spent time together at a face-painting booth. As was the case with so many others, Kathy found Sheri's zeal for life—her sheer joyfulness—irresistible.

Kathy, her husband, Bob, and their four children lived in a nice house in Fenton. The backyard was larger than some city parks, and the basement featured a spacious, comfortable recreation room with a wraparound couch. The place was perfect for kids, and Sheri would drop off her boys almost on a weekly basis while she went to work or took care of other business.

Garett and Gavin loved hanging out at the LaPlante home. They'd shoot hoops in the backyard with Kathy and

Bob's son, Alex, who was about a year older than Garett. They'd grab big pillows from the living room and slide down the stairs from the kitchen on them. They'd watch cartoons on the television in the recreation room, or they'd settle in with popcorn for a full-length movie. (Their favorites were *Indiana Jones*, *Star Wars*, and *Transformers*.) They'd play the SpongeBob SquarePants edition of Monopoly or Super Smash Bros. Brawl on the video game console. On Sundays in the fall, they'd try to catch a Chicago Bears game on TV. Both boys thought that Bears linebacker Brian Urlacher was just about the best player in the entire NFL.

It was actually more fun for Garett and Gavin to hang out at the LaPlante house than it was their own house in Columbia Lakes. Neither Kathy nor Bob was in the least uptight, and they were more than happy to let the boys have the run of the place. The boys didn't have to worry about their dad getting upset with them for making a mess or talking too loudly.

Sheri would sometimes come by with the boys and hang out herself for a couple of hours. She'd sit in the kitchen and talk with Kathy over a cup of coffee. Or she'd play Guitar Hero with Kathy and Bob's son, Austin, who was a bright and sociable kid just then entering his mid-teens. She was especially fond of the song "No Sleep till Brooklyn" by the Beastie Boys, for which she'd lay down a backing drum track to Austin's lead guitar track.

Occasionally Chris, too, would come by and all of the adults would go out for the evening, entrusting care of the boys to Kathy and Bob's daughter, Audrey. Sheri was always fashionable, and she'd enjoy getting dolled up for these evenings out. She'd put on makeup, some super-cute ensemble, and her latest pair of high heels. Sheri loved high heels, *really* high ones. Kathy sometimes marveled that she was even able to stay upright on them.

Sheri appreciated the kindness that the LaPlante family showed her, and she was always looking for ways to reciprocate. One day she marched into their house with a measuring tape and announced that she intended to remodel the kitchen, which was beginning to look rather the worse for wear. She ordered new appliances and oversaw their installation, and then she and Kathy repainted the walls and cupboards a nifty black and white. Once everything was done, the room looked stunning.

Kathy had mixed feelings about Chris, with whom she worked fairly closely at Joyce Meyer Ministries. She handled international travel arrangements for the ministry, which involved booking hotels and planes for out-of-country conferences. She'd then feed this information to Chris so that he could make proper provisions for security, and sometimes she'd also travel with him to these conferences. She'd found that he could really turn on the charm when dealing with foreign dignitaries and other people whom he wanted to impress. In more routine interactions with coworkers, however, he tended to be cold, abrupt, and dismissive. The guy could change color as easily as a chameleon.

Kathy's husband, Bob, was pastor of the St. Louis Dream Center, which was an inner-city church run by Joyce Meyer Ministries. It would be hard to imagine anyone better suited for such a position. Bob was smart, practical, and humble. He had the sort of deep religious faith that didn't require much in the way of personal advertising. It simply shined through.

Bob had fashioned a decent relationship with Chris over the years, if not an especially deep one. "Whenever he was away at conferences, we'd instant-message one another," he said recently. "Just small talk, nothing heavy. We never really graduated much beyond small talk. It was sort of the framework that we operated within."

Chris had cultivated a highly stylized look by this point. It was the Chris Coleman cool-guy look. His head was shaved and he sported a blond goatee. He wore aviator sunglasses and designer jeans. He carried himself with a certain swagger, a studied aloofness. "That was Chris," Bob said. "He was the spy, doing this secretive security work that none of us fully understood. All of our kids admired him. He was the cool uncle kind of guy."

* * *

Religion continued to play a critical role in Sheri's life. And during the spring of 2006, she'd started to attend a new church in the St. Louis area. It was called Destiny Church. Sheri loved the worship and the fellowship at Destiny, which she believed to be deeply inspirational. She was convinced that she'd found her true spiritual home.

From the outside, Destiny Church seems anything but inspirational. Located in a dreary stretch of suburbia, and facing busy Interstate 270, it's a modern cinder-block building with high, narrow windows. Apart from a small cross perched atop a slender, tapered pole at the front of the building, the overall effect is one of bland functionality.

Sheri seems not to have been bothered by any of this. She'd faithfully attend the 6:00 p.m. service on Saturdays, almost always bringing her two sons with her. Chris would often join them, and before long so, too, would Kathy LaPlante and her youngest child, Alex.

In early 2007, Sheri left Joyce Meyer Ministries and became the personal secretary of Phil Stern, who was a founding pastor of Destiny Church. Among other tasks, she did preparatory work for the church's mission teams, and she also accompanied them on various trips to Asia and Latin America. After one of these trips, she somehow finally found time to undertake—and complete—training to become an emergency medical technician.

Sheri would eventually also work for a year as the receptionist at Destiny Church, which was a position that Pastor Phil Stern thought suited her to a T. "She was the sort of very bubbly person that you definitely wanted up front," he said recently.

In November 2007, Sheri, Garett, and Gavin, along with Kathy LaPlante and her daughter, Audrey, drove up to Chicago for a weekend.

Mario was running a valet service out of a local restaurant at the time, and he was surprised when they dropped by to see him. He'd had no idea that they were coming. He gave

Garett a big hug and Gavin a kiss on the top of his head. (He realized that Gavin wasn't a big fan of hugging.)

Mario introduced them to the owner of the restaurant, Frankie, who insisted on paying for everybody's meals. Sheri and the gang had a nice dinner, and the next day they toured Chicago and took in a performance of the Blue Man Group.

During the drive home, Sheri really opened up to Kathy. She talked about her parents' divorce and her estrangement from her dad, and about how her older cousin, Joe Miglio, had become a kind of father figure to her. She talked about Chris's frantic work schedule and about how she hated that he was away from home so often. She said that she'd discussed this with Chris and that he'd seemed open to the possibility of leaving Joyce Meyer Ministries and perhaps starting up his own security company somewhere in the Columbia area.

She also talked about Chris's parents, Ron and Connie Coleman. She said that she'd never really felt loved or accepted by them. That they'd accused her of getting pregnant on purpose so that Chris would have to marry her.

She showed Kathy a tiny tattoo that she'd gotten on her left ankle years before. She said that she'd love to get a matching tattoo on the other ankle but that she didn't dare do so. Chris hadn't wanted her to get the first, and he'd be enraged if she went ahead and got yet another. Chris's father, the Reverend Ron Coleman, didn't approve of tattoos.

Heaven forbid that Sheri should do anything that ran contrary to the Reverend Ron's wishes.

CHAPTER NINE

Insofar as her in-laws were concerned, Sheri was probably fighting a losing battle. It seemed highly doubtful that she'd ever succeed in winning their affection. Ron and Connie seem to have disliked her from the very start, and to have disliked her more with each passing year.

Despite realizing that she failed to meet their approval, Sheri continued to drive down to Chester with Chris and the boys several times monthly. She'd visit with Ron and Connie in their home. She'd participate in family cookouts. She'd go to Wednesday evening services at Grace Church. She'd sometimes help out at the church's summer camp for children in Peaceful Valley, Missouri.

Several former members of Grace Church have fond memories of Sheri. They say that they always found her to be a real sweetheart, laughing, joking, trying to put a smile on everybody's face. They say that her mere presence was almost guaranteed to brighten up a room.

But Ron and Connie appear to have been immune to Sheri's charms. A couple of the former church members say that Connie in particular seemed to have disliked her. They say that she'd often curl up her lips when Sheri spoke. That she'd make snide comments behind her back. At one church-related gathering, Sheri mentioned that she'd been a cheerleader in high school and jokingly suggested that she might consider trying out for the St. Louis Rams cheerleading squad.

"So disgusting," Connie supposedly commented when Sheri was out of earshot. "Who does she think she is?"

Sheri had several marks against her. Ron and Connie disliked her for getting pregnant in the first place and marrying their oldest son. According to some people, they disliked her for her Italian Catholic background. But perhaps the thing that rankled them most was her indomitable spirit. Sheri could be fiercely stubborn. Once she'd committed herself to something, she wasn't easily knocked off course. Here was a young woman, after all, who'd joined the Air Force upon graduating high school over the protests of her older brother. Who'd started a new life in the culturally unfamiliar precincts of southwestern Illinois. Who'd converted to a faith that went against the grain of her family background. Who'd kept alive a cold war with her dad despite his desperate wishes for détente.

Sheri wasn't inclined to bend to people's wills. In a thousand and one ways, she must've conveyed this to her in-laws. She could be sweet and solicitous, but in the end she'd almost certainly do things her own way. She wouldn't be brought fully under Ron and Connie's control.

In their eyes, this was perhaps her most grievous sin.

Ron and Connie had apparently grown accustomed to having people brought under their control. Over the years, according to the former members, they'd turned Grace Church into their own private fiefdom. They'd turned it into something resembling an authoritarian cult.

The ex-members say that it hadn't started out this way. Somewhere along the line, however, Ron had gotten hungry for power. He'd insist that churchgoers submit to him completely. He'd bridle at the slightest challenge to his authority, suggesting that disobeying him was tantamount to disobeying God. That anyone who dared question him was in an obvious state of spiritual rebellion.

Ron ruled the church like a paranoid dictator, the ex-members say. He didn't trust anyone. He was always on the lookout for signs of dissent among the flock. He'd insist that his handpicked elders accompany churchgoers on even the most innocent of excursions, such as a bus trip to St. Louis for a show. And then he'd insist that the elders report back to him as soon as possible. The only catch here was that he apparently didn't trust them much more than he trusted anybody else. On more than one occasion, he called elders into his office and berated them for not being sufficiently compliant to him.

According to some ex-church members, Ron deployed a number of other mechanisms for keeping potential dissidents in line. One of these was threatening them with outright expulsion. "This is my church," he'd say. "If you don't like the way I'm running things, then you can leave." Or perhaps his favorite line: "If you don't like it here, there's the door. Don't let it hit you on the butt on your way out."

Another mechanism, according to ex-church members, was old-fashioned fear. He'd apparently insist that Grace Church was the only true church and that anyone not fully in tune with its teachings—or its pastor—was putting their eternal salvation at risk. He'd back this up with stories of people who'd left the church only to lapse into lives of terrible sin and despair.

Another was the threat of ostracism. People who departed the fold were apparently treated as total outcasts. They were cut off entirely from friends and family members within the church, who weren't permitted so much as to acknowledge their existence. By some accounts, this meant shunning departed members even during casual encounters at the grocery store, the gas station, and so forth.

Still another mechanism involved the allocation of voluntary positions at the church. Positions of this sort—whether in the choir, Sunday school, or elsewhere—were much sought after by church members. They carried with them a certain status or prestige. They gave the people who held them a decided edge in the congregational pecking order. But Ron would apparently award these positions only to people who demonstrated unflinching allegiance to him. And if their allegiance should show any sign of faltering, he'd threaten to strip them of the positions and award them to others more evidently in line with the program.

Ron was reportedly much influenced by a book entitled *Sheep, Goats and . . . Wolves*, which seems to have been mandatory reading for his church elders. Written by an evangelical minister named Mark T. Barclay, the book claims that there are three different kinds of people within any Christian congregation. The "sheep" are meek and docile, the "goats" stubborn and uncooperative, and the "wolves" dangerous and subversive.

Some people felt that Ron only wanted sheep in Grace Church. He had no use whatsoever for goats or wolves. He wanted nothing less than total control.

Hardly an eloquent presence in the pulpit at the best of times, Ron's preaching seems to have gotten progressively worse as his appetite for power grew. According to some ex-church members, he'd sometimes resort to angry shouting and screaming.

They recall that he also loved to play the role of the reluctant prophet, thrust against his will into a position of terrible responsibility. "Do you think I want this job?" he'd sometimes say, or words to the same effect. "I have no choice in the matter. God's called me to it. He's made me your pastor. He's entrusted me with the care of your souls. So, of course, I have authority over you."

Connie was also a licensed minister by this point, and churchgoers would commonly refer to her as Pastor Connie. She'd preside over women's retreats at the church, and also women's Bible studies. She'd sometimes take to the pulpit, though not nearly as often as her husband would. Some ex-members say that she was actually a better preacher than Ron, calmer, more scriptural—not nearly as condescending. As often as not, she'd sit quietly in the front pew during services unless convinced that she'd received some word of knowledge or encouragement from the Holy Spirit. Then she'd stand up and face the congregation and share whatever word she'd received. While doing so, she'd often speak in tongues.

The ex-members say that Connie, too, had changed for the worse over the years. Once as nice as pie, she could now be spiteful and manipulative. She was quick to take offense at seemingly harmless remarks, and she harbored long grudges.

Connie had always tried to model herself after Joyce Meyer, and both she and Ron remained huge fans of Meyer's ministry. Like Meyer, Ron and Connie taught a prosperity Gospel and tried to give their preaching a practical slant. The admiration may very well have been mutual. Joyce Meyer had known Ron and Connie since her earliest days as an evangelist, and there were rumors that she'd donated $100,000 to help pay off the last of Grace Church's debt.

Ron and Connie were thrilled that their oldest son, Chris, had landed so high-profile a position with Meyer's ministry. They enjoyed the prestige that this gave them as Chris's parents. It made them feel like real insiders. They'd gossip about Joyce Meyer's personal foibles, and her likes and dislikes. They'd talk about what a shopaholic she was, and how Chris would get tired simply carrying her bags from the shopping mall out to the parking lot. They'd talk about how Joyce would sometimes buy things for Chris, such as a nice shirt or a pair of designer jeans.

By this point, Chris was not only the head of security for the ministry but also Joyce Meyer's personal bodyguard. He'd accompany her everywhere. He was her veritable shadow. "I guess I'm pretty close to Joyce," he bragged to his parents, "'cause I know her bra and panty size." He once confided to his mother that the job of bodyguard mostly amounted to looking the part. "The bald head, being beefed up, never smiling—it's all intimidation, 99 percent of it," he said.

Chris apparently didn't confide to his mother a crucial component to looking the part. Once no more than 165 pounds sopping wet, he was now heavily muscled and pushing the 190 mark. The guy was buff. Was this merely because of his daily workouts at the gym, or was he also taking steroids?

Ron and Connie seem to have been proud of all three of their sons. Their second oldest, Brad, was now married with a couple of kids, and working full-time as a guard at Menard Correctional Center and part-time with the Chester Police Department. Their youngest, Keith, had done a stint as a Marine in Iraq, and Ron apparently enjoyed referring to him as "a real killing machine."

But their favorite was Chris. He was their oldest and the one for whom they'd always had the highest expectations. In their eyes, Chris could scarcely do wrong.

Their only misgiving about Chris seems to have been his choice of a spouse. Besides her other defects, Sheri apparently wasn't docile enough for their tastes. She wasn't sufficiently compliant.

Sheri was no sheep.

CHAPTER TEN

In January 2008, Sheri told Chris in no uncertain terms that she wanted him to quit his job at Joyce Meyer Ministries. She told him that his long absences from home were putting too great a strain on their marriage. She told him that the job simply wasn't worth all of the trouble.

Chris seemed to agree. He told Sheri that he'd seriously pursue the idea of leaving the ministry and starting his own video-surveillance company, or perhaps opening a gym in Columbia. He said that he looked forward to spending more time at home with her and the boys.

But it didn't happen. Instead he got another handsome increase in salary, which meant that he was now making $100,000, and he decided to stay put. He arranged for someone from the office to send flowers to Sheri on Valentine's Day, since he was away at yet another in a seemingly endless series of out-of-town conferences. The job, which had initially seemed so promising, was now an open sore in their marriage.

On the whole, however, the marriage still seemed solid.

In late February 2008, Joe Miglio's daughter, Jenna, flew in from Chicago for a visit. She rented a car at the airport and drove across the Jefferson Barracks Bridge to the house in Columbia Lakes. Sheri was at her receptionist's job at Destiny Church when she arrived, and Garett and Gavin were at school. Chris was home alone, packing for another ministry-related trip.

Jenna hung out in the living room and watched *America's Best Dance Crew* on MTV. Chris joined her after he'd finished packing, and the two of them chatted for a while. They talked about the dance show, which Chris said that Sheri also enjoyed watching. They also talked about Eastern Illinois University in Charleston, where Jenna was enrolled for the second semester of her freshman year.

It occurred to Jenna that she'd never before spoken so much with Chris. She found the experience actually quite pleasant.

When the show was over, they got some takeout and joined Sheri for a late lunch at Destiny Church. This, too, proved very nice. If Sheri and Chris were experiencing marital problems, they certainly gave no indication of it. Jenna thought that everything seemed just fine between them.

Jenna and Sheri saw Chris off at the airport after lunch, then picked up Garett and Gavin from school. The boys were thrilled to see Jenna. She'd always been one of their favorites.

The two boys seemed to be flourishing during the winter of 2008. Gavin had turned eight on January 25, and older brother Garett was scheduled to celebrate his tenth birthday on April 30. Both boys attended Parkview Elementary School, which was a large cinder-block building located just a short jaunt up Veterans Parkway from Illinois Route 3 on the outskirts of Columbia.

They seemed quite happy at school for rambunctious boys their age, and they were popular among their classmates—especially Gavin, the more sociable of the two. He'd sometimes even hang out with the girls in his grade during recess.

Both boys loved to play sports, and Gavin baseball in particular. He was already gearing up for the upcoming season. Every spring Sheri would sign the boys up for the Columbia Khoury League, which played its games at American

Legion Memorial Park. This was a vast tree-lined space with ten baseball diamonds, located three blocks off North Main Street in the old section of town.

Garett played baseball, too, but his favorite sport by far was football. Both he and Gavin played for the Columbia Blue Jays Peewee team on a field right next to their school. Gavin played center and Garett defensive tackle. Garett's coaches and teammates had nicknamed him "the Claw," because he'd often grab a ball carrier by the jersey and hang on until he'd dragged him to the ground. Whenever he'd tackle a smaller kid especially hard, he'd help him up and apologize. "Sorry," he'd say. "Are you okay?"

Jenna's older brother, Joseph, had photographs of the boys that he always carried in his wallet. They were wearing their royal blue football uniforms in the photos, with COLUMBIA printed across the jerseys and white piping on the sleeves. Garett's uniform number was 18, and Gavin's 16. Each boy was down on one knee, his white helmet lying on the grass beside him and a football tucked under his right arm. Gavin in particular—teeth bared, eyes narrowed—seemed to be aiming for a menacing pose.

Joseph loved these photographs. He thought that the boys looked so very much at home in them, so perfectly happy.

Sheri would make a special point of attending all of their games, and so would Chris if he wasn't on the road with Joyce Meyer. He'd sometimes also help to coach their teams, and he'd always congratulate them for their effort and reward them afterward with sno-cones.

In fact, when Chris was home, he seemed an exemplary father. He'd take the boys out for treats, watch sports with them on TV, and play catch with them in the driveway. Both he and Sheri would take them across the river to Destiny Church for Saturday evening services.

And every single evening that he was home, he'd take Garett and Gavin upstairs to their bedrooms and say prayers with them. Then he'd tuck them into bed and kiss them good night.

* * *

In early May 2008, Chris took the boys to see *Indiana Jones and the Kingdom of the Crystal Skull.* Vanessa Riegerix's fiancé, Chris Beutler, and her son, Brandon, joined them at the movie theater. Afterward Chris took Beutler aside and told him that he and Sheri were mired in debt, and that it was all Sheri's fault. He said that Sheri would routinely charge a thousand dollars to his credit card at the mall. "I'm making one hundred grand a year," he added, "and I've gotta drive around in a clunker."

Sheri, Chris, and the boys visited Vanessa and Beutler's house a couple of weeks later, over the Memorial Day weekend. They played board games and cards, and then Vanessa got into the hot tub with Garett, Gavin, and her own son, Brandon. After a great deal of coaxing from Vanessa, Sheri finally put on a swimsuit and joined them.

It was then that Vanessa noticed that Sheri had a lot of bruises. They were large, nasty bruises, mostly on her upper legs. Vanessa's fiancé noticed them, too, and over the next several weeks both he and Vanessa also noted that Sheri was always careful to cover herself up. She'd wear jeans or long skirts with long-sleeved blouses. She'd never wear anything even remotely revealing.

"Why the long clothes?" Vanessa's fiancé would ask.

Sheri would try to deflect the question, joking about how she was getting so fat that she needed to cover herself up.

It didn't occur to Vanessa at the time that Chris might have been physically abusing Sheri. Vanessa admired Chris. She'd assumed him to be an ideal husband and father. She'd put him on a pedestal.

But there seemed little question that Sheri was being abused by Chris.

One evening a week or so after the Memorial Day weekend, Sheri sent her good friend, Meegan Turnbeaugh, a text message. "Chris is gone right now," the message read. "But he just beat me up. I'm okay, though."

Meegan was aghast. She'd never seen this side of Chris. She'd never even imagined that he had such a side. She showed the text message to her husband, Lonnie, and then phoned Sheri right away.

"Pack your things, Sheri," she said. "Come over to our house with the boys right now. Come over or I'll come and get you."

"No, no," Sheri said. "I'm okay, really. Anyway, Chris is off on a trip for a few days."

"I'm serious," Meegan said. "Let me come over and get you and the boys. It's no trouble at all."

"Honestly, I'm okay," Sheri said. "There's nothing to worry about."

Meegan tried her best to convince Sheri that there was indeed something to worry about. That getting beaten up by your husband was serious business. But Sheri held her ground, insisting that the danger had passed and that she and the boys were just fine.

Whenever she'd meet Sheri for lunch over the following months, Meegan would broach the topic indirectly. She'd ask Sheri how things were going at home. How she and Chris were getting along. She was careful not to push too hard. She was careful to respect Sheri's privacy. She simply wanted to assure her friend that the communication lines were open.

Sheri would generally seem upbeat. She'd suggest that everything was going well. Meegan couldn't tell for sure if this was really true or if her friend was merely putting on an act.

Sheri's three best friends—Meegan, Vanessa, and Kathy LaPlante—weren't close with one another. They inhabited separate spheres of Sheri's life. Though they both worked at Joyce Meyer Ministries, Meegan and Kathy didn't hang out together with Sheri. Meegan would mostly do girlfriend-related stuff with her—taking dance classes, shopping for clothes—whereas Kathy would do church- and family-related things. And Vanessa was the good friend from the neighborhood who knew Meegan and Kathy hardly at all.

Sheri would confide something to one of them, and then something else to another. The three friends never had a chance to compare notes. They never had a chance to put it all together.

* * *

On July 6, 2008, Sheri, Chris, and the boys went to Kathy and Bob LaPlante's house for a barbecue. Everybody had a good time, and Sheri seemed especially upbeat. She told Kathy and Bob that Chris was now well into the planning stages for his own security business, which would finally allow him to leave Joyce Meyer Ministries and spend more time at home.

Shortly afterward Chris went to see Joyce Meyer's son, David L. Meyer, who was his immediate superior at the ministry. He told David that his and Sheri's tenth wedding anniversary was soon coming up. He said that they wanted to celebrate by having a real church wedding and renewing their vows. Toward this end, he asked David for some time off. He asked if somebody else could handle the next international trip, which was scheduled for Ethiopia in September. David refused the request, saying there was simply nobody else properly trained to handle Chris's job. Chris asked if he could at least meet Sheri on the last stop of the trip so that they could spend some precious hours together on their anniversary. Again David said no, saying this was impractical and they'd have to wait for a more convenient time.

Chris wasn't happy that he'd been turned down, especially since he'd amassed plenty of vacation time over the previous several years. Why shouldn't he be permitted to use some of it for an occasion as important as his tenth wedding anniversary?

For the first time, he began to feel truly disgruntled about his work situation. He complained to friends that, due to a shortage of seats on Joyce Meyer's private jet, he'd sometimes have to sleep on the floor. He complained that Joyce would often awaken him by throwing her empty water bottles at him and then order him to fetch her fresh ones. He complained that Joyce and her husband, Dave, would order him to shovel their driveway in the winter, and that their sons, David and Daniel, would sometimes also order him to shovel theirs. He complained about having to lug Joyce's heavy shopping bags from the mall out to the parking lot.

He said that he felt unappreciated, exploited. He was supposed to be the head of security, for heaven's sake, and yet there were times when he was treated like a mere lackey.

He also seemed to have developed some deep ambivalence toward both Joyce Meyer personally and her ministry, which was linked in his mind to his growing ambivalence toward Sheri. He'd complain to Vanessa's fiancé, Chris Beutler, about his "shotgun marriage" and being forced to spend endless hours every week "protecting some millionaire lady I don't even like while my old lady gets to sit at home in this nice big house." He'd suggest that Meyer's ministry was nothing but a scam, saying he found it incredible that there were people making only "fifty grand a year [who'd] write her a check for $10,000."

But he'd sometimes also profess admiration for Joyce Meyer, saying he felt privileged to have the opportunity to work for her. Joyce, after all, was a great evangelist who was spreading God's Word throughout the entire world. Of course he felt privileged to work for her.

For all of his misgivings, however, Chris stayed on with the ministry, and the idea of starting his own security company went nowhere. Perhaps the money and the prestige were too much for him to give up. Perhaps he thought that he was truly serving a sacred cause in protecting Joyce Meyer from harm.

Perhaps he was afraid of disappointing his mom and dad.

In early August 2008, Sheri and Vanessa made a road trip to Chicago. Garett and Gavin were down in Chester for a summer camp at Grace Church at the time, and Vanessa's son, Brandon, was spending the weekend with his father. This meant that the two women had the car all to themselves.

Sheri seemed excited about the idea of spending a couple of days in Chicago with one of her very best friends. She was wearing her cowgirl boots with stiletto heels, which were her favorite boots in the whole world. She almost always wore them when she was excited at the prospect of a little adventure.

The weekend got off to a flying start. They met Sheri's cousin, Enrico Mirabelli, and his wife for a late lunch on their first day in town. Then they toured the Loop district and did some shopping on the Magnificent Mile.

They'd planned on meeting up with Mario for drinks later that evening, and so after they'd finished shopping they drove over to Sheri's mom's place, where Mario was living at the time. But then something odd happened. Sheri asked Vanessa to wait out in the car while she went inside to see them. This was unlike Sheri, who'd normally never leave a friend stranded even for a moment. Was she somehow uncomfortable with the idea of Vanessa meeting her mom and Mario in their home? Or was there perhaps something that she simply wanted to discuss with them in private?

They met Mario at a sports bar a couple of hours later, which worked out very nicely. Vanessa found him warm and convivial, if not quite as chatty as his younger sister. They then went to the hotel where they'd planned on staying, only to encounter an apparent mix-up.

Their names weren't on the reservation list, and all of the rooms were already booked. Chris was supposed to have taken care of this, using travel points that he'd accumulated over the previous year. He'd assured Sheri a day or two earlier that he'd done so.

They found a room at another hotel easily enough, but Sheri seemed miffed. She seemed to think that Chris's failure to make the reservation hadn't merely been an oversight. That it reflected instead some deeper, more serious problem. Out of the blue, she mentioned the name of a guy whom she'd dated for a short while prior to getting married.

"If Chris ever leaves me, I'll go back to him," she said.

The comment caught Vanessa off guard. She'd always thought of Sheri and Chris as the ideal couple. She and her fiancé would jokingly refer to them as "Barbie and Ken with their perfect kids."

The more she mulled it over, the more convinced Vanessa became that she'd had it wrong. Sheri and Chris weren't in fact the ideal couple. Hadn't she herself seen signs of fissure within their marriage, which she hadn't at the time recognized as such? She'd noticed, for example, a certain chilliness between them of late whenever Chris returned home from a Joyce Meyer–related trip. They wouldn't hug or hold hands. They wouldn't communicate much affection at all. She'd also noticed that Chris had started to poke fun at Sheri, calling her dumb and immature. This had struck Vanessa as curious, though she hadn't made much of it. The Sheri she knew was fun loving and goofy, certainly not dumb. And certainly no less mature than Chris himself was.

And then there were those bruises that she and her fiancé had noticed over the Memorial Day weekend, just a couple of months previously. Was it possible that Chris had inflicted those, and that Sheri had worn nothing but jeans or long skirts for several weeks afterward in an effort to cover up still more bruising?

"Listen, Sheri," Vanessa said. "You know I'm your friend, right?"

"Of course," Sheri said.

"So if there's ever anything you want to talk about, please come to me, okay? You know I'm always here for you."

"I know that," Sheri said.

Vanessa knew better than to force the issue. She knew that Sheri had definite boundaries insofar as her private life was concerned. She'd let you know only what she wanted to let you know.

The two friends finally succeeded in putting the botched hotel reservation behind them, and the next day they had a great time shopping and sightseeing. They felt so good on the drive home that they scheduled another trip to Chicago for the following year.

A couple of months later, in early October 2008, Chris came over to Vanessa's house in a state of obvious agitation. He went into the kitchen and started to bang a fist against the countertop. Neither Vanessa nor her fiancé had ever seen him nearly so upset.

"Whoa, Chris," Vanessa said. "What's the problem?"

"The problem?" he said. "I want a divorce. That's the problem."

Vanessa and her fiancé managed to calm Chris down. They pulled out some chairs and sat with him at the kitchen table.

"A divorce?" Vanessa. "Are you serious?"

"Yeah, I'm serious," he said.

"But why?" Vanessa said.

"I'm sick and tired of the way she's spending money," he said.

Vanessa realized that Sheri could spend a lot of money. She realized that shopping was one of her real passions. But surely that wasn't cause enough for something as drastic as a divorce.

"Is that it, Chris?" she said. "Just money problems?"

"That's it," he said.

"Then that's something you guys should be able to work out," Vanessa said. "I'd hate to see you break up just over money."

Chris seemed to consider this for a while. He sat silently at the table with his chin in his hands.

"Okay, I'll wait," he finally said. "I'll wait until after the Christmas holidays to see if anything changes."

"If you'd like, I'd be happy to talk with Sheri about it," Vanessa said.

Sheri telephoned Vanessa two days later. She was crying so hard that she could barely speak.

"What's wrong, Sheri?" Vanessa said.

"Chris is going to leave me," Sheri said, trying to stifle sobs.

"I'll be right over," Vanessa said.

Vanessa went over and sat with Sheri in the living room. As much as she hated to see her friend so distressed, she decided that the time was right for some straight talk.

"Listen, Sheri," she said. "Chris came over and talked with me a couple of days ago."

"Oh?" Sheri said, still shuddering with sobs.

She apparently hadn't been aware of this.

"He told me that you're spending way too much money," Vanessa said. "And let's be honest, Sheri. We both know how much you love to shop."

"Uh-huh," Sheri said.

"I told him that this was something you guys should be able to work out," Vanessa said. "That people shouldn't split up just over money."

Sheri sat up straight. She'd stopped crying now and was wearing a determined expression.

"I'll do whatever it takes to save my marriage," she said.

Vanessa had no doubt that Sheri meant this. However, she didn't want the conversation to end without once again emphasizing that her door was always open.

"Is there anything else, Sheri?" she said. "Anything else you think we should talk about?"

"I don't think so," Sheri said.

"Because you know you can always come to me, right?"

"Thanks," Sheri said. "But I'll be okay."

CHAPTER ELEVEN

Sheri still kept in touch with Tara Lintz, her best friend from high school. Tara was her number one friend on Myspace, and they'd also chat over the phone occasionally.

Tara was divorced now, and still living in the Tampa–St. Petersburg area. She'd held various jobs over the years, including a stint as a hostess at a gentleman's club. For the past five years, she'd been working as a cocktail waitress at the Derby Lane dog track in St. Petersburg.

Tara also knew Chris. She'd visited him and Sheri in Quantico years before, and gone up to see them once at their former home in Affton. And more recently, she'd met up with them while they were vacationing at Disney World. She and Chris might also have exchanged the occasional flirtatious e-mail, though the evidence here is far from clear.

In mid-October 2008, Sheri contacted Tara with big news. Joyce Meyer was scheduled to give a three-day conference in Tampa, beginning on November 6. The featured musical act would be the Australian Christian singer-songwriter Darlene Zschech. Sheri strongly suggested that Tara attend the conference. She'd thought for quite some time that her old high school friend was leading too worldly a lifestyle. She thought that Tara might benefit spiritually from hearing Joyce Meyer preach.

Sheri told Chris that Tara might be at the conference and half-jokingly warned him against meeting up with her. She realized that Tara had a certain way with men.

Chris traveled to Tampa ahead of time so that he could see to all of the necessary security arrangements. Once in town, he got in touch with Tara. They met for dinner and drinks, and did so again the next evening. Then they began to spend every available moment together. They were convinced that they'd fallen in love. They couldn't stand the thought of being out of each other's sight.

They had lots of photographs taken of themselves during those evenings in Tampa. In some of the photos they're nuzzling up against one another in the moonlight. In others they're smooching over a bottle of wine. In all of them, they're smiling fantastically. They look like newlyweds enjoying an especially romantic honeymoon.

They seem to have had sex for the first time on November 5, although Tara would later claim that this didn't happen until mid-December. And once the conference was over, on November 8, Chris asked Joyce Meyer if he could stay behind in Tampa for a few days "to visit with friends."

It's not difficult to imagine why Chris might have become infatuated with Tara. She was gorgeous and sensual. She was hedonistic, uninhibited. And he thought that she appreciated him in a way that Sheri never had, and perhaps never could. She gave him her undivided attention. She told him all the things about himself that he wanted to hear. She told him that he was handsome and witty, and great in bed. She told him that she loved his job with Joyce Meyer Ministries.

It didn't hurt that Tara had entered the picture just when Chris's marriage had hit a rough patch. He was sick of Sheri's reckless spending. And sick of her nagging him about his job. Couldn't she realize that it was no ordinary job? That he was serving a divine purpose in helping Joyce Meyer propagate the Gospel? And perhaps he was also sick of married life with Sheri in general. After ten years, everything had gotten stale and cramped and tired. There was nothing stale or cramped about Tara. With her, every moment was thrilling, intoxicating, wondrous. It was as if he'd been reborn all over again.

Perhaps his mom and dad had been right all along. Perhaps Sheri had indeed trapped him into getting married. Perhaps they really weren't meant for one another.

And Tara's infatuation with Chris? Likewise, the reasons for this aren't hard to fathom. He was eager to please, and no less appreciative of her than she of him. He was indeed a decent-looking guy, and he projected a sort of macho charm. And there seemed no question that he had a fabulous job. He'd told her himself that he played flag football with Kurt Warner, and would sometimes chauffeur the star quarterback around the St. Louis area. He'd told her that he had the cell phone numbers of Joel Osteen and other evangelical celebrities in his company BlackBerry. This was heady stuff for a thirty-plus woman who still entertained dreams of the high life.

Tara Lintz might've been gorgeous, but she also had a limited shelf life. She didn't have much to fall back on once her looks began to fade. And Tara wasn't getting any younger. She'd been stuck at that dog track far too long. Chris might've represented her one last good chance at a slice of happiness.

And there was possibly something else besides. Chris belonged to Sheri, which might very well have affronted Tara's sense of entitlement. Hadn't she been the more attractive of the two in high school? Hadn't it been she who'd had the pick of all the guys? Why should Sheri now have something that she didn't? It must've galled her. It must've made her want Chris all that much more. Sheri wasn't really her best friend. She was actually more like a sibling rival.

Upon returning home from the Tampa conference, Chris went into the basement of the family home on Robert Drive. He opened his Dell laptop and created a document that he entitled "All About Tara." The document was a lover's memorandum of sorts, a testimony to his mounting obsession with Tara Lintz.

He listed every detail that he thought relevant about her. He listed her birthday and also her dog Gizmo's birthday. He listed her height and her weight, and her bra, panties, and jeans sizes. He listed her favorite sports teams, her favorite songs and albums, and her Netflix user account. He listed her favorite brand of perfume and her favorite flavor of ice cream.

Her favorite flowers were tulips and pink roses. Her secret fantasies seemed to consist mostly of having sex on the beach or just about anywhere else outdoors. And she loved jewelry, especially rings featuring a "circle diamond or diamond cross."

He wrote that November 5, 2008, was "the day Tara changed my life." And that his and Tara's future daughter would be named Zoe Lynn Coleman.

Chris and Tara were convinced that they'd each found their perfect match. They were like lovestruck teenagers. A single moment without being in contact was much too long for either of them. They text-messaged back and forth almost constantly. They exchanged racy pictures. They cooed to each other over the phone.

They also talked earnestly about the new life that they planned on having together. They began to plot the particulars.

They'd get married in Florida, hopefully no later than a year or so from then. Then Tara would relocate to the St. Louis area so that Chris could keep his job with Joyce Meyer Ministries. Tara wouldn't have it any other way. The job was one of the things that most impressed her about Chris. She loved the six-figure salary, the prestige, the international travel. She loved its aura of glamour. Tara wasn't cut out to be a hostess at a dog track in St. Petersburg forever.

They'd live in some nice suburban community not unlike Columbia Lakes, though perhaps within easier driving distance of an upscale mall. They'd spend their evenings watching movies and listening to music, and their nights perhaps experimenting with new sex positions. When the time was right, Chris would get his vasectomy reversed and they'd have their love child. They'd have Zoe Lynn, the daughter that they'd been dreaming about.

There were two things holding them back. The first of these, of course, was that Chris was still married to Sheri. Somehow he had to divorce her, and the sooner the better. Tara insisted that he waste no time setting the gears in motion.

Then there was the second thing, which Chris was aware of but Tara wasn't. If he got divorced from Sheri, he'd jeopardize his job at Joyce Meyer Ministries. Joyce Meyer frowned on her employees getting divorced, especially if it was a consequence of their own sexual immorality. If Chris ended his marriage to Sheri, and the ministry found out about the affair with Tara, he stood a good chance of being fired. At the very least, he'd be reassigned to another position of considerably less prestige within the ministry.

So Chris was in a bind. He had to divorce Sheri or risk losing Tara. But if he did indeed divorce Sheri, he risked losing the very job that had helped make him so attractive to Tara in the first place. Which meant that he might lose her anyway.

Quite a bind, indeed. Surely there was some sort of a solution.

On Friday, November 14, 2008, at 8:37 p.m., Joyce Meyer, her husband, Dave, and their sons, David and Daniel, received an e-mail on their ministry computers. Chris received the identical e-mail on his work-issued laptop. The e-mail was entitled "Fuck Chris," and was created by the Google account "destroychris." The subject line read, "Fuck Chris's Family. They are Dead!!!"

"I'm sure this will make it to someone in the company," it began. "If you jackass's [*sic*] are like any other company this will be someone's account. Pass this on to Chris!!!

"Tell Joyce to stop preaching the bullshit or Chris's family will die," it went on, the writing becoming more erratic. "If I can't get to Joyce then I will get to someone close to her and if I can't get to him then I will kill his wife and kids. I know Joyce's schedule so then I know Chris's schedule. If Joyce doesn't quit preaching the bullshit then they will die. During the Houston conference I will kill them all as they sleep. If i dont' hit there then i will kill them during the booktour or the trip to India. I know where he lives and I know they are alone. Fuck them all and they will soon die! Tell that mother fucker next time to let me talk to Joyce. She needs to hear what I have to say and now she will."

Two minutes later, at 8:39 p.m., Chris received a separate e-mail from the same account whose subject line read, "Go to Hell!"

"Your family is done!" it said.

Roughly a minute later, he received a follow-up e-mail.

"They will be done while you are gone at the Houston Conference," it read. "I know you will be out of town."

And two minutes after this, Joyce Meyer's son, Daniel, received an e-mail from the same account with the subject line, "Houston Death."

"Tell Chris his family is dead!!" it began. "I know his schedule and they will die. Next time that mother fucker will let me talk to Joyce."

Then, about two minutes later, he received another one.

"Tell Chris his family is dead," it read. "They don't deserve to live with someone that protects the SOB Joyce."

The next day, Saturday, November 15, at 5:33 p.m., two additional e-mails from the "destroychris" account showed up at the ministry. "Fuck u all!" was the subject line of rather the more substantial of the two.

"I know you all got my fucking email," it read. "You think i am full of shit. Just wait. I will shoot there asses with my 40. Kill them all, I am so sick of bitches like her taking everyone's cash so she can fly her jet and pamper her white ass. Fuck you all. Tell Chris I will kill them. He has no idea when but it will happen. I'm sure you mother fuckers are going to try putting your pussy ass security team at the house or police. Whatever. I kill them then i am coming after Chris, then you Danny, then David. I may not be able to get to Joyce but i'll get the rest of you mother fuckers. Fuck you all. I know when you read these. Just wait you will see. Fuck you all!! Tell that bitch Joyce to give my money back and talk to me and this will all stop. Until then everyone will die starting with Chris's wife and kids. I know his fucking schedule, everytime Joyce is gone he is gone.

"You mother fuckers are probably wondering how i got your e-mails. You stupid fucks. Just like every company, so fucking predictable. Dumb asses!!!"

The e-mails created quite a stir within the ministry. Were they merely somebody's idea of a joke? The online equivalent of crank phone calls? Or was the person who'd sent them deadly serious? Did he really harbor deep grievances against Joyce Meyer? Grievances so severe—so gnawing—that he'd resort to murdering the family of the man who was charged with protecting her?

Such a scenario wasn't entirely beyond the realm of possibility. Joyce Meyer was controversial, after all. She had enemies: people who regarded her prosperity Gospel as a travesty of faith, as a thinly disguised scam for ripping off the poor and the vulnerable. Perhaps such a person had tried to confront her at a conference only to be turned away by Chris Coleman. Perhaps he'd thought that Chris had treated him rudely, and he'd subsequently built himself into a rage. And if this was so, who could tell who this person might be? In his capacity as Joyce Meyer's bodyguard, Chris would've turned away plenty of people over the years, quite possibly without any one of them in particular standing out in his mind.

Chris told his bosses that he'd report the e-mails to the police, and the following Monday he went to the Columbia Police Department and did so. The Columbia PD advised him to file a report with the proper authorities in Jefferson County, Missouri, which was where Joyce Meyer Ministries was located. In the meantime, just to be on the safe side, they said that they'd provide extra patrol in his Columbia Lakes neighborhood.

* * *

As the days passed, Chris became more and more hostile toward Sheri. The very sight of her repulsed him. She was an obstacle to his happiness, an albatross around his neck. The boys were in the way too. They reminded him of their mother. They reminded him of precious time wasting away. Living in Columbia Lakes with his family was now an intolerable burden. He yearned for a fresh start with Tara. He thought of no one else but her. She dominated his every waking moment.

Tara resented Sheri every bit as much as Chris did. She seemed to be growing more possessive by the hour. She hated the idea of Chris and Sheri living together under the same roof. She hated the idea of Chris showing the least bit of affection to another woman, even if that woman happened to be his wife.

Tara needn't have worried much on this particular score. The last thing that Chris was showing Sheri nowadays was affection. He was belligerent and insulting toward her, and sexually remote. He'd taken to spending most nights on a couch in the basement, where he'd exchange text messages and erotic pictures with Tara before falling asleep.

During the early evening of November 25, 2008, Chris cornered Sheri in the family kitchen. He told her that their marriage was through and that he planned on divorcing her. This time he said nothing about her spending habits. Instead he said that she and the boys had gotten in the way of his job with Joyce Meyer Ministries.

He was careful not to mention Tara Lintz.

CHAPTER TWELVE

Sheri was frantic. She was beside herself. What Chris had told her made absolutely no sense. *He wanted to divorce her because she and the boys had gotten in the way of his job?* Surely he realized that if he went ahead with a divorce, he'd be putting his job with Joyce Meyer Ministries at grave risk. Anybody who'd ever worked at the ministry knew that Joyce Meyer disapproved of her employees getting divorced.

What, then, was really going on? Was Chris having an affair? His behavior of late certainly suggested as much, but Sheri couldn't be sure. All she knew for certain was that she still loved him, and that she fully intended on keeping him.

The next day, November 26, she text-messaged Vincent Hall, who was an assistant pastor at Destiny Church. The church had a bulletin board that was used for prayer requests, and Sheri wanted Pastor Hall to post an anonymous message on it requesting prayer for a troubled marriage. She knew that Chris would be furious if their actual names were mentioned.

"Vinny," she wrote, "can you please put Chris and I on the prayer bulletin in the prayer room and keep it confidential?"

Pastor Hall responded right away, promising that he'd take care of it.

"Don't put our names," Sheri insisted in a follow-up text.

"God knows who it is. Chris told me our marriage is over and he wants to leave me. I'm not giving up! He'll be so mad if I tell anyone. I just want people to pray."

Pastor Hall was stunned. He knew Sheri and Chris quite well. He and his wife had recently spent an evening at their house playing Monopoly and eating pizza. He'd had no idea that their marriage was in trouble.

"I'm speechless," he texted back, adding that he thought it a good idea for Sheri to discuss the matter with another pastor at the church who had a special "anointing" to help couples in troubled marriages.

"It won't help," Sheri wrote. "I'm so confused and I'm not getting the whole story. He told me he's leaving me for his job! But if Joyce finds out she'll fire him. This all hit me yesterday and I'm just scared . . . I don't know what is going on! I feel like the doctor just told me I have cancer and I'm going to die."

"I'm so sorry, Sheri," Pastor Hall responded. "I never saw anything wrong in your marriage."

He encouraged her to "stay strong" and promised that he'd keep her in his prayers.

Sheri had stopping working in a paid capacity at Destiny Church by this point. However, she still showed up several times weekly to do volunteer work in the church's youth department. A few days after her text-message exchange with Pastor Hall, she discussed her marital problems in person with Larry Bridges, a minister in the youth department and somebody whom Sheri counted as a friend.

Then, on December 8, she sent Bridges a cautiously optimistic text message suggesting that she and Chris had achieved some sort of a breakthrough and were now in the process of resolving their difficulties.

"Just want to let you know it's going to be okay with Chris and me," the message read. "He's got some things to work through but he's willing to work it out. Thanks for your prayers! It's going to be super tough but it will work."

Sheri's optimism proved short-lived. On December 10, Chris seemed to have blown his top once again and threatened to leave her. Making matters worse, Sheri's brother, Mario, had apparently run into legal problems and was facing the prospect of jail time.

"Please pray for me!" Sheri text-messaged Larry Bridges the next day. "Yesterday things got worse and I just found out that my brother's going to jail!"

"For sure," Bridges responded.

Sheri's life had become an emotional roller coaster.

In mid-December 2008, Chris traveled with Joyce Meyer to Florida. He dropped Meyer off for a vacation cruise and then rendezvoused with Tara Lintz at a hotel in Orlando. They went to a New Kids on the Block concert later that evening, and Chris assured Tara that he was no longer sleeping with Sheri.

The next day they exchanged promise rings, signaling their lasting commitment to one another. They talked some more about their prospective wedding. They were giddy with excitement.

Back home in Columbia Lakes, Sheri once again considered the possibility that her husband was having an affair. She needed to talk with somebody about it. She needed to unburden herself. And so she gave her old friend Tara Lintz a call.

Tara apparently lent her a sympathetic ear.

Chris's youngest brother, Keith, was also experiencing marital conflicts at this time. He'd recently left his wife, Angela, for another woman, which probably didn't sit well with Ron and Connie Coleman. Their three sons were supposed to be men of character, after all. Hadn't they grown up listening to Ron as he preached the clear, undiluted truth of the Gospel?

Their middle son, Brad, might not have had the sturdiest character, either. On December 18, 2008, Chris's brother Keith e-mailed Sheri the oddest of videos.

The video opens with Brad shooting a deer with a bow and arrow, but not fatally. However, rather than dispatching the wounded animal with a knife or another arrow, Brad and a friend strangle it to death. All the while, the deer is writhing in agony on the ground. The person shooting the video can be heard chortling in the background, as if the entire scene were a real hoot.

It's not entirely clear why Keith sent the video to Sheri, who wasn't in the least interested in hunting. Perhaps he thought it so humorous that he simply couldn't resist sharing it.

The same day that she received it, Sheri forwarded the video to Meegan Turnbeaugh. Meegan was hardly impressed. She and her husband, Lonnie, were accomplished hunters. Treating an animal in such a manner was appalling to them.

Meegan phoned Sheri at once, and for the first time in their friendship she raised her voice in anger. She wanted Sheri to appreciate just how offensive the video truly was.

"This is animal abuse," she said. "Do not ever send me anything like this again. If an animal is wounded, you put the poor thing out of its misery. You don't prolong its suffering by choking it to death."

Sheri played the video for Kathy LaPlante the next day.

"Isn't that the sickest thing?" she said.

"Yes, it is," Kathy said.

It was December 21 now and Chris was still in Florida, most likely spending as much time with Tara as possible. Sheri reached him by phone that evening and they had an ugly confrontation. Chris once again insisted that he wanted a divorce, saying he no longer loved her. Sheri pleaded with him to reconsider, but Chris was adamant. He said that Sheri and the boys were keeping him from "realizing God's destiny for his life."

Sheri packed up the boys and drove to Chicago, where she stayed with relatives. The next morning she contacted Phil and Linda Stern, the founding pastors of Destiny Church, and filled them in on her marital woes. She decided that she might also contact Joyce Meyer and her husband, Dave, upon returning home from Chicago. She'd suffered passively long enough. Now it was time for a more aggressive approach.

Later that same day, at 8:50 p.m., Sheri initiated an exchange of text messages with Larry Bridges, the youth minister at Destiny Church.

"Things just got way worse with Chris and I," she wrote. "Please continue to pray. I'm so scared."

Bridges assured her that he would indeed continue to pray. He told her to let him know if there was anything else that he could do.

"Thanks!" Sheri responded. "I let Phil and Linda [Stern] know and Joyce and Dave will know soon. I'm tired of hiding it. I need people praying . . . I'm not giving up on my marriage!! I love Chris way too much! This all seems like a horrible dream."

Bridges agreed that the marriage was worth "fighting for."

"I know Chris is in Florida and has been," Sheri went on. "So I took the kids and went to Chicago . . ."

Bridges encouraged her to keep in touch with him.

"I'll be at the church next week," Sheri wrote. "I'm going to try to go to prayer every day."

About ten minutes later, Sheri also exchanged text messages with Pastor Vincent Hall from Destiny Church.

"How are things?" Pastor Hall asked her.

"Not good, not good at all," Sheri wrote. "Chris is in Florida. He told me he doesn't love me and it's pretty bad."

Hall said that he was sorry to hear that. He asked if there was anything beyond praying for her that he and his wife, Jaimee, could do to help.

"Needless to say I'm pretty messed up right now," Sheri wrote. "I've talked to [Chris]. Some things were better but just got way worse today. I did just talk to Phil [Stern] though. Just pray. Chris and I need that more than anything and I need that more than anything."

Hall told her to feel free to drop by his and Jaimee's house if she ever thought that she needed to talk.

"Very cool," Sheri wrote. "I really, really appreciate it."

Chris was finally back from Florida when Sheri returned home. It was a miserable reunion, with Chris angrily demanding a divorce and Sheri insisting that under no circumstances would she ever let him go.

"Chris, I'm never going to divorce you," she told him. "I will not leave. What are you going to do? Kill me?"

Chris kept quiet about Tara Lintz, of course. However, he did talk about Joyce Meyer—so appreciatively that Sheri apparently began to wonder if this was the heart of the problem. Had her husband fallen in love with his boss? Had he become so emotionally attached to Joyce that his marriage now meant nothing to him?

Sheri held off contacting Joyce and Dave Meyer for the time being. Instead she continued to reach out to people from Destiny Church. Early on December 24, she e-mailed Karen Dossey, a friend from the church with whom she'd done volunteer work in the past. She wrote that things were going badly and asked Karen to give her a call.

Karen called and knew at once that things were indeed going badly. Sheri sobbed and whimpered over the phone. Her old spunk seemed to have been knocked right out of her. She told Karen that Chris wanted a divorce. That he'd repeatedly said that she and the boys had gotten in the way of God's plans for his life. Now Karen also began to cry. What a terrible thing for a wife to hear from her husband!

Karen was so concerned after hanging up that she spoke with one of Destiny Church's staff pastors about Sheri's situation. This was the same pastor who presumably had a special anointing to help couples in troubled marriages. He told Karen that he was already aware of the situation.

Christmas day was brutally hard for Sheri. She tried her best to put on a happy face for the sake of the boys. She tried to pretend that nothing was wrong.

Chris spent much of the day in the family basement, cooing over the phone with Tara.

On December 26, the day after Christmas, Sheri initiated yet another exchange of text messages with the Destiny Church youth minister, Larry Bridges.

"I think I know what's going on with Chris," she wrote. "And I'm so disgusted I'm not sure where to even go with it."

Bridges asked her if she'd be more comfortable speaking with a woman about this. He suggested Linda Stern.

"I'm talking to Linda," Sheri responded. "Chris is emotionally attracted to Joyce. As a man, how does that happen and how do I confront it?"

"It happens by time spent," Bridges opined.

"Yeah," Sheri wrote, "and he's with her more than me."

The next day, December 27, she phoned Kathy LaPlante, who'd always been one of her most supportive friends. She told Kathy what she'd already by then told several other people. Chris wanted a divorce, insisting that his marriage and family were interfering with his true purpose in life.

Later the same day, at 11:30 p.m., she communicated via text message with a young woman, Stephanie Jones, who was a worship leader at Destiny Church.

"Can you pray for me?" Sheri wrote.

"Of course, friend!" Stephanie responded. "What's up?"

"Chris wants a divorce," Sheri said. "He said me and my kids are in the way of his job."

Stephanie said that she was sorry to hear this. She said that Sheri should feel free to call on her for help at any time.

"Thanks so much!" Sheri wrote. "I just need as many prayers as I can get now."

Two days later, she text-messaged another young woman, Christine Cincotta, who was a Joyce Meyer Ministries employee and a longtime friend. She wrote that Chris wanted to divorce her, ostensibly because she and the boys had become detrimental to his life and his work. She knew that Christine herself had gone through a divorce not so long ago, and she asked her how she'd managed to cope with it.

Sheri was talking with just about everybody now, but none of it seemed to be making much of a difference. Her marriage was still in a shambles.

CHAPTER THIRTEEN

On January 2, 2009, Chris contacted the Columbia Police Department, saying he'd just found a disturbing letter in his mailbox at home. Officer Steve Patton drove over to the house on Robert Drive and spoke with both Chris and Sheri. They showed him the letter, which was typewritten on a plain sheet of paper.

"Fuck You," it read. "Deny your God publically or else! No more oppurtunities. Time is running out for you and your family! Have a goodtime in India MOTHER FUCKER!"

Officer Patton knew that Chris worked as head of security for Joyce Meyer Ministries, and that a month and a half earlier he'd reported getting some threatening e-mails in connection with his job. He also knew that the Columbia PD had subsequently increased patrols in the vicinity of the Coleman residence. He asked Chris about the reference to India in the letter: "Have a goodtime in India MOTHER FUCKER!"

"What does this mean?" he said.

Chris explained that he'd be traveling to Bangalore, India, with Joyce Meyer for a conference that was scheduled for January 15–18. He said that the person who'd been threatening him might pick this time to strike at his family.

Later that day, Patton discussed the matter with Joe Edwards, the chief of the Columbia PD. Edwards decided that the department would keep an even closer watch on the Coleman house for the time being.

Kathy and Bob LaPlante dropped by the house in Columbia Lakes a couple of days later, and Chris told them about the threatening letter. He said that he'd reported it not only to the police but also to Mike Cole, a Joyce Meyer Ministries employee who was charged with handling sensitive affairs of this sort. Kathy and Bob asked Chris if he was worried. Did he think that the threat was serious?

"No," he said. "It's probably just some crackpot."

The following week Sheri and Christine Cincotta, her friend from Joyce Meyer Ministries, visited the Ameristar Casino Resort Spa in downtown St. Charles, Missouri. Over dinner, Christine asked Sheri how things were going on the home front.

Sheri said that things were going badly. Chris still wanted a divorce. They bickered constantly and very rarely slept together. She said that Chris had joined her in bed one night and turned it into something ugly. He'd told her not to get the wrong idea. He'd gotten into bed with her, he'd said, not because he loved her but simply because he was feeling horny.

Sheri said that she'd been trying to talk Chris into going for counseling but that he'd wanted no part of it.

"I don't need counseling," he'd said. "All I need is to get out of this marriage so I can realize my true destiny."

At some point over the next several days, Sheri began to zero in on the truth. It wasn't any sort of attraction that Chris felt toward Joyce Meyer that was ruining her marriage. Nor was it her spending habits or her nagging Chris about his frequent absences from home.

Rather, it was her best friend from high school.

It was Tara Lintz.

Perhaps Sheri overheard one of Chris's phone conversations with Tara or glimpsed one of his text messages. Or perhaps she noticed some telltale look in Chris's eyes when Tara's name came up in conversation.

Sheri still wasn't absolutely sure. The more she thought about it, however, the more sense it seemed to make. Hadn't matters taken a decided turn for the worse when Chris returned home from the Tampa conference in November? The marriage certainly hadn't been perfect before then, but neither had it seemed so utterly doomed. Was it possible that Chris and Tara had slept together in Tampa and that they'd been swooning over one another ever since?

Of course it was possible. Sheri knew Tara. She knew that Tara was the envious type. That she couldn't stand anyone having something that she herself didn't have. But would she actually go so far as to try stealing her onetime best friend's husband? As loathsome as this was, Sheri wouldn't put it past her.

And to think that she herself had contacted Tara about the conference in Tampa and suggested that she attend! She'd done so, of course, out of genuine friendship. She'd thought that Tara might benefit spiritually from hearing Joyce Meyer preach. She'd thought that the experience might transform her life, just as Sheri's had been transformed. The irony was almost too cruel to contemplate.

Chris wouldn't give it a rest.

He continued to pester Sheri about the divorce even while away on the trip to India in mid-January. He'd text-message her practically every hour, repeating all of the spiteful things that he'd been saying for weeks now. She and the boys had become a terrible hindrance to him. They were interfering with his job, standing in the way of his destiny. He needed to leave them behind and make a fresh start with his life.

This in itself was hard enough for Sheri to deal with. Making it all the harder was the threatening letter that Chris had reported to the police. Hadn't the person who'd written it insinuated that he might strike out at her and the boys while Chris was away on the India trip? Chris had told her that there was nothing to worry about. That the letter writer was probably just some harmless crank. But what if this wasn't so? What if the threat was serious and Garett, Gavin, and she were right then in grave danger?

Sheri was grateful that Chief Joe Edwards had made good on his promise to provide increased patrols in the neighborhood. Every time that she looked out the front window, she could see a police car cruising by. It was a welcome sight.

She was also grateful that her friend Jessica Wade had agreed to keep her and the boys company for the week. Jessica was a sweet young woman who was part of the youth ministry staff at Destiny Church. She'd often spend time at the house on Robert Drive, looking after Garett and Gavin during the day and sometimes staying overnight when Chris was out of town. Never had Sheri been more appreciative of her company than now.

Jessica realized that Sheri was having marital problems. She couldn't help but notice it. With every new text message from Chris, Sheri would become visibly upset. Sometimes she'd break down and cry.

Finally, while sitting on the couch together one evening, Sheri decided that she'd open up to Jessica about her problems.

"I'm pretty sure my husband's having an affair," she said.

"Oh?" Jessica said.

"And I think I know who he's having it with," Sheri went on. "Would you like to see a picture of her?"

"Okay," Jessica said, though she wasn't entirely sure that she did indeed want to see any such picture.

Sheri fetched a laptop and pulled up the picture of a sultry young woman on Facebook.

"That's her," Sheri said. "Her name's Tara."

A few days later, Stephanie Jones came by the house for a visit. Sheri had text-messaged Stephanie during the frantic days immediately after Christmas, when she'd been notifying almost everybody she knew about her marital situation. Stephanie had come by wanting to know if the situation had shown any signs of improving.

Sheri said that it hadn't. If anything, the situation had gotten considerably worse. She was now quite certain that

Chris was having an affair, and that the other woman was her very own best friend from high school.

She went into another room and returned with a copy of her Largo High School senior yearbook. She opened it to a picture of an attractive girl with thick, curly hair and pudgy cheeks.

"I'm pretty sure that's Chris's mistress," she said, jabbing at the picture with an index finger. "Tara Lintz. She lives in the Tampa area."

A day or two later, Sheri had a sudden thought. If Tara was in fact having an affair with Chris, perhaps she was doing so only out of boredom. Perhaps she'd come across him in Tampa at a time when she'd had nothing else going on in her life, and one thing had simply led to another.

And if this were so, perhaps the thing to do was to set her up with somebody else. Sheri knew how much Tara craved excitement. Chances were that she was already getting tired of Chris. If she were to meet somebody new, she might forget about him altogether.

The question, then, was who that somebody new might be. Did Sheri know anyone who could serve as appropriate bait? She thought about it for a while and finally settled on Chris's youngest brother, Keith. She realized that Keith had recently split up with his wife over another woman. However, insofar as she knew, he hadn't yet made a serious commitment to this other woman, which meant that he was still available. Sure, it was a long shot, but right then she didn't have any better plan in mind. She got in touch with Keith and gave him Tara's contact information.

Keith apparently wasted little time making his move. He contacted Tara and sent her a sexually provocative photograph of himself. The plan came to naught, however. Tara didn't bite. She simply ignored Keith's overture. She already knew who she wanted. Why settle for anything else?

Chris was in a foul mood when he returned from the India trip, which had also included a one-day stopover in Beijing.

He said that he was exhausted from all the travel and didn't want anybody bothering him.

The next day he announced to Sheri that he planned on going to the Super Bowl, which was scheduled for February 1. He said that an old friend from elementary school had gotten tickets and that it was an event that he simply couldn't afford to miss.

Sheri asked which teams were playing in that year's Super Bowl. Chris said that the game featured the Pittsburgh Steelers versus the Arizona Cardinals, with the Steelers the heavy betting favorite. Sheri asked where the game was being played.

Chris said that it was being played at Raymond James Stadium.

Sheri knew exactly where Raymond James Stadium was located. She'd spent her teenage years practically in its shadow.

The stadium was located in Tampa, Florida.

Sheri knew one thing for certain: the last place in the world where she wanted Chris to go was Tampa, Florida. Tampa was Tara Lintz country. If they were indeed having an affair, she couldn't permit them to be within easy range of each other. She had to find some way of keeping them geographically distant. Otherwise she stood little chance of salvaging her marriage.

Sheri tried to reason with Chris. It made no sense for him to go to the Super Bowl, she said. Hadn't he just returned home from a lengthy mission trip to Asia? Didn't they have important issues to work out? Wouldn't his free time be better spent with her and the boys?

And when she got nowhere reasoning, Sheri begged and cajoled. She told him that she loved him and that she missed him when he was on the road. Couldn't he please do her this one small favor and stay home?

She apparently said nothing to him about Tara Lintz. Mentioning Tara's name might have ignited a terrible confrontation. It might have spelled the end.

Chris was indifferent to Sheri's concerns, unmoved by her pleading. He told her that he planned on leaving her for good as soon as he got back from Tampa. He said that he didn't love her and that he never had.

Sheri stewed about it for a day or two, then decided that she'd play her trump card. She'd contact Joyce and Dave Meyer's son, Daniel, and inform him that Chris wanted a divorce. If nothing else, this would force Chris's hand. If he insisted on going ahead with the divorce, Joyce Meyer would almost certainly reassign him to a less prestigious position with the ministry. She might even fire him altogether.

Sheri phoned Kathy LaPlante and asked for Daniel Meyer's cell phone number. Kathy did a bit of digging around and got the number, and Sheri dialed it. She told Daniel that Chris wanted a divorce and that he'd been threatening to leave her and the boys for quite some time. Daniel promised that he'd alert his parents to the matter as soon as possible.

Joyce and Dave Meyer met with Chris the next day and asked him about his marriage. Was it true that he and Sheri were experiencing problems—that he'd been talking about divorcing her? Chris said that there were indeed problems with the marriage. He said that Sheri was very controlling and that he hadn't found a way to make her happy. Joyce and Dave asked him if he'd agree to undergo marriage counseling with Mike Shepherd, a pastor connected to their office.

Chris agreed. He could hardly do otherwise. He fully understood the likely consequences of declining the counseling and simply going ahead with a divorce. He stood to lose his precious job, which meant quite possibly also losing Tara Lintz. She might be decidedly less impressed with him if he were fired from Joyce Meyer Ministries or perhaps reduced to being a mere security guard.

Chris phoned Sheri after his meeting with Joyce and Dave. He was furious with her. Why had she blabbed to the Meyers? Why had she betrayed him? Didn't she realize how important his job was? That it was a vital part of God's plan for his life?

Sheri called Kathy LaPlante and told her what had happened. She said that Chris was on his way home and that she was frightened.

"Are you afraid that Chris will hurt you?" Kathy asked.

Sheri sobbed.

"Talk to me," Kathy said. "Do you want me to come over?"

"No, no," Sheri said. "It's just I know he's so angry with me."

However, when Chris arrived home, he was anything but angry. He was sweet and conciliatory. He told Sheri that he'd be happy to undergo marriage counseling. That he'd do whatever it took to save their marriage. He told her that he loved and cherished her and the boys.

He kept up the façade over the next several days. He was kind and considerate toward Sheri. He held her hand while they sat on the couch watching a Chicago Bulls game on TV. He helped her wash the dinner dishes. He reminded Sheri of the nice, slightly shy young man whom she'd fallen in love with at Quantico.

Sheri was pleased that she'd taken the trouble to contact Daniel Meyer. After being at Chris's mercy for so long, she finally had some leverage of her own.

She was also cautiously optimistic. Perhaps Chris was really serious about making the marriage work. Perhaps they'd turned the corner after all.

In the end, Sheri rewarded Chris for his good behavior. She told him that he could attend the Super Bowl with her blessing.

On January 30, 2009, Sheri text-messaged Vincent Hall, the assistant pastor from Destiny Church.

"Chris is in Florida going to the Super Bowl," she wrote.

"What!" Pastor Hall responded. "That's cool. Joyce Meyer tickets?"

"Nope, not Joyce tickets," Sheri wrote. "A friend of his got some through work. Some guy he's known since grade school who lives in Florida."

Pastor Hall asked how her "situation" was going.

"Going good," Sheri wrote. "Chris said he wants to do

whatever it takes to make it work and, to tell you the truth, ever since he decided that, things have been better than ever. I'm a bit leery because he did this before, but I'm just trusting God."

Pastor Hall congratulated her on this positive development. He promised that he and his wife would continue to pray for her.

"It got so bad, I told Joyce," Sheri went on, exaggerating a little. She hadn't actually spoken with Joyce Meyer herself.

"Oh?" Pastor Hall wrote. "How did she react? I bet she was a little pissed, huh?"

"[Chris] was pissed, to say the least," Sheri responded. "But that was the breaking point. She forced him into counseling."

It took some late fourth-quarter heroics by the Pittsburgh Steelers to prevent the Arizona Cardinals from pulling off a major upset in that year's Super Bowl.

While Chris was still in Florida, Sheri sent him a provocative photo of herself—nude from the waist up—by her cell phone. She probably hoped that this would inject some spice into their faltering marriage.

But the move backfired. Chris was with Tara when he received the photo on his BlackBerry. Tara took the BlackBerry and, posing as Chris, sent Sheri a text message. "Honey, you've really got to stop this," she wrote. "I'm not in love with you anymore."

CHAPTER FOURTEEN

As February passed, Sheri's friends hoped that the worst was behind her. They hoped that the counseling was proving effective and that her marriage was back on track. Sometimes it seemed that such was the case.

Kathy LaPlante would catch glimpses now and again of the carefree, vibrant young woman whom she'd known before all of the marital strife had set in. Sheri would drop off her boys at Kathy's house on Saturday mornings before heading off to her new part-time job at Buckle, a fashionable footwear and accessory shop at South County Center. Sheri was always working at some part-time job nowadays. Before Buckle, it had been Buffalo Wild Wings. And before that . . . Kathy could scarcely remember. She marveled at Sheri's energy. The boys, the house, the jobs, the endless volunteer work at Destiny Church—how in the world did she cope?

After finishing work, Sheri would sometimes talk Kathy into going for a drive. She'd play Natasha Bedingfield's "Pocketful of Sunshine" over and over again as they cruised the backcounty roads. Or she'd talk Kathy into going for a walk and all the while enthuse about her latest personal project. She'd already gotten certified as an emergency medical technician. Now she had her mind set on becoming a personal trainer. Sheri always had something new on the go. It was all Kathy could manage simply to keep track of it all.

Kathy would catch glimpses of the old sparkle, but she still worried. She'd seen and heard too much not to worry. Sheri still had the long-familiar ring tone on her cell phone for Chris. Every time that he'd call, the phone would play the song "Lucky" by Colbie Caillat. But Kathy couldn't help but wonder. Was the ring tone a sign of hope or delusion? Was it celebrating a genuine renewal in Sheri's marriage or, rather, disguising the grim truth of ruin?

Kathy and her husband, Bob, would lie in bed some nights and discuss Sheri and Chris's marital problems.

"Do you think I should talk with him?" Bob would ask.

Bob would've been happy to talk with Chris, and he possessed the sort of personal presence that commanded respect. But Kathy was fearful that this might only aggravate the situation. Chris might resent Bob trying to talk with him. He might construe it as unwarranted interference in his domestic affairs. And who could tell what consequences this might have for Sheri?

"I don't think so," she'd say. "That might not be the best thing for Sheri right now."

And so Kathy worried. She prayed that the young woman whom she'd grown to love as much as a sister would somehow emerge from her troubles in good shape.

Meegan Turnbeaugh worried too. She'd meet Sheri for lunch and receive conflicting reports. Sometimes Sheri would suggest that things were improving between her and Chris. At other times she'd seem less sure. Once she confided that Chris had recently told her that she was ruining his life. That he found it incredible that he couldn't divorce her.

It was a delicate equilibrium. Meegan wanted to find out exactly where matters stood with the marriage, and yet, she also wanted to respect Sheri's privacy. All she could do was continue to meet with her and trust that Sheri would tell her anything that really needed to be told.

Chris also worried. But his worries were of a different order.

Tara had been turning up the heat of late, wanting to know exactly when he planned on divorcing Sheri. The sooner they divorced, the sooner he and Tara could get married. She'd already enrolled in a bridal gift registry. She'd been scouring the real estate and help-wanted listings for the St. Louis area.

She'd given him a deadline for serving Sheri with divorce papers, and the time was fast approaching.

The deadline was May 4, 2009.

But how could he divorce Sheri? If he did, he'd almost certainly lose his prestigious job with Joyce Meyer Ministries. He hadn't mentioned this to Tara, of course. He knew how much his job meant to her. It was one of the things that she found most attractive about him. She wouldn't be in the least pleased if she thought that he stood a chance of losing it.

Chris was still in the same bind. He wanted to divorce Sheri, but he also wanted to keep his job. He couldn't accomplish the first objective without imperiling the second.

Making matters worse was this stupid marriage counseling. Which, of course, was Sheri's fault. Everything wrong and complicated about his life was Sheri's fault. Why on earth had she betrayed him and blabbed to Daniel Meyer? Why hadn't she just kept her mouth shut?

Of one thing he was certain: Sheri had won this battle, but she wouldn't win any others. He'd make damn sure of that.

Chris and Tara had gotten a credit card in both their names by this point. It was yet one more secret that they were keeping from Sheri. They planned on using it to pay for Tara's travel expenses whenever they hooked up at a Joyce Meyer–related event. They'd have a chance to get together again in early March, when Chris was scheduled to participate in a charity football game in Arizona.

Chris had apparently also gotten a separate credit card in his own name, which he'd use primarily to purchase gifts for Tara. She was easy to shop for. He knew all of her clothing sizes and her favorite perfumes, music, and flowers. He knew just about everything in the world that gave her pleasure. He'd already bought her a vibrator and quite a few expensive items of intimate apparel. She loved receiving these gifts from him. He got a huge kick out of sending them to her.

Chris could hardly wait until their next tryst in Arizona. He was counting down the days.

In the meantime, he kept in constant contact with Tara. He text-messaged her countless times daily. He called her at every opportunity. He exchanged personal pictures with her. He always told her how much he loved her, and she always responded in kind. It was so new and fresh—so thrilling. He'd never experienced anything like it.

Chris was careless, though. He was doing all of that calling and text-messaging on a company-issued phone. This was bound to arouse suspicion, and eventually it did.

Sheri's longtime friend Christine Cincotta was in charge of cell phones at Joyce Meyer Ministries, and she couldn't help but notice that Chris's phone expenses were skyrocketing. Christine knew that Sheri and Chris had been experiencing marital strife. She'd discussed the situation at some length with Sheri over dinner during their visit to the Ameristar Casino in January. She wondered if Chris's skyrocketing bill was connected somehow to the strife, and so she pulled his phone records and noticed that he'd been calling a particular number in Florida time and again.

Christine took this information to Daniel Meyer, who dialed the Florida number. A woman answered, and Daniel hung up without speaking to her. He then went and asked Chris about it. Chris said that the number in question belonged to an old high school friend of Sheri's and her husband. He said that he'd been in regular contact with the husband in recent months about his, Chris's, marital problems. The guy had been helping him to sort things out.

This seemed to satisfy Daniel. He didn't bother to check with Sheri on whether Chris was telling the truth.

The next day Chris purchased his own BlackBerry. From then on he'd make sure to use it to contact Tara.

Chris loved that new BlackBerry. It afforded him a whole new avenue of communication with Tara. It helped to bridge the physical distance between them. They'd always enjoyed exchanging pictures, even the occasional risqué one. But with Chris's new BlackBerry, they could get as risqué as they wanted without fear of anyone at Joyce Meyer Ministries finding out.

He'd send her nude pictures of himself lying on the couch in the basement, standing in the shower, fondling his genitalia in the tub. And she'd send him pictures of herself posing provocatively in bra and panties or nothing at all. Their favorite pictures were those where they'd be standing in front of a mirror with the camera capturing not only their naked bodies but also their gleefully narcissistic grins.

One day Chris thought that he'd try something even more risqué. He'd make a video of himself for Tara. He set up a webcam in the family basement and sat down in front of it. "Just got finished texting you, and I've still got a hard-on," he said. "Want to see it?" He stood up, chuckling, so that his erection was in full view. "Just wanted to make a video, see where it'll go," he said, practically giggling now. "Love you. See you."

Throughout all of this, Chris still managed to come across as a caring father. He'd take the boys upstairs to their rooms in the evening. He'd say prayers with them and tuck them into bed.

And then he'd kiss them good night.

CHAPTER FIFTEEN

In mid-February 2009, Sheri spent the better part of a day with Jessica Akers, another friend from Destiny Church. She and Jessica had gotten to know each other the previous year when they'd gone on a mission trip together to Cambodia. Jessica was now heading off on a trip to China, and Sheri had wanted to take her shopping at South County Center as a sort of send-off.

Before hitting the mall, they met for breakfast at the IHOP restaurant in Fenton, where Sheri opened up about her and Chris's recent marital problems. Jessica had heard through the grapevine that they'd been experiencing difficulties. She asked Sheri if they'd been going to marriage counseling. Sheri said yes but that Chris had been lukewarm about it from the start and now wanted to stop going altogether. She said that she'd continue to go by herself if she had to.

Jessica asked about the boys, Garett and Gavin. Was Chris concerned about the impact that their marital problems might be having on them? Sheri said that he seemed indifferent to considerations of this sort. She said that he still seemed intent on getting a divorce.

She wasn't prepared to let that happen, Sheri added.

A few days later, Sheri spoke privately with Chris after work. She said that she had a terrific idea. How about a family vacation to Disney World in Orlando? They'd gone there once before and had a great time, and they were certainly long overdue for some family fun. They could schedule it for mid- to late July, when things would be less hectic at Joyce Meyer Ministries.

She managed to talk Chris into it, and that evening she contacted Disney World and made reservations for a weekend in July. Sheri was delighted. She thought that this might very well prove the perfect tonic for their marriage.

But Chris couldn't keep his mouth shut. Later the same evening, he called Tara and told her about the trip. Tara was furious. She couldn't stand the thought of Chris enjoying a weekend at Disney World with Sheri and the boys. And hadn't she given him a May 4 deadline for serving Sheri with divorce papers? Was he trying to stall? How could he meet the deadline and then, two months later, accompany his family on this ridiculous vacation?

She told him to cancel the trip. Chris whined and pleaded. It was too late to cancel, he said. He and Sheri had already shelled out a nonrefundable deposit. Never mind that, Tara said. Leave it to her. She'd figure out some solution.

The next day, pretending to be Sheri, she spoke with a customer service representative at Disney World and apparently put on quite a performance. She canceled the vacation and also succeeded in having the deposit refunded. Hadn't people in high school always told her that she showed promise as an actress?

Then she called a travel agency and booked a luxury cruise for her and Chris to St. Thomas in the Virgin Islands. She scheduled it for July and charged it to the credit card that she shared with Chris. Who could tell—with any luck, this might even prove to be their honeymoon cruise.

Chris wasn't certain how he'd explain the cancellation to Sheri. But then again, maybe he wouldn't have to.

Sheri created quite a stir within her circle of friends in late February 2009 when she changed her status on Facebook from married to single and went back to using her maiden name. Did this mean that marriage counseling hadn't worked? That she and Chris had split up and a divorce was imminent?

What had actually happened was that an unknown person had gotten access to her Facebook page and was leaving harassing messages: "You're not good enough for Chris." "You don't deserve him." "Why don't you just let him go?"

Sheri wasn't certain who this person was, but she definitely had her suspicions. On February 25 she text-messaged a friend from Destiny Church, explaining that she'd changed her name and marital status in the hopes of throwing her harasser off track.

"Just want to let you know not to pay attention to the new and improved info on my Facebook page," she wrote. "There is no truth to it. It will be back to normal soon."

"What do you mean?" the friend responded.

"I changed my name and marital status," Sheri wrote.

"Oh. Why is that?"

"Crazy lady won't leave me alone. She's obsessed with Chris, so I figured if she thinks I'm not married to him anymore she'll leave me alone. She's obsessed with my Facebook page. Have no clue how she even sees it."

Sheri's strategy proved ineffective, however. She continued to receive harassing messages, sometimes several per day. She finally decided that she'd had enough and deactivated her Facebook account altogether.

At just about this same time, Sheri's dad, Don Weiss, was desperately trying to reestablish contact with her. Don hadn't spoken with Sheri since their last falling-out a couple of years earlier, but he hadn't given up on his dream of once again becoming a part of her life.

Mario had told him in early February that Sheri had a Facebook account, and so he'd opened his own account and sent her a "friend request." She'd ignored it, and she'd also ignored a subsequent request that he sent her.

Then she deactivated her account.

Don thought at the time that she'd deactivated it because of him. That she couldn't abide the idea of his trying to communicate with her.

He saw it as yet another lost opportunity. He wondered how many more opportunities he'd have.

Chris flew to Arizona in the first week of March for quarterback Kurt Warner's annual flag football charity event. Warner was with the Arizona Cardinals now, and so the event had been moved out of St. Louis and was being held at the Cardinals training facility in Tempe. This particular year it was being billed as the Ultimate Football Experience.

Chris was part of the eight-man Joyce Meyer Ministries team, which was quarterbacked by none other than Kurt Warner himself. Chris caught several touchdown passes from Warner over the two-day event, though during one play from scrimmage he seemed to have hurt his knee. He text-messaged Sheri saying that he was taking oxycodone to relieve the pain.

It's hardly surprising that Tara Lintz was on hand for the occasion. She and Chris had been salivating for weeks over the chance to get together in Arizona. Rather more surprising is that she was so conspicuously present. According to one eyewitness report, neither she nor Chris made even a token effort to disguise that they were a couple. At one point she was standing on the sidelines, whispering into his ear and stroking his stomach. Apparently, just about everybody saw them together, including Joyce Meyer's son Daniel.

One can only imagine how thrilling all of this must've been for Tara. Here she was in sunny Arizona, cavorting with sports celebrities and watching as her new flame pulled in perfectly thrown passes from the legendary Kurt Warner. It must've made her feel that much more appreciative of Chris. It must've made her feel that much more appreciative of his job with Joyce Meyer Ministries.

They wouldn't have a chance to get together again until April 15, when Chris was scheduled to accompany Joyce Meyer on a trip to Hawaii. April 15 was five weeks away, which must've seemed to them an eternity. How could they possibly survive the wait?

Chris spent the next several weeks on tour with Joyce Meyer Ministries. There were stops in Hong Kong, Singapore, and Manila, and then a series of events in Southern California.

Vanessa popped over one day while Chris was still on the road. She noticed that there were curtains on the big bay window at the front of the house. She was relieved to see that Sheri had finally taken her advice. She'd pleaded with her for weeks to cover up that bay window.

"Don't you get scared?" she'd said. "Especially with these threatening messages you and Chris have been getting. I mean, people can look right in."

"I never get scared," Sheri had answered.

Vanessa asked her about the curtains now. Why had she decided to put them up? Sheri said that she'd talked it over with Chris and he'd agreed that it was probably a good idea.

When Chris finally returned home from the Joyce Meyer tour, he was gruff and resentful toward Sheri. He was colder than the winter weather. He went back to marriage counseling but only so as not to jeopardize his job. He knew that this was what Joyce Meyer required of him.

One day Sheri phoned Kathy LaPlante with some disturbing news. She said that Chris had come upstairs from the basement the night before and joined her in bed. He'd then flipped her on her back and started to have sex with her. Sheri said that she'd asked him what he was doing. "Shut up and just lie there," he'd answered.

Kathy was horrified. Had Chris actually raped Sheri?

"What did you do?" she asked.

"Nothing," Sheri said. "I just lay there. I was desperate for his affection."

Another day not long afterward, Sheri phoned Kathy at work. She said that she'd just dropped Garett and Gavin off at school and was now driving to Chicago to see her mother. She said that she'd arranged for her neighbor, Vanessa, to pick the boys up.

"But why, Sheri?" Kathy said.

"I've got to talk to my mom," Sheri said, and then she broke down crying.

Kathy tried to calm her. She asked what was wrong. She pleaded with Sheri to turn the car around and head back, saying she was obviously in no condition for such a long drive.

"If anything happens to me, Chris did it," Sheri said.

But Sheri's friends sometimes picked up mixed signals from her. Toward the end of March, Meegan Turnbeaugh treated her to lunch at The Cheesecake Factory in the Chesterfield Mall. Meegan had been so busy of late that she hadn't seen much of Sheri, and she was anxious to catch up. She asked Sheri how things were going on the marriage front. Had there been any noticeable improvement?

Yes, Sheri said. There had indeed been some improvement. She said that Chris had resisted marriage counseling at first but now seemed to have warmed up to it. She said that he seemed committed to resolving their differences and was attending Destiny Church with her and the boys on a regular basis.

Meegan was relieved to hear this. The storm had apparently subsided. Sunny days for Sheri lay just ahead.

It also seemed that way to Christine Cincotta, the friend from Joyce Meyer Ministries. At the beginning of April, Christine and Sheri went on a shopping expedition to Lexington, Kentucky. Along the way, Sheri spoke several times with Chris over the phone. She seemed so relaxed during these conversations, and so genuinely happy, that Christine wondered if the marital conflict was a thing of the past. She certainly hoped so.

The waiting was killing Chris. He hadn't seen Tara since the charity football event in Arizona, and their scheduled rendezvous in Hawaii still seemed so far away. He wanted to do something special for her—something that would show her how much he loved her despite the distance separating them.

Finally it hit him. He had the perfect idea. He'd make a video of himself masturbating in the shower and send it to her. She was certain to love it. She'd know that it was a gift from the heart.

He locked himself in the bathroom, stripped down, and got into the shower with his webcam. He positioned the webcam just so and stood in front of it, showing off his bulked-up frame, his scraggly blond goatee, his shaved head. He turned on the shower faucet and rubbed shampoo into his scalp. "If I had hair, I'm washing my hair," he said. He waved and broke into a big grin. "I love you, baby. Can you see me? Oh, yeah, you can." He took a disposable razor from a ledge in the shower stall and shaved. "I love you," he said. "You're the only person I've ever done anything like this for before." He lathered up a washcloth with a bar of soap. "You know that?" he said. "You're the only person I've done a lot of things for. This is crazy. I love it, though." He scrubbed himself with the soapy washcloth. "Tara, I just got cleaned," he said. "Tara, Tara. Can't wait to see you in Hawaii. Hawaii!" Then he began to masturbate. He moaned and groaned and worked himself into a fit of ecstasy. Five minutes later, still heaving and sighing from all of the exertion, he waved good-bye to the camera.

Kathy and Bob LaPlante dropped by the house on Robert Drive early in the afternoon on Saturday, April 4. They were concerned about Sheri and Chris. They were concerned about the boys. They wanted to see how things were going.

Kathy thought that Sheri and Chris seemed comfortable together that Saturday afternoon. She wondered if they'd reached some sort of rapprochement—if the marriage counseling was finally making a positive difference.

But Kathy knew better than to get her hopes up too high. She'd thought several times previously that they'd been making progress only to hear of some new crisis in their marriage. She remembered the frantic phone call that she'd received from Sheri not long before. *If anything happens to me, Chris did it.* The words haunted Kathy. She couldn't get them out of her mind.

Kathy and Bob were also concerned about those threatening messages that the Colemans had received in recent months. It seemed to them that Chris and Sheri were treating the whole business much too casually.

"Look, Sheri," Kathy now said. "You've been getting death threats and you don't even have drapes on your rear windows."

Sheri shrugged.

"Come on, guys," Bob said. "You've got to take this seriously. You should install a security system in the house."

"Smith & Wesson is our security system," Chris said. "That's all we need."

Bob couldn't figure it out. The guy sounded so flippant.

There was one thing that Bob and Kathy did know: Sheri carried a gun with her at all times. She normally carried it in her purse but she also sometimes put it inside her bra. A couple of weeks earlier, while they were shopping at West County Center, Sheri had patted her bra and said to Kathy: "I'm packing."

"Okay," Kathy had said. "But why are you packing at West County Center?"

Quite a few people at Destiny Church also knew that Sheri carried a gun. She'd shown it to Pastor Vincent Hall one day, saying she carried it mainly for the protection of the church. You could never tell when some lunatic might show up and threaten the congregation, she'd suggested.

She'd also shown it to Vanessa Riegerix once or twice. She'd told Vanessa that she always slept with it on her nightstand.

Sheri phoned Kathy LaPlante late in the evening on April 12, Easter Sunday. She said that she and Chris had entertained the Coleman clan at the house on Robert Drive earlier that day. Ron and Connie had been there. So, too, had Brad and his wife, and Keith and his new girlfriend.

Sheri said that the Colemans spent the better part of the visit bashing Keith's estranged wife, Angela. She said that she could scarcely believe how cruel they were. Why would they say such terrible things about Angela? Sheri added that they'd probably say even worse things about her if Chris ever succeeded in getting his divorce.

Kathy didn't doubt that this was so. She'd heard that Ron and Connie had never especially cared for Sheri. She'd heard that they'd sometimes ask Chris: If Sheri hadn't gotten pregnant, would you ever have married her?

Pastor Vincent Hall and his wife, Jaimee, had a baby boy. They'd been looking for somebody to take care of him on Tuesdays so that Jaimee could go back to work part-time. Since they lived fairly close to the house on Robert Drive, they'd asked Sheri if she'd be open to the idea of doing so. She'd initially said yes, but then she got back to them shortly after Easter and said that she'd checked with Chris and he was opposed to the arrangement. He'd told her that Tuesdays just wouldn't do. Sheri said that he was adamant about it.

No, Tuesdays just wouldn't do. They wouldn't do at all.

CHAPTER SIXTEEN

On April 15, 2009, Chris accompanied Joyce Meyer on the trip to Hawaii. This was the opportunity that he and Tara had eagerly anticipated for weeks.

They rendezvoused in Chris's hotel suite, ordered room service, and then had sex in the shower.

The next morning Chris was struck with a sudden inspiration. Why not make a video of him and his sweetheart frolicking in the hotel suite? It would serve as a sort of cinematic tribute to their love.

He fired up his webcam and did a quick scan of the suite, all the while chuckling like a schoolboy.

"Here we are, in our hotel room in Hawaii," he said.

He walked toward the bathroom, where Tara was standing nude by the sink.

"And here's Tara, naked," he said.

Tara turned so that she was facing the camera. She flashed a big movie-star smile.

"And what are we doing here in Hawaii, Tara?" he said.

"We are in Hawaii being bad," she said.

She ducked coyly behind the bathroom door.

"Hey, why are you hiding?" he said.

His voice sounded oddly high-pitched.

"Because I can," she said.

She giggled and peaked around the corner.

"Are you nervous?" he said.

She stepped out from behind the door, still wearing her big smile.

"Does this make you nervous?" he said.

She giggled and struck several provocative poses. Chris chuckled as he filmed her. He turned the camera on himself occasionally, making certain to get plenty of footage of his own private parts.

Then he went on a walk-through of the hotel suite, providing narration along the way.

"Here's the shower where we had sex yesterday," he said.

He filmed the tangled sheets on the bed, the glorious view outside the windows. He returned to the bathroom and took some bonus shots of Tara. She gushed and giggled while assuming various poses.

"And that ends the tour of our hotel room in Hawaii," Chris finally said. "Good-bye."

"Bye," Tara chimed in.

Chris returned home after a few days. Then he and Sheri went to marriage counseling with the Joyce Meyer pastor, Mike Shepherd.

Sheri hoped that this was a good sign. She hoped that Chris's willingness to attend counseling meant that he harbored some affection for her. He was still cold and distant around the house, still averse to sleeping with her. But at least the counseling was something.

Sheri's friends mostly worried. Sometimes they thought that she seemed happy and confident. Sometimes they weren't so sure.

They noticed that Sheri had been ducking out of social engagements of late. She'd canceled various shopping trips and luncheon dates. She'd even begged off attending the birthday party that Meegan Turnbeaugh was throwing for her husband, Lonnie. The party had been in the works for quite some time. Meegan had booked a country music band to play at it.

This was so unlike Sheri. Normally she'd be the last person to bail out on an event of this sort.

Sheri phoned Vanessa during the early evening on April 24. Vanessa was just then in the process of dropping off her son, Brandon, at his father's house.

"Hey, what's up?" she said.

"I'm at Garett's baseball game," Sheri said. "I was wondering if you guys wanted to come down to the house after I get home. You know, we could talk, maybe have a few drinks."

Something about her tone of voice suggested to Vanessa that this was important to Sheri.

"Sure, we'll come down," she said. "Call me when you get back from the game."

About an hour later, Vanessa and her fiancé went over to the house on Robert Drive. They could tell almost at once that something was amiss.

Chris looked as if he'd gotten a good head start in the drinking department. He was already pretty intoxicated. Vanessa was surprised. She'd never known him to have more than a casual beer or two.

The beer ran out before long, and Chris talked Vanessa's fiancé into driving him to the gas station for another case.

When they returned, Chris asked Vanessa if she liked his new look.

"What do you mean?" she asked.

"My hair," he said. "What do you think of it? You like it?"

Vanessa had noticed when they first came in that he was letting his hair grow out, but she'd refrained from commenting on it.

"Actually, Chris," she now said, "I like the bald look a lot better."

Vanessa could sense that Sheri wasn't quite herself. She seemed nervous, anxious.

"Are you okay?" Vanessa asked her.

"Sure," Sheri said. "I'm fine."

Garett and Gavin came inside from the backyard and joined the adults in the living room for a few minutes. Then

Chris abruptly ordered them to bed. His sternness of voice surprised Vanessa. Normally he'd be gentler with the boys; he'd take them upstairs himself and kiss them good night.

Chris went into the kitchen and returned with a bottle of whiskey that he'd brought home from one of his Joyce Meyer trips. He took a few slugs and then offered the bottle to Vanessa.

"Here," he said. "You want to try some of this?"

"No thanks," Vanessa said. "I'm not in the mood tonight."

They adjourned to the basement at midnight, where they spent half an hour or so talking about nothing in particular. Chris seemed chattier than usual, probably because of the booze. Sheri simply seemed tense.

Then Chris got out of his chair and announced that he was going upstairs for another beer.

"Chris," Sheri said. "Would you mind getting me one too?"

He stood in the middle of the floor and glared at her.

"Get off your ass and go get it yourself," he snapped. "Quit being lazy."

Sheri tittered nervously. She seemed embarrassed that Chris had insulted her in front of her friends. Vanessa was tempted to tell him off right then and there. How dare he treat Sheri so disrespectfully!

"Come on, Chris," Vanessa's fiancé said. "Sheri's your wife. Go get her a beer."

Chris chuckled, and then sat down again.

Vanessa's fiancé reached over and nudged her leg. "We'd better go," he whispered.

Vanessa stood up and said that it was getting late. She thanked Sheri for inviting them over.

Sheri got up and clutched Vanessa's arm.

"Please don't go," she pleaded. "Can't you stay just a little longer?"

"I'm tired, hon," Vanessa said. "We'll talk tomorrow, okay?"

Vanessa didn't get much sleep that night. She couldn't stop thinking about the terrible awkwardness of the evening.

Why had Chris behaved so nastily? And why had he been drinking like there was no tomorrow? Chris and Sheri weren't ordinarily big drinkers. Vanessa had never seen Chris drunk before, and Sheri only once. She'd overindulged at Vanessa's house one night a couple of years earlier and crawled into the bedroom closet. "Show me some lingerie," she'd said.

Normally Vanessa and her fiancé would have a good time hanging out with Sheri and Chris. But this had been different. It had been weird, heavy. It nagged at Vanessa most of the night.

The next day Sheri sent Vanessa a text message.

"Vanessa," it read. "You're like family. We'll always be together."

"The feeling is mutual," Vanessa responded. "You're like a sister to me."

CHAPTER SEVENTEEN

On Monday, April 27, Chris dropped by the Columbia Police Department and spoke with Officer Shawn Westfall. He told Westfall that he'd just retrieved another threatening letter from the mailbox at his house and thought that he should report it without delay.

"Fuck You," the typewritten letter read. "I am giving you the last warning! You have not listened to me and you have not changed your ways. I have warned you to stop traveling and to stop carrying on with this fake religious life of stealing people's money. You think you are so special to do what you do protecting or think you are protecting her. She is a bitch and not worth you doing it. Stop today or else. I know your schedule! You can't hide from me ever. I'm always watching. I know when you leave in the morning and I know when you stay home. I saw you leave this morning. I will be watching. You better stop traveling and doing what you are doing. THIS IS MY LAST WARNING! YOUR WORST NIGHTMARE IS ABOUT TO HAPPEN!"

After Chris had left the station, Officer Westfall conferred with Justin Barlow, one of the Columbia PD's only two full-time detectives. Westfall knew that Barlow lived catty-corner to the Coleman residence in the Columbia Lakes subdivision. He told him about this most recent letter and asked him if he'd noticed any suspicious-looking characters lurking about the neighborhood. Barlow said that he hadn't noticed anything or anyone out of the usual.

However, Justin Barlow did have an idea for dealing with the situation, and later the same day he ran it by Joe Edwards, chief of the Columbia PD. Since he lived almost directly across from the Coleman residence, he said, why not set up a video surveillance camera in the window of his three-year-old son's second-floor bedroom? They could train the camera on the Coleman mailbox, so that anybody leaving another threatening letter would almost certainly be nabbed.

It was a generous proposal, especially since Barlow didn't know the Coleman family personally. He'd waved to Chris a number of times several years before but had never received a wave in return. Then he'd stopped trying, assuming that the guy simply wanted to be left alone.

Chief Edwards signed off on the idea. Hadn't he always encouraged the people working under him to go that extra step in solving crimes?

Barlow then advised Chris of the plan. He gave him his cell phone number and told him to get in touch if he ever felt concern about the safety of his family.

Chief Edwards and Barlow contacted a colleague from the Illinois State Police, who installed the surveillance camera on Tuesday, April 28. Now only a phantom could leave anything in the Coleman mailbox without being detected.

Chris apparently spent most of that same Tuesday chauffeuring Kurt Warner around St. Louis. The star quarterback had come up from Arizona for a one-day visit.

On Wednesday, April 29, Chris's youngest brother, Keith, got in touch with Sheri. He said that he was concerned about this most recent threat letter and offered to stay over at the house whenever Chris was away on Joyce Meyer–related business.

Sheri declined the offer, saying that everything was under control. The police had installed a surveillance camera across the street, and Chris was just then in the process of installing his own home security system, which would consist of both indoor and outdoor cameras.

On Thursday, April 30, Meegan Turnbeaugh contacted Sheri in the early afternoon. They were supposed to have dinner together that evening, but Meegan had just found out that she'd be working later than expected. They rescheduled the dinner for the following week, on Tuesday, May 5.

Later that same day, Chris finished installing his home security system. He informed Justin Barlow that he only needed a power source to activate the cameras. Barlow offered to contact the Illinois State Police for assistance in this regard, but Chris turned him down. He said that he'd take care of it himself.

On Friday evening, May 1, Kathy and Bob LaPlante and their children went to the house on Robert Drive for dinner. Sheri made hamburgers, and everybody had a good time. Kathy thought that things seemed much improved between Sheri and Chris. She hoped that their marriage was now back on track.

There was only one sour note in the entire evening. At one point, while they were alone in the kitchen, Sheri began to tell Kathy about the circumstances that had caused her to shut down her Facebook account several weeks earlier. Chris overheard her from the living room and called out in a stern voice: "Let's not talk about that this evening."

Chris took Kathy and Bob down to the basement after dinner and showed them the digital video recorder for his new home security system. He said that the system was now fully operational and that, just the previous evening, one of its outdoor cameras had caught a masked figure putting yet another threat letter into their mailbox.

On Saturday morning, May 2, Chris went to a hair salon in Columbia for a trim. He'd been letting his hair grow out over the past several weeks and worried that it might be getting a little shaggy. Sheri met him at the salon after getting her passport photo taken for a mission trip that she was planning on taking with Destiny Church. Chris asked her if she'd remembered to smile for the camera.

Later that day, Sheri, Chris, and the boys dropped by the LaPlante house while on their way to Destiny Church for

Saturday evening services. Sheri needed to pick up some paperwork from Kathy that was connected to the upcoming mission trip.

Toward the close of evening services at Destiny Church, there was an altar call for troubled marriages. Sheri and Chris went to the front of the sanctuary and knelt at the altar. Pastor Vincent Hall put a hand on Chris's shoulder and prayed for both him and Sheri. He prayed that God would perform a miracle in their lives and make their marriage strong and healthy.

While leaving the church after services, Pastor Hall saw Sheri and Chris in the main hallway. They were sitting at a table with Garett and Gavin.

CHAPTER EIGHTEEN

On Monday morning, May 4, Chris phoned the office and said that he needed to take the day off. Joyce Meyer found this odd. She couldn't remember Chris ever calling and asking for time off.

He took the boys to school, did some grocery shopping, and spent the rest of the day at home.

Vanessa Riegerix saw Chris later that afternoon while she was at the school waiting to pick up her son, Brandon. She was chatting with some other parents when Chris pulled up in his Ford Explorer. Normally he'd get out and join the conversation, but today he simply sat in his vehicle. Vanessa waved to him, and he gave her a halfhearted wave in return.

Vanessa drove Brandon home, and along the way she saw Sheri standing in the driveway of the house on Robert Drive. She honked and waved. Sheri smiled and waved back at her.

Vanessa fixed Brandon a snack, and then Garett and Gavin came over. They almost always came over within a few minutes of getting home from school. The three boys went outside and played football, but Gavin soon decided that he'd had enough. He didn't enjoy playing football as much as Garett and Brandon did.

"I'm done with this," he said. "Let's play something else."

Garett pleaded with him to reconsider.

"Come on, Gavin," he said. "Just a little longer. We can't play football with just two guys."

But Gavin's mind was made up. He said that he wanted to go bike riding, and Vanessa said that she'd be happy to join him.

Vanessa and Gavin rode their bikes up and down the street and around the block for about fifteen minutes, and then the two Coleman boys went home for dinner.

They came back at 6:30 or so, and Garett asked Vanessa if he and Gavin could spend the night at her house.

"Of course you can," Vanessa said.

This had been the plan all along. Every year on May 4, the Coleman boys would sleep over at Vanessa's in celebration of both Brandon and Garett's birthdays, which were less than a week apart: Garett's was on April 30, and Brandon's on May 5.

"Go home, Garett, and tell your mom and dad to pack your clothes," Vanessa said.

Garett went home and came back a few minutes later. His shoulders were slumped and he was wearing a big frown.

"My dad said we can't do it," he said. "We can't sleep over. He said tonight's not a good night."

Vanessa was surprised. The annual sleepover had become something of a ritual with the boys. It had never posed any sort of a problem before.

"I ought to go down and tell your dad to give me your clothes," she said. "I can take you both to school with Brandon in the morning."

"But my dad said no," Garett repeated. "He said we have to be home by eight thirty."

Vanessa thought that Garett seemed nervous. She decided against pushing the matter any further.

The three boys played outside until 8:25, and then Garett and Gavin walked home and went inside their garage. Vanessa stood and watched as they closed the door behind them.

Sheri spent most of Monday, May 4, doing volunteer work at Destiny Church. She got back at shortly past four and parked in the driveway. She saw Vanessa driving past with Brandon and waved hi.

Just then Chris pulled up with Garett and Gavin. The boys said hi to her and raced off to Vanessa's house. They were always in a big hurry to get over there after school so that they could play with Brandon. Sheri went into the house and began to prepare pasta and chicken for dinner.

Tara called Chris at this point, wanting to know if he'd gotten around to serving the divorce papers to Sheri. Today was May 4, after all, which was the deadline that she'd assigned him for doing so.

But, of course, there were no divorce papers. Chris hadn't even bothered to contact a lawyer in this regard. Divorcing Sheri simply wasn't in the cards—not if he wanted to keep his high-profile job with Joyce Meyer Ministries.

Chris couldn't tell Tara this, though. And so he lied. He said that he'd found some serious typos in the papers, and the lawyer was having them redone. He promised Tara that he'd serve them to Sheri the very next day. She told him to make sure that he did.

And she wished him good luck.

Garett and Gavin came home for dinner, and afterward the entire family went out for sno-cones. Chris played catch with Garett in the driveway upon returning home, then both boys left to play with Brandon again.

A short time later, Garett came back and asked if he and Gavin could spend the night at Vanessa's house. He reminded his mom and dad that they always slept over at Vanessa's on May 4 in celebration of his and Brandon's birthdays.

Chris said no. He said that it wasn't a good night for a sleepover. He told Garett to make sure that he and Gavin were home by 8:30 at the very latest. Then he changed into his gym clothes and drove to a fitness club in Waterloo for a workout.

Chris got back from the gym at roughly 8:00 p.m., and Garett and Gavin came home for the evening shortly afterward. They came in through the garage door, because Gavin had his bike with him and they always kept their bikes in the garage.

The boys played some video games before going upstairs to shower. Gavin had gotten poison ivy while camping with friends a couple of days earlier, and Sheri applied some steroid cream to it.

Then Chris said prayers with them, tucked them into their beds, and kissed them good night.

Sheri and Chris spent the rest of the evening watching television together in the living room. They watched *Batman Returns* on a movie channel and then switched over to the Los Angeles Lakers–Houston Rockets NBA game.

And all the while Chris text-messaged Tara. It didn't matter to him that Sheri was right there. He couldn't help himself. He texted and texted and texted.

Tara reportedly told him that she was at a karaoke bar in St. Petersburg.

PART FOUR

May 5, 2009

CHAPTER NINETEEN

6:56 a.m.

Detective Justin Barlow and Officers Jason Donjon and Steve Patton assembled in the second-floor hallway of the house on Robert Drive. Their hands were shaking. Their voices were stricken with horror.

"Oh, my God," they kept saying. "Oh, my God."

Justin Barlow called the dispatcher on his cell phone, saying there were multiple victims. "One adult and two juveniles," he said. Patton called Joe Edwards, the chief of the Columbia Police Department, and Donjon called the crime scene unit at the Illinois State Police's District 11 headquarters in Collinsville.

They then split up again, each man going into the rooms that he hadn't yet seen. They were careful not to touch the walls or the furniture or anything else of potential evidentiary value.

Donjon went into Garett's room and felt for a pulse on the boy's neck. This was the first time that he'd ever seen a deceased child. He had two young boys of his own and a slew of nieces and nephews. Seeing Garett lying there filled him with dread.

It was even worse when he next went into nine-year-old

Gavin's room. The little boy was wearing Spider-Man pajamas, which Donjon's sons also wore. And the spray-painted message on the bedsheets was staring right at him: FUCK YOU. It was like a punch to the heart.

Donjon took several deep breaths, trying to calm down. He could feel his heart beating through his entire body. Then he felt for a pulse on Gavin's wrist. He bent down and put his ear next to the boy's mouth, checking for breath. But there was no pulse, of course. There was no breath.

Donjon lingered in Gavin's room for a moment longer. He was convinced that Satan had been there earlier that morning, but now he desperately wanted to feel some presence of God.

The three men congregated once again in the hallway outside the bedrooms.

"Oh, my God," Donjon kept saying.

"I can't believe this," Steve Patton said.

"Man, oh, man," Justin Barlow said.

They heard somebody yelling from downstairs. Donjon's first thought was that it was the killer. Then he made out the words and realized that it was Chris Coleman.

"What's going on?" Chris was yelling. "What's going on?"

Barlow and Patton exchanged a glance. They also recognized the voice.

"We can't let him up here," Donjon said. "It's a crime scene."

Donjon was thinking that they'd have to fight Chris to prevent him from coming up. How awful, he thought. They'd have to fight the guy who'd just lost his wife and two little boys.

They ran downstairs. Chris was standing in the kitchen with a perplexed look on his face.

"Chris, you can't go upstairs," Barlow said. "Let's go outside."

Donjon and Patton likewise told him that he couldn't go upstairs, that it was best right then if he simply left the house.

"What's going on?" Chris said again. "What happened? Why can't I see my family?"

Donjon thought that there was something terribly wrong here, something weird. Why wasn't the guy struggling to get upstairs? Why wasn't he pressing them for specific details about what had happened to his family?

Barlow went over and placed a hand on Chris's back. He turned him around and led him outside through the garage door.

Now Steve Patton also thought that there was something terribly wrong. The guy had turned around too easily. He hadn't tried to see his family. He'd been altogether too compliant. *If it were* my *house,* my *family,* Patton thought, *it would take a helluva lot more than three cops to stop* me *from going upstairs.*

Patton and Donjon also went outside through the garage door. Chris was sitting in the driveway a few feet from the door.

Justin Barlow bent down and put a hand on his shoulder. "Chris, they didn't make it," he said.

"What do you mean, 'They didn't make it'?" Coleman said.

"Chris, they didn't make it," Barlow repeated.

Chris sat there in the driveway and started to cry. However, to Steve Patton, the tears seemed forced. They stopped at the bridge of Chris's nose. *The guy has just found out that his entire family's dead,* Patton thought, *and this is the best that he can muster?*

"I gotta call work," Chris now said. "I gotta call my dad."

He repeated this several times. Then, still sitting in the driveway, he contacted Joyce Meyer Ministries via his BlackBerry and told somebody there that his family had just been killed. Next he contacted his father and told him the same thing.

"I don't know what's going on," he blubbered into the phone. "They're not telling me anything."

Jason Donjon called the dispatcher and asked him to get in touch with the Columbia PD's chaplain. Then he retrieved gloves from his squad car and went around to the rear of the house, where he secured the open window.

Steve Patton made eye contact with Justin Barlow and took him aside at the edge of the driveway.

"You want to know your chief suspect?" he told Barlow. "That's him right there. Chris Coleman."

Justin Barlow couldn't have agreed more.

Emergency medical technicians Gary Hutchison and Jared Huch arrived on the scene at 7:01 a.m. Hutchison was an ash-blond guy of about forty, Huch somewhat younger, with a shaved head. Both men had seen more than their fair share of human carnage over the years.

They got out of their ambulance and saw Chris Coleman sitting in the driveway with his hands on his head. He appeared to be crying. Steve Patton walked over and told them that it was a triple homicide and that two of the victims were young boys. Then Justin Barlow escorted them inside the house.

Immediately upon entering, Hutchison and Huch were hit with the acrid odor of freshly spray-painted obscenities. They saw the message that was scrawled on the kitchen wall next to the doorway.

FUCK YOU
I AM ALWAYS
WATCHING

Then the message that was scrawled on the adjoining kitchen wall:

I SAW
YOU
LEAVE

And then the message on the living room wall:

FUCK YOU
BITCH
PUNISHED

And finally the message on the wall of the staircase leading up to the second floor:

U HAVE
PAID

They went into Gavin's room and saw the poor little boy lying facedown on his bed with FUCK YOU spray-painted on his sheets. His lips and eyelids were purplish in color, indicating that he'd been without oxygen for a significant period of time. His skin was cold and mottled. Huch pulled on Gavin's left arm, which was extended toward the near wall. The limb remained rigid upon being released, with no pliability whatsoever. This was rigor mortis, a certain sign of death. There was clearly no point in trying to resuscitate the boy.

Huch went back outside at this point to see if Chris Coleman needed attending to, while Hutchison went into Garett's room. He initially thought that the splotch of red on the blanket was blood but soon realized that it was yet more spray paint. Garett was cold to the touch, with discoloration around his mouth. Hutchison pulled on his left arm; it proved just as stiff as his younger brother's.

Hutchison went down the hallway and into the master bedroom. A lamp sat on a small dark-stained desk. Toiletry items cluttered the top of a dresser. Sheri lay facedown on the circular bed, half of her body purplish red in color, her face shrouded by hair. A comforter and several articles of clothing were bunched on the floor at the foot of the bed. Hutchison managed to pull Sheri's hair aside, which gave him a better view of her face and neck. There was a large, angry bruise on the left eye and discoloration around the right. And there were double ligature marks around the neck, suggesting that she'd been strangled not just once but twice.

Hutchison pulled on her left arm, and the stiffness of the limb told the whole story. Sheri was obviously dead, and most likely had been for quite some time. A recently deceased body would have exhibited far more plasticity or pliability.

There was nothing more for Hutchison to do. Now it was simply a matter of waiting for the folks from the coroner's office to arrive.

CHAPTER TWENTY

Columbia police chief Joe Edwards had just finished shaving when Steve Patton called. Edwards had been planning on taking his nine-year-old twin daughters to school before heading off to the station.

"Joe, you know Chris Coleman's house in Columbia Lakes?" Patton said.

"Sure," Edwards said.

He knew, of course, about the threatening messages that Chris had reported to the police department.

"You've got to get up here right away," Patton said.

"What's going on?" Edwards said.

"Coleman's wife and two sons," Patton said. "They've all been killed."

"You gotta be kidding me," Edwards said.

Justin Barlow called seconds later with a fuller description of the nightmarish scene at the house on Robert Drive, and then the dispatcher also called.

Edwards brought his daughters around the corner to a neighbor, who agreed to see them off to school. The two girls could tell that something was terribly amiss.

"Daddy, what's wrong?" they said.

Edwards jumped into his car and sped to the Columbia Lakes subdivision. Along the way he called his deputy chief, Captain Jerry Paul, who was midway through his usual morning run. He told Paul to get into uniform as quickly as possible and meet him at the Coleman house.

When Chief Edward arrived at the house, Justin Barlow and Steve Patton came over to his car with a full report. Their faces were pale and haggard, their eyes bloodshot. They looked to Edwards as if they'd just taken a walk through hell.

The departmental chaplain, Jonathan Peters, arrived a minute or two later and conferred with Chief Edwards and Justin Barlow. Peters was a big guy with a mustache and a goatee. Besides serving as chaplain for the Columbia PD, he was pastor of a Baptist church in town. Edwards and Barlow asked him to speak with Chris Coleman and make sure he realized that his wife and two children had just been killed. After all, there was still a chance that Chris hadn't fully understood what Barlow had meant when he'd told him that his family hadn't made it.

Chris was still sitting in the driveway with his hands on his head. Chief Edwards and Chaplain Peters walked over and hunkered down on either side of him. Peters put an arm around his shoulders and then, as gently as he could, gave him the dreadful news. Chris blinked back tears but otherwise seemed remarkably calm. He started fidgeting with his BlackBerry, which had been lying on the grass beside him. He'd pick it up and look at it. Then he'd put it down, only to pick it up and look at it again. Edwards and Peters both found this response highly peculiar.

Chief Edwards asked Gary Hutchison and Jared Huch to put Chris in the ambulance. He asked Chaplain Peters to sit with him there in the event that he needed consoling. Then he went to the rear of the house with crime scene tape to make sure that the entire property was secured.

At this point, Jason Donjon was still in the backyard guarding the open window through which he and Justin Barlow had entered the house half an hour earlier. He was frantic, desperately worried about his own two young sons. He lived just blocks from the Colemans, in a house that was almost identical in layout to theirs. Was there a monster on the prowl

Gavin, Sheri, and Garett. (Courtesy: Mario DeCicco)

Garett and Gavin. (Courtesy: Mario DeCicco)

Gavin, Mario, and Garett at a Chicago White Sox game. (Courtesy: Mario DeCicco)

Angela DeCicco and Gavin.
(Courtesy: Mario DeCicco)

Sheri, 1995. (Courtesy: Mario DeCicco)

Tara Lintz and Chris Coleman. (Columbia Police Department)

Spray-painted grafitti on the living room wall of the Coleman house. (Columbia Police Department)

The Coleman residence in Columbia Lakes after the triple homicide. (*Republic-Times* photo by Corey Saathoff)

A curbside memorial outside the Coleman residence in Columbia Lakes. (*Republic-Times* photo by Corey Saathoff)

Chris Coleman is escorted from the Columbia police station on the evening of his arrest. (*Republic-Times* photo by Paul DeBourge)

Joyce Meyer addresses the media after her deposition. (*Republic-Times* photo by Alan Dooley)

Joyce Meyer leaves the Monroe County Courthouse with her new bodyguard. (*Republic-Times* photo by Alan Dooley)

Ron and Connie Coleman arrive at the Monroe County Courthouse for a pre-trial hearing. (*Republic-Times* photo by Alan Dooley)

Some of Sheri's family members address the media during a trial recess. Left to right: Attorney Jack Carey, Joe Miglio, Mario DeCicco, and Angela DeCicco. (*Republic-Times* photo by Alan Dooley)

Detective Karla Heine prepares to escort Tara Lintz into the Monroe County Courthouse. (*Republic-Times* photo by Alan Dooley)

Brad Coleman (second from left) and Keith Coleman, with their wives on a balcony outside the Monroe County Courthouse. (*Republic-Times* photo by Alan Dooley)

Chris Coleman leaves the Monroe County Courthouse in the back of a police car after the guilty verdict. (*Republic-Times* photo by Alan Dooley)

Police officers celebrate the guilty verdict. Front row, left to right: Detective Kelly Cullen, US Marshal Justin Barlow, Sergeant Dave Bivens, and Special Agent Byron R. Workman. Back row, left to right: Chief Joe Edwards, Detective Sergeant Jason Donjon, and Officer Steve Patton. (Columbia Police Department)

The gravesite at Evergreen Cemetery in Chester, Illinois. (The photo was taken on Garett's birthday.) (*Republic-Times* photo by Alan Dooley)

in the neighborhood? Was Donjon's family also potentially at risk?

He'd tried calling home on his cell phone but no one had answered. He'd tried calling his mother-in-law's cell and then his wife's, without getting through to either one of them. He'd finally managed to contact a neighbor, who said that she'd go over and check on his family, but he hadn't heard back from her yet. He was seriously considering leaving his post at the window and running home when Chief Edwards came into the backyard with the crime scene tape.

Edwards asked Donjon how he was holding up, and then they talked for a few moments about the terrible situation. Edwards said that Chris Coleman was sitting in the ambulance just then. He asked Donjon if he realized that Chris had been home earlier that morning and that he'd apparently left at 5:40 or thereabouts for a predawn workout at a gym in south St. Louis County.

No, Donjon said. He hadn't realized that. He knew that Chris was head of security for Joyce Meyer Ministries and that the job involved a lot of traveling. He'd assumed that the guy was just returning from an out-of-town trip when he'd pulled into the driveway shortly before 7:00 a.m.

Donjon had wondered why Chris hadn't been more curious when they'd told him that he couldn't go upstairs to see his family. Now he thought that he understood. The guy had been home just a short while earlier. He already knew what he'd find upstairs. He knew that his wife and two sons were dead.

Donjon felt immense relief. There wasn't a monster at loose in the neighborhood after all. The monster was sitting in an ambulance out front, surrounded by cops.

Chief Edwards put crime scene tape around the perimeter of the yard and then returned to the front of the house. He saw Chris Coleman sitting on a gurney inside the ambulance, with Chaplain Peters sitting across from him. They appeared to be praying.

Edwards decided that he had little choice but to reach out

for help. The Columbia PD consisted of only two detectives and fourteen sworn officers in total, and a tragedy of this magnitude was more than the department could reasonably be expected to handle on its own. He got on his cell phone and called his old buddy Bill Baker, who was commander of the Major Case Squad of Greater St. Louis.

The Major Case Squad had been created in 1965 precisely for the purpose of helping smaller police departments in the St. Louis area with homicide investigations. It was made up of roughly 430 criminal investigators, all of whom were drawn from these smaller departments and any of whom might be tapped at a moment's notice to assist with an investigation. The squad operated on an ad hoc basis. Upon request from a local police chief, the commander would activate it and then assign a deputy commander to take charge of the case. The deputy commander would typically be somebody with a proven track record in criminal investigations.

"Listen, Bill," Edwards said. "We've got a horrible situation down here. I need all the help I can get."

"Of course," Commander Baker said.

Baker realized that Chief Edwards wasn't prone to flying into panic mode. If he said that he needed help, then he *really* needed it.

"But do me a favor," Edwards said. "Don't send me some deputy commander who's only worked a few of these. I need the best of the best."

"How about Major Jeff Connor?" Baker said.

Edwards knew Jeff Connor, who was based out of the Granite City PD. If Connor wasn't the best of the best, he was certainly in the running for the distinction.

"Sounds good," he said.

Chief Edwards hung up and conferred with Captain Jerry Paul, who'd just then arrived on the scene. Paul was a tall, handsome guy in his early forties with a highly courteous style. Even in the most stressful of situations, he'd never raise his voice or show frustration. He was utterly unflappable.

Edwards asked Paul to grab a notebook and join Chris Coleman and Chaplain Peters in the back of the ambulance.

"Tell Coleman anything he needs, we're here for him," Edwards said. "Anything he asks for, write it down. Anything you see or hear that might be of relevance, write it down."

Captain Paul sat in the back of the ambulance and waited until Chris and Peters had finished praying. Then he asked Chris if he'd mind talking about what had happened that morning.

Chris said that he got out of bed at about 5:40 and went downstairs to the living room, where he put on his gym clothes. He'd laid them out there the previous evening, he said, so as not to disturb Sheri and the boys while getting ready for his early-morning workout. Then he drove across the Jefferson Barracks Bridge and went to a Gold's Gym in south St. Louis County. While crossing the bridge on the drive home, he grew concerned when he couldn't reach Sheri on his cell phone, and so he called Justin Barlow and asked him to go over to the house and see if everything was all right.

Chris was still wearing his gym outfit: blue shorts, sneakers, and a sleeveless sweatshirt. Chaplain Peters noticed that there were two scratch marks as well as a red blotch on the inside of Chris's right forearm. He caught Jerry Paul's eye and gestured toward the marks.

"What happened to your arm?" Paul asked Chris.

Chris didn't answer Captain Paul's question. Instead he raised his arms and examined them and then rested them on his knees. A moment or two later, he seemed to become agitated. He raised his right arm and pounded it against the heavily padded part of the gurney.

Ron Coleman arrived a short while later and sat next to his son in the ambulance. He fully realized by now that Sheri, Garett, and Gavin had been killed, and yet, he seemed more miffed than anything else. He seemed to think that the police were responsible for the killings, suggesting that they hadn't taken the threatening messages that his son had reported to them as seriously as they might have.

"They haven't done anything to prevent this from happening," he said.

Father and son then talked amiably for several minutes.

They talked about Connie, who'd recently been diagnosed with lupus. They talked about other family matters. And all the while, Chris fiddled with his BlackBerry, picking it up and studying it and sometimes pecking on the keyboard.

Captain Paul found all of this quite odd. He realized that people responded to tragedy in strikingly different ways. But Ron and Chris Coleman seemed so calm and untroubled—so remarkably matter-of-fact—that anybody observing them would have been hard-pressed to know that a tragedy had actually taken place. Were they in shock? Had the grim truth of the killings not yet fully sunk in? Or were they merely indifferent to it?

Joyce and Dave Meyer arrived, accompanied by a pastor from their ministry. They came into the ambulance and asked Chris what had happened. They prayed with him and offered their condolences. Chaplain Peters left soon after, but Captain Paul remained in the ambulance.

The Meyers stayed for about forty-five minutes. Shortly before they left, Ron Coleman asked Chris about Sheri's family.

"Do they know about this yet?" he said.

Chris shrugged.

"How do I get hold of Sheri's mom?" Ron asked.

Chris said that he wasn't sure. He didn't have contact information for her in his BlackBerry.

The pastor who'd accompanied the Meyers said that he'd try to call Sheri's mom on Ron and Chris's behalf. Then Dave Meyer gave Captain Paul his cell phone number, saying he'd be happy to help out in any way that he could.

Ron Coleman saw the Meyers off. When he returned to the ambulance, Chris said that there was one person whom definitely should be contacted right away. This was Tara Lintz, who lived in Florida and was Sheri's very best friend from high school.

"Okay," Ron Coleman said.

He typed Tara's number into his cell phone from Chris's BlackBerry.

"Dad, call her," Chris said.

CHAPTER TWENTY-ONE

The phone call came at 7:45. Major Jeff Connor had just finished knotting his tie and was about to head off to work at the Granite City PD, where he was deputy chief of police.

It was the personnel officer for the Major Case Squad of Greater St. Louis. He briefed Connor on the triple homicide in Columbia Lakes and told him that Chief Joe Edwards of the Columbia PD had requested the squad's help.

"It's a high-profile case, Jeff," he said. "Can you command it?"

"Absolutely," Connor said.

He went into the kitchen and told his wife that he'd just been activated to the Major Case Squad. She reminded him that their oldest child was scheduled to graduate college that Saturday. She knew from long experience that once he took command of a case, it tended to dominate his time and attention. He'd usually be away from home for a week at a stretch. Connor promised her that he'd do everything possible to make the graduation. He kissed her good-bye, then drove out to Interstate 55 and headed south toward Columbia.

Jeff Connor was the sort of cop who inspired confidence in those about him. Raised in a tough working-class section of Granite City, he'd joined the local police force in 1986 and had always comported himself with class and professionalism. He was also tall and handsome, devoutly Pentecostal, and streetwise. Whenever Connor arrived on the scene, his fellow cops somehow expected that things would turn out all right.

Connor took a personal stake in the crimes that he investigated, as if the victims were his own family members. Exiting the interstate and merging onto Illinois Route 3, he couldn't help but feel anger and revulsion. He hated to imagine the sort of person who'd go into two little boys' rooms, and also their mom's, and kill them while they slept.

Justin Barlow directed him by cell phone to the Coleman residence in Columbia Lakes. Once he'd arrived, both Barlow and Chief Edwards told him what they thus far knew about the case.

The victims were Sheri Coleman and her two sons, eleven-year-old Garett and nine-year-old Gavin. Sheri's husband and the boys' father, a guy named Chris Coleman, worked as head of security for Joyce Meyer Ministries. He'd reported receiving disturbing e-mails on his work laptop in mid-November, and then two equally disturbing letters in the mailbox at the front of his driveway on January 2 and April 27. The e-mails and letters threatened terrible harm to Coleman's family unless he stopped working for Joyce Meyer and publicly renounced her ministry. Justin Barlow lived diagonally across from the Coleman residence, and after the second letter was retrieved from the mailbox he installed a video surveillance camera in the window of his son's second-floor bedroom. The camera was trained directly on the mailbox so that anyone leaving a threatening letter was certain to be spotted.

Then just that very morning, at 6:43, Coleman phoned Justin Barlow, saying he was crossing the Jefferson Barracks Bridge on his way home from an early-morning workout at a gym in south St. Louis County. He said that he was worried about his family, since he'd tried calling Sheri on his cell phone and she hadn't answered. Barlow went over to the Coleman house on a welfare check, and shortly afterward Sergeant Jason Donjon joined him there. The two men found an open window at the rear of the house and called for backup. They entered the house through the window, searched the basement, and climbed the stairs to the main floor, where grotesque messages were scrawled on the walls in red spray paint.

Chris Coleman pulled into the driveway at 6:56, thirteen minutes after he'd called Barlow, which seemed rather slow driving for someone who professed to be worried about his family. Officer Steve Patton arrived immediately after and told Coleman to wait outside until the police had finished inspecting the house. Then Barlow, Donjon, and Patton went upstairs and found the bodies of Sheri and the two boys in their bedrooms. All three appeared to have been strangled to death by a ligature of some sort, and the killer or killers had spray-painted FUCK YOU on the bedsheets of nine-year-old Gavin.

Barlow, Donjon, and Patton heard Chris Coleman calling out from the kitchen, asking what was going on. They hurried downstairs and told him that he'd have to leave the house. He turned around meekly at Barlow's prodding, went outside through the garage door, and sat in the driveway. Barlow put a hand on his shoulder and said, "Chris, they didn't make it." Coleman said, "What do you mean, 'They didn't make it'?" He began to cry but at no point did he ask the officers what precisely had happened to his family. About this he seemed remarkably disinterested.

The paramedics arrived next and confirmed that Sheri and the boys were indeed dead. They also noted that their bodies were stiff and discolored, suggesting that they'd been dead for several hours or longer.

Major Jeff Connor took all of this in and recognized at once that Chris Coleman had to be counted a serious suspect.

"Where's Coleman now?" he asked.

"Sitting in the ambulance with his father," Chief Edwards said. "Jerry Paul's with them."

Major Connor moved quickly. He realized that the first several hours of any investigation were of crucial importance. He told Chief Edwards that he wanted Chris transported in the ambulance to the Columbia police station for questioning.

"We'll sit him down in an interrogation room," Connor said. "That way we get him out of his comfort zone."

The next item of business was neighborhood trash collection, which was scheduled for later that same day. Connor and Chief Edwards called the sanitation department with instructions to hold off collecting it until further notice. There was a chance, after all, that the killer had disposed of some vital piece of evidence—the ligature, say—in one of the trash bins lining the curb.

About twenty investigators with the Major Case Squad had arrived on the scene by this point. Major Connor organized them into two teams. The first team undertook an extensive canvass of the neighborhood, knocking on doors and asking people if they'd seen or heard anything unusual over the previous twelve hours or so. The second team scoured the neighborhood for physical evidence, emptying trash cans, pulling off sewer lids, picking through shrubbery.

Connor also began to formulate a strategy for dealing with the media. A satellite truck from St. Louis was already on the scene, with others sure to follow. He had no doubt that this case would receive far more coverage than any he'd been involved in until now.

The ambulance left for the police station at about 8:45 a.m. Captain Jerry Paul rode in the back with Chris and Ron Coleman.

They parked behind the station, and Jerry Paul led the Colemans up the rear staircase, thinking that he'd sit with them in his second-floor office while awaiting further instructions from Jeff Connor. However, upon reaching the top of the stairs, he realized that this probably wasn't a good idea. The second floor was already teeming with additional investigators from the Major Case Squad, who'd converted the large conference area on the floor into a command post. Illinois State Police detective Dave Bivens was there, and so were a dozen other men whom Paul recognized.

Paul took the Colemans downstairs again and into Officer Josh Bayer's office, which was located behind the dispatch center toward the front of the station. It was a nice, private space with a couple of desks, some swivel chairs, a bulletin board, and a window.

Chris sat down on one of the swivel chairs and inadvertently turned over his right arm, revealing the scratches and the red blotch.

"What happened to your arm?" Ron Coleman asked.

Chris studied the arm for a moment, then leaned forward and put both arms between his knees.

"I don't know," he said. "It must've happened when I hit the arm against the gurney in the ambulance."

Jerry Paul knew that this wasn't true. Both he and Chaplain Peters had seen the marks on Coleman's arm prior to his striking the gurney. Even if they hadn't, Coleman had struck the heavily padded part of the gurney, which surely wouldn't have caused damage of this sort.

The three men sat for a while in Officer Bayer's office. The seconds seemed to tick by slowly. Ron Coleman would occasionally step out into the corridor leading to the dispatch center in order to make a phone call.

One of the first people he called was Tara Lintz.

The Major Case Squad had managed to get an address and a home phone number for Sheri's mom, Angela. They'd contacted the Chicago area police, who'd sent a couple of officers over to her house with the terrible news, but she hadn't been home.

Now, at roughly 9:30 a.m., the Case Squad succeeded in getting her cell phone number, and they decided that they should try to call her themselves. They certainly didn't want her to learn about the murders through the news media. The only question was who exactly should be given the assignment of making the call.

For Chief Joe Edwards and Major Jeff Connor, there seemed only one obvious choice. This was Detective Karla Heine.

Karla Heine was a petite, attractive woman in her late thirties. She'd joined the Columbia Police Department in 2004 after spending ten years in law enforcement in Cahokia,

Illinois. She was smart and insightful, with an impressive reserve of human empathy. Along with Justin Barlow, she made up the Columbia PD's tiny, two-person detective squad.

Karla had first heard about the killings at 7:15 while en route to a sex-abuse prevention class in St. Louis. She'd just crossed the Poplar Street Bridge into downtown St. Louis when she phoned Chief Edwards. The Cardinals were playing a home game that afternoon, which she'd planned on attending with some of her D.A.R.E. (Drug Abuse Resistance Education) students. She wanted to check with the chief to see if this was still all right.

"Hi, Joe," she said. "Just reminding you about the Cards game today. Is it still okay if I go after my class?"

"No, Karla," Chief Edwards said. "No class, no baseball game. You've gotta come right back."

"What's going on, Joe?" she said.

"A triple homicide, with two kids involved," Edwards said. "It's the Coleman family in Columbia Lakes."

Karla turned her car around, sped to Columbia Lakes, and helped out with the neighborhood canvass. Then she followed the ambulance to the police station and got down to work preparing search warrants. And now she was being asked to make the worst of all imaginable phone calls.

She went into a private office with Major Jeff Connor and got through to Angela, who was just then running an errand in her car. Karla identified herself and tried to find the right words. But, of course, there were no right words.

"I'm so sorry," she said. "Something terrible has happened to your daughter."

Karla couldn't bring herself to go into details. She couldn't begin to say anything about the two young boys. The situation was simply too horrible. She handed the phone to Major Connor.

Connor told Angela what had happened. He told her that her daughter and two grandsons had been murdered earlier that morning.

CHAPTER TWENTY-TWO

Major Jeff Connor had a crucial decision to make. To whom should he assign the job of interviewing Chris Coleman?

In any criminal investigation, there are few things more important than the initial interview of a key suspect. This is where a case is often made—and sometimes lost. Connor and his team didn't have the luxury of formulating a precise game plan for the interview. There simply wasn't time. The suspect was right there in the police station, practically staring them in the face. They needed to start questioning him at once, and with the right people doing the questioning they might even get a confession.

Connor opted for Justin Barlow and Illinois State Police detective Dave Bivens. He'd worked with both men on the Major Case Squad many times before. He knew that they were smart and confident and that they functioned well in tandem. He also knew that they were quick-witted enough to make adjustments on the fly, which was important when conducting an interview with almost no advance preparation.

There were additional advantages to having Justin Barlow involved. He had firsthand knowledge of the crime scene, and he'd had an opportunity to develop some measure of rapport with Chris Coleman. Moreover, Columbia Lakes was his home turf. The murders had been committed directly across the street from where he himself lived. Major

Connor knew that Barlow wouldn't rest until this case was solved.

Captain Jerry Paul escorted Chris into a small gray room on the second floor of the police station. Two signs on adjoining walls advised that the room was "monitored by audio and video surveillance." Chris was carrying a bottle of water and still wearing his gym clothes. He sat in a straight-backed chair next to a long narrow table. He heaved a sigh and laid his BlackBerry on the table.

Captain Paul left the room, closing the door behind him. Chris rocked from side to side and began to sob. He wiped his eyes, and then clamped his hands on top of his head. The big round clock on the wall behind him read 10:05 a.m.

Justin Barlow and Dave Bivens came into the room. Barlow still had on the Chicago Bears cap that he'd worn to the Coleman house earlier that morning. Bivens was the older of the two by a decade or so and was wearing a shirt and tie with tan khakis. He projected an aura of confidence, which was the hard-won result of a long tenure in criminal investigation.

They sat across from Chris and read him his Miranda rights. Barlow assured him that the police would stop at nothing in solving the case. He said that there were already thirty-five investigators working on it. He asked Chris if he was doing all right. Was there anything that he needed right then?

Chris said that he felt cold and wouldn't mind a blanket. Barlow thought this rather odd. The room was stiflingly hot. He and Bivens had come in just moments before, and already perspiration was streaming down their faces. Still, he called the front desk on his cell phone and requested a blanket.

Barlow leaned forward in his chair and looked Chris in the eye. He asked him what had happened that morning. His tone of voice was friendly, solicitous.

Chris said that he got up at 5:30 and slipped into his workout clothes. He said that he left for the Gold's Gym in south St. Louis County at 5:43 and tried calling Sheri while he was driving away ("to wake her up, get her going"). He said that he text-messaged her several times from the gym and then tried calling her again on his way home. "She didn't respond," he said, "so that's when I called you."

Barlow asked Chris if he could see his BlackBerry. He scrolled through it and checked on the calling and text-messaging activity that morning.

Chris had called Sheri's cell phone at 5:43 a.m., immediately after leaving the house. He'd text-messaged her at 6:23 ("I've got about five minutes to go on cardio, then I'll be home"), and twice more at 6:27 ("Hello, are you up?" "Time to get the kids up"). Then he'd called her at 6:34, and again at 6:53 and 6:58.

Barlow and Bivens asked him to spell out the precise route that he'd taken to the gym that morning. Then somebody came into the room with a blanket. Chris took it and draped it over his arms and shoulders. He took special care to cover up the telltale scratches on his right arm. Was this perhaps why he'd claimed to be cold?

Barlow asked him about his job with Joyce Meyer Ministries. Had there been any other threats beyond those that he'd reported to the police?

"No, not really," Chris said. "Except sometimes people will get angry with me." He went on to explain that in his capacity as head of security, he'd occasionally have to get physical with overzealous conference attendees. He added that he himself had "built the security department from the ground up."

Chris seemed calm now, almost unemotional. He leaned forward in his chair with his feet flat on the floor and his hands clasped between his legs. Nothing about his manner suggested that his wife and two little boys had just been murdered.

Barlow asked him about the video surveillance system that he'd installed in the house on Robert Drive. Was it now fully operational?

Indeed it was, Chris said. He went on to describe the

placement of the cameras, their lens angles, and so forth. The surveillance system seemed a source of some pride to him.

Barlow thought this odd too. Hadn't somebody presumably just broken into the guy's house and murdered his family? So, why hadn't he volunteered right off the bat that the surveillance system was operational? It would seem something that he'd want the police to know about.

Barlow asked him what Sheri had thought of his high-ranking job with Joyce Meyer Ministries.

Chris said that he and Sheri had sometimes argued about it, mostly because of the extensive traveling. He said that she would've preferred him to have "a regular eight-to-five job."

He began to sob. It sounded forced, contrived.

"We're going to work this out and get through this, okay?" Barlow said. "The best thing you can do is to help us."

Up till this point, Dave Bivens had mostly watched and listened while scribbling on a yellow notepad. Now he chimed in, asking Chris for more detail about his employment with Joyce Meyer.

Chris described Meyer as a television evangelist whose ministry reached people in "forty-two languages" and spanned "three-quarters of the world." (It sounded as if he were reading from a promotional brochure.) He said that he'd worked for her since 1998 and that he was responsible for ensuring her safety wherever she went.

"Do you have her cell number?" Bivens asked.

"Yeah, I've got it," Chris said. "But usually I don't give it out."

"This might be a time when you can make an exception," Bivens said. "Joyce will probably understand."

Bivens asked him about the previous evening. What exactly had he, Sheri, and the boys done?

Chris said that they had dinner together and then went out for sno-cones. He drove to a gym in Waterloo for a workout, and after returning home he said prayers with the boys and helped tuck them in for the night. He and Sheri watched TV for a while in the living room before going upstairs. They got undressed and brushed their teeth, then he went back down and made sure that all of the doors and windows were locked. Finally they went to bed.

"What did Sheri wear to bed?" Bivens asked.

"Nothing," Chris said. "She sleeps in the nude."

The two cops left the room now, telling Chris that they wanted to get a soda. On his way out the door, Dave Bivens placed his notepad on the edge of the table.

Once they'd left, Chris retrieved the notepad and flipped through it. Then he put it down and began to sob. "Oh, man," he said, covering his eyes with his hands. He dried his tears with a Kleenex, stiffened his back, and took a drink of water. He crossed his legs and examined the scratch marks on his right arm.

Seconds later, he picked up his BlackBerry and began to peck away at the keyboard.

Barlow and Bivens hadn't actually wanted a soda. Rather, they'd each received a text message from Major Connor, advising them that critical new information was developing and asking them to step out for a moment.

The critical new information involved Tara Lintz.

Major Connor had assigned an investigator the job of monitoring Internet activity in connection with the case, and something interesting had just emerged. An anonymous individual had posted a comment on a media blog suggesting that Chris Coleman had a girlfriend named Tara Lintz in the Tampa–St. Petersburg area.

"Hang tight for a couple of minutes," Major Connor told Barlow and Bivens after they'd come out of the interrogation room. "Let's see where this goes."

While they waited, Detective James Newcombe of the Major Case Squad contacted the St. Petersburg PD, who managed to get him Tara's home phone number. He called her and identified himself. She seemed nervous, hesitant.

"Do I need a lawyer?" she asked.

"I don't think so," Newcombe said. "Why? Have you done something wrong?"

She said that she knew about the murders. Her boyfriend Chris Coleman's father had called and told her.

Newcombe didn't want to push her too hard just then. He realized that the telephone was a poor substitute for a face-to-face interview, especially in a case of this magnitude. So he thanked her for her trouble and promised that he'd keep in touch.

He then contacted the St. Petersburg PD again, and the dispatcher put him through to Detective Shannon Douglas of the homicide division. He briefed Douglas on the situation and asked her if she'd go and see Tara in person. Detective Douglas said that she'd get on it right away.

Major Connor gave Barlow and Bivens a nod of encouragement. They now knew something of potentially major significance that they hadn't known before. Chris Coleman did indeed have a girlfriend in Florida.

Deborah Von Nida arrived at the house on Robert Drive at 11:00 AM. Von Nida was a supervisory investigator with the Madison County Coroner's Office, and she'd been called to the scene because of her expertise in taking core body temperatures.

Von Nida and her team went into Sheri's room first. They rolled her over so that she was lying on her back. When they did so, her left leg stuck up in the air and remained there. Rigor mortis had fully set in. Her limbs had no more flexibility than rusty old pipes. Much of her skin was a ghastly purplish-red. They took her core temperature by inserting a thermometer into her liver.

They took Garett's temperature next but decided against taking Gavin's, since they noticed that he had strands of hair in the crook of his left arm at the elbow. They realized that this might constitute important evidence, which they didn't want to risk compromising by moving or disturbing Gavin in any way.

Superficially at least, the hair resembled Sheri's.

The CSI people from the Illinois State Police had been cooling their heels outside the house, waiting for a search warrant. Now that the warrant had finally been issued, they went inside and got down to business.

With state police sergeant Michael Grist taking charge, they scoured the house from top to bottom. They searched for fingerprints and footwear impressions. They searched for telltale DNA evidence. They scraped flecks of paint off the walls. They bagged hairs, fibers, and other potentially incriminating items.

The murders had obviously been committed by strangulation, so they searched for ropes, coils, or anything else that might've been deployed as a ligature.

Sergeant Grist asked CSI investigator Abby Keller to videotape the residence. She started in the backyard, where there was a trampoline, three bales of hay, and a small patio with a barbecue and garden furniture. Then she went inside and videotaped the main floor, which was dominated by the ugly, spray-painted scrawls. Otherwise, everything seemed perfectly in order. There was a tan couch in the living room, with a remote controller lying on it and several cushions carefully propped up. A kitchen wall was decorated with a montage of family pictures and children's artwork.

Keller next went upstairs and into the master bedroom. Sheri was lying on her back now, her left leg sticking grotesquely in the air. The surfaces of a dresser and a small table were cluttered with toiletry items and knickknacks.

She went into Garett's room and then Gavin's. She videotaped the two little boys lying in their beds and the jumbles of toys beneath their windows. She videotaped the Chicago White Sox pennant that hung on the wall behind Garett's dresser.

Finally she went down to the basement, where there was a family room and an office. A metal desk in the office was jam-packed with boxes and pictures of the boys in their baseball uniforms.

Keller videotaped everything.

This was supposed to have been Sheri and Chris's suburban dream home.

CHAPTER TWENTY-THREE

The big clock on the wall behind Chris now read 11:30 a.m.

Justin Barlow and Dave Bivens came back into the interrogation room with a couple of sodas. They sat across from Chris and hunched forward in their chairs. This time it was Bivens who took the lead. He asked Chris if he'd spoken with Sheri prior to leaving the house for the gym earlier that morning.

"No," Chris said. "She was still asleep."

"Did you go into the kids' rooms?" Bivens asked. "See them before you left?"

"No."

"The doors to their rooms were closed?"

"They're usually open a crack."

Bivens asked Chris some more questions about his home security system and also about the threat letters that he'd reported to the police. Chris seemed calm and confident in responding.

"So it's fair to say some people think Joyce Meyer Ministries is just a scam?" Bivens said. "To get money from people?"

"Oh, yes, definitely," Chris said.

Bivens asked about Chris's father's church in Chester and about Chris's own religious beliefs.

Chris said that his dad was pastor of the nondenominational Grace Church in Chester, and that he and Sheri had regularly attended Destiny Church in the St. Louis area. He added that they'd been there with the boys just this past Saturday evening. He said that his own religious beliefs corresponded with those of Destiny Church. "Jesus died on the Cross for us, saved us from our sins. We believe that," he said.

Bivens decided that now was the time to zero in on the subject of Chris's marriage. He asked him if he and Sheri had ever seriously quarreled.

Chris conceded that they'd gone through a rough patch a while ago and had even "talked about divorce a little." He said that matters had improved since they'd started seeing a Joyce Meyer pastor for counseling.

"Did Sheri get pregnant right away after your marriage?" Bivens asked.

"Pretty much, yeah," Chris said.

"Was the pregnancy planned?" Bivens asked.

"Oh, no," Chris said.

"Is your sex life okay?"

"Oh, yeah."

"When was the last time you guys had sex?" Justin Barlow asked.

Chris mulled this over for a few seconds.

"Sunday, I think," he said.

"You're sex life was healthy?" Barlow asked.

"Yeah, sure," Chris said.

Bivens asked him when they'd last had a serious argument, and Chris answered that it was probably sometime in January.

"I just got back from India and we argued about money, I guess," he said. "I make over $100,000 per year. She doesn't need to work but she wants to."

He smiled at this. He chuckled.

Barlow and Bivens took Chris for a bathroom break and then left him alone for a few minutes while they conferred with Major Connor, who'd been watching the proceedings on a monitor in an adjoining room. Connor suggested that they turn up the heat, which was exactly what the two detectives had intended on doing.

While sitting alone in the interrogation room, Chris bent over in his chair and sobbed. He laced his fingers and sniffled. He picked up his BlackBerry and pecked away at the keyboard.

Barlow and Bivens returned to the room with a third cop, who asked Chris if he'd agree to sign "consent to search" forms for his BlackBerry, personal computers, and so forth. Chris signed the forms and the cop left with the BlackBerry in hand.

Bivens took a drink of soda. He sighed and crossed his legs.

"Look, Chris," he said. "We're trying to find out what in the world could've caused this to happen. Were there any real problems in your relationship with Sheri?"

"No, not really," Chris said. "Mainly just communication."

"Have you been seeing somebody other than your wife?" Bivens asked.

"No," Chris said. "I've talked a lot lately to a woman named Tara, but that's it."

"Anything else? Just talk?"

"Just talk."

Bivens asked him about Tara. What was she like? Chris said that she was easygoing. He said that she was Sheri's number one friend on Myspace.

"Was Sheri jealous about you talking with Tara?" Bivens asked.

"No, not really," Chris said. "But she did tell me to stay away from her once."

Bivens edged his chair closer. He told Chris that he wasn't in a very good position. That he needed to be honest with them.

"What do you make of it?" he said. "What happened? Who do you suspect?"

Chris blubbered and wiped his eyes.

"I don't know," he said. "I wish I did. I should've been there this morning."

Now Justin Barlow rejoined the fray. He assured Chris that investigators in the field were already coming up with critical evidence and that an arrest was inevitable.

"I'm a religious guy myself," he said. "What do you think should happen to the person responsible for doing this?"

"I don't know," Chris said. "Like anything else, put them away."

He sounded whiny, pathetic. The ex-Marine sounded like a complete weakling.

"I need your help, Chris," Bivens said. "There's something you're not telling us, a big piece of the puzzle. Help me out. What is it?'

"I'm trying," Chris said. "I'm racking my brain. I don't know what else to tell you. I've got nothing to hide. I've told you everything."

"What are you not telling us, Chris?"

"I don't know. I'm getting frustrated. I've told you everything."

Bivens decided that they'd circled the truth long enough. Now was the time to home right in.

"When you left the house this morning, was your wife alive?" he asked.

"Oh, yeah," Chris said.

"What if I tell you I don't believe you," Bivens said. "I think she was dead, Chris."

"What can I say?" Chris said. "She was alive, lying on her side right beside me."

"Listen, man," Bivens said. "She was not alive when you left this morning. Physical evidence doesn't lie. The children weren't alive. Tell us, Chris."

"Yes they were," Chris said, shuddering with sobs.

"No, Chris. I can't buy what you're saying. She was not alive when you left. Period. We both know you're not telling the truth. Just looking in your eyes . . . I've been doing this a long time. We've got to go forward, Chris. We can't turn back the clock. We know she wasn't alive. There's got to be an explanation."

"No. I don't know what else to tell you."

"Were you involved in her death?"

"No!"

"Did you arrange for someone else to be involved in her death?"

"No!"

"Things happen, Chris. We're all human. We have breaking points. Sometimes our body just reacts. We do something we can't control or understand. Then afterward we think, 'Oh, my goodness. What just happened?' Tell you the truth, Chris. That's what I'm leaning toward here."

"No!" Chris said, his voice rising in exasperation.

"Can't turn back the clock," Bivens repeated. "Gotta come to terms. People are going to say, 'What kind of monster would do this?' Come clean now, Chris. This is your chance to tell us. We all make mistakes. This is something people can understand. Come clean now so people can have a more favorable view of you."

"No," Chris said. "I don't know what else to tell you. I didn't do anything. I'm not going to make something up just to make you happy."

He sounded like a petulant nine-year-old accused by his parents of stealing from the cookie jar.

"You can't make me happy, Chris," Bivens said. "Nothing you could say. It's a very unhappy situation. The physical evidence is conclusive. It says she was dead before five thirty. Physical evidence doesn't lie, Chris."

"No," Chris said. "I've told you everything I know."

"We both know that's not true, Chris. We've reached the point of truth. We haven't treated you badly, have we?"

"No, and you've got no reason to."

Bivens and Barlow exchanged weary glances.

"Chris, we're gathering evidence right now," Barlow said. "Come clean. We have the resources to determine time of death."

"I don't know what else to tell you," Chris said.

"You tell us something we know not to be truthful, we gotta assume you're not being truthful about anything," Bivens said.

"I don't know what else to tell you," Chris insisted. "I'm tired, worn-out, in shock."

"I know that, Chris," Bivens said. "I know you're grieving right now. I know you're in tough shape. I'm feeling for you. How did it get to this point, Chris?"

Chris rubbed his eyes. He gave Bivens an imploring look.

"You've asked the same question about twenty times," he said.

"I know that, Chris," Bivens said. "I know the answer's on the tip of your tongue. Tell us, Chris."

"I don't know what to say."

"She was deceased when you left, Chris. Are you saying my physical evidence is wrong?"

"She was lying there right beside me."

"But she was deceased, Chris."

"She couldn't be. She was lying right there."

Bivens took a deep breath. He shifted in his chair.

"You're a religious man, Chris," he said. "You believe in forgiveness. Own up and tell us what happened."

"You keep asking me the same stuff," Chris said, his voice now a full-fledged whine. "I'm not going to make stuff up to please you."

"I need your help, Chris," Bivens said. "Help me to understand what happened. Were you having an affair?"

"No."

"Doing anything your wife wouldn't approve of?"

"Maybe just some sexual kind of stuff with Tara."

"Like what?"

"You know, talk about what she was like, what I was like."

"Did you want it to go farther?"

"No, I didn't want to hurt the kids. Maybe under different circumstances . . ."

At this point Barlow and Bivens received another text message from Major Connor advising them that more information had just come in from the field. They told Chris that they'd be back in a couple of minutes and stepped outside.

After they'd left, Chris stood up and stretched. He seemed grateful for the break.

The new information once again involved Tara Lintz. Detective Shannon Douglas of the St. Petersburg PD had just visited with Tara, who hadn't seemed in the least reluctant to talk. She'd told Douglas that she and Chris had been having a hot and heavy affair. That they'd been exchanging long-distance sex pictures. That they'd planned on getting married and that Chris was supposed to have served Sheri with divorce papers.

He was supposed to have done so that very day.

CHAPTER TWENTY-FOUR

Barlow and Bivens returned to the interrogation room and sat down across from Chris. They wore expressions of grim determination. The clock on the wall now read 2:00 p.m.

They wasted no time on preliminaries. Barlow got it started.

"Listen, Chris," he said. "St. Petersburg Homicide is talking with Tara right now. I'm not bullshitting you. We know you guys are having an affair. We know about the sex pictures. We know you met up with her in Hawaii."

Chris seemed nonplussed.

"I didn't know it was an affair," he said.

"You didn't know it was an affair?" Barlow said. "How many times have you had sex with her? You've lied to us, Chris. Why shouldn't we assume everything you've told us is a lie?"

"I just didn't want to upset my dad," Chris said.

"Did Sheri know?" Barlow pressed on. "Did she know about the pictures?"

"I don't know," Chris said.

"Tara says you told her you had divorce papers drawn up," Barlow said. "Is this true?"

"No."

"Anything else, Chris? Remember, we've got St. Petersburg

Homicide talking with Tara right now. Anything else that's going to cause you trouble?"

"There's nothing to get in trouble about."

"How long you guys had this relationship?"

"Since the Joyce Meyer Tampa conference this year," Chris said. "February or March."

This, of course, was false. The Tampa conference had taken place in early November of 2008.

"Would Joyce Meyer's husband know about this?" Barlow asked. "Would he have seen Tara at any of these conferences?"

"He never talked to me about it," Chris said. "Danny talked to me. He said, 'Hey, whatever you've got going on, stop it.' "

"These personal pictures of yourself," Barlow said. "You sent them from your own phone?"

"Yes," Chris said.

Barlow gave Chris an appraising look. He decided that he'd once again try to play the religious angle.

"If you're not remorseful and truthful, Chris, no way you're going to heaven," he said. "You're going straight to hell. You know that, Chris. We're getting to the bottom of this. We already know who the first victim was."

"I've already told you—" Chris started to say.

"Chris," Barlow said, interrupting him. "You gotta level with me, Chris. Tell the truth now. What are you going to do? Admit to it once all the evidence is in? How does that make you look, Chris? A demon? A monster? So tell us now."

Chris put his hands over his face.

"Let's talk about your kids, Chris," Barlow went on. "You owe them that. Tell the truth. Are they responsible for any trouble between you and Sheri?"

"No," Chris said.

"Look at me, Chris," Barlow said. "What about your two boys? What happened to them?"

"It's horrible," Chris said.

He bent his head and whimpered.

"Garett and Gavin didn't deserve this," Barlow said. "You gotta own up to it. We know what happened. We just don't know why. Only you know why. Tell us. It's your last chance to make good for your two dead children."

"I already told you," Chris said.

"Come on, Chris. Level with me. Did you and Sheri get into a tussle last night?"

"No. Nothing happened. We watched TV together. I laid down on the couch with her."

"If your two boys were here now, would you apologize to them?"

"No . . . well, for what happened to them."

The comment soundly oddly detached. He might just as well have been talking about a couple of kids whom he'd never met.

"What happens when we find your DNA under one of the boy's fingernails?" Barlow asked.

"I wrestle with them," Chris said.

"No," Barlow said. "This wouldn't be play wrestling, Chris. This would be from your boy trying to defend himself. You've gotta appreciate what your kids have been through."

"Yeah, they've been through a lot," Chris said.

He said this so softly that Barlow thought they might finally be on the verge of a breakthrough.

"So tell me, Chris," he said.

But there was no breakthrough, just more whining.

"I don't know what to tell you," Chris said. "I don't know where to go from here. I don't have anything to give you."

"It's not just you, Chris," Barlow said. "Think of the grandparents, all of the people who love these kids. They'll want to know why."

"That's your guys' job. To find out why."

"We will find out, Chris. But you can help us."

Chris clasped his hands and stared straight ahead. His biceps bulged.

"Did you hire somebody to kill your family, Chris?" Barlow went on. "You did, didn't you?"

Chris bristled at the question.

"No!" he protested. "They're my wife and kids. I didn't hire anybody to kill them."

"Did Sheri know about your affair with Tara?" Barlow asked. "Did she threaten to expose you?"

"No," Chris said. "Talk to Mike [Shepherd]. He's been counseling us."

"Does Mike know about the affair with Tara?" Barlow asked.

Chris had no answer for this.

"What about Joyce Meyer's son, Danny?" Barlow asked.

"No," Chris said. "Maybe he just knows about the pictures."

Dave Bivens hadn't yet said a word during this latest round. Now he leaned forward and locked eyes with Chris.

"So you're telling us somebody was waiting outside your house to murder your family?" he said. "Is that your explanation?"

"I don't know what to tell you," Chris said.

"I do," Bivens said. "You're a security professional. But you don't notice somebody lurking in your bushes. Come on, man. Let's get real."

He was loud now, insistent. The measured coaxing and prodding obviously hadn't worked.

"Did you love your children?" Bivens went on.

"Yes," Chris said.

"How much?" Bivens asked.

Chris threw his arms up. He gasped and sputtered.

"As much as you can," he said.

"I'm positive you didn't see anything," Bivens said. "There was nothing there, only you. Help me understand. Come on, man. Your family deserves an explanation."

"I don't know," Chris said. "They were alive when I left home."

"No!" Bivens said. "All three were dead when you left for the gym. Gavin, Garett, your wife—all three of them gone. Dead. No doubt about it."

"No," Chris said.

He sounded pathetic. There was no real conviction to his voice.

"They were all dead when you left, Chris," Barlow said, jumping back in.

"No way they could've been," Chris said.

"There is a way, Chris," Barlow said. "So tell us. Only you know the explanation. You gotta tell us."

"No," he said.

"What about the two boys?" Barlow said. "You picked them up in their cribs when they were babies. You were playing catch with them last night. They went to bed thinking everything was all right."

"I don't know," Chris said.

It went on like this for a while longer, and then Bivens left the room. Barlow let fifteen seconds tick off the clock before continuing.

"You think we're trying to make you feel bad?" he said.

"You're making me feel horrible," Chris whined. "You're blaming me for everything."

Barlow asked him some questions about the affair with Tara. He asked him again if Sheri knew about the affair.

"I don't know," Chris said.

"Did Sheri know Tara?" Barlow asked. "Were they friends?"

"Yeah, from high school."

"Would Sheri be angry if she found out?"

"I don't know."

"Would she yell?"

"Maybe. Yell or cry."

Barlow let several more seconds tick off the clock.

"I'm the one who found those boys, Chris," he said. "I don't know about you, but I can't get the images out of my mind."

"I know," Chris whimpered. "I know."

"You can pray for forgiveness, Chris," Barlow said. "That's a start."

Dave Bivens returned and sat down again.

"How do you think they died?" he said.

"I don't know," Chris said. "You guys haven't told me."

"I don't know if you overreacted or if you're just a vicious person," Bivens said. "We need your help. We're just running in circles."

"I already told you everything," Chris said.

"Do you want us to find out what happened?"

"Yes, of course."

"You'll do what you can to help us?"

"Yes."

"You'll submit to a handwriting sample?"

"Yes."

Now Barlow left the room. Bivens took a sip of soda. He decided that he'd give it one more shot.

"I'm you're friend," he said. "I'm not here to hurt you. I'm here to see if we can get some explanation, some healing—closure. I'm not here to bury you, man. You're confusing me for an enemy, I think."

Chris merely sat there.

"What would you think?" Bivens went on. "If you were in my shoes?"

"I don't know," Chris said.

"There was a tiny time frame when the murders could've been done after you left for the gym," Bivens said. "Then Tara popping up, saying you're having an affair. What would you think if you were in my shoes? That you're not being truthful?"

"I guess," Chris said.

"So let's be honest," Bivens said. "Come on, man."

Once again, Chris merely sat there.

"You will not sleep well," Bivens said. "If you have any conscience, any soul whatsoever, this is going to bug you until the day you die."

"Of course," Chris said. "Because my wife and kids are dead."

"What else can you tell me?"

"I've told you everything I can think of."

They sat in silence for ninety seconds. Chris sniffled. He bent over in his chair and rested a hand on his forehead.

"What do I do now?" Bivens said.

"I don't know," Chris said. "I'm tired."

"You hungry?" Bivens said. "Want me to get you something to eat? I'll get you anything you want."

"No, I'm okay," Chris said. "Can I go? Finish the rest of this tomorrow?"

The clock now read 3:20 p.m.

The interview was essentially over. Barlow and Bivens had performed skillfully. They'd pulled out all the stops. They'd never once lost their cool. They'd shaken Chris. They'd rattled his cage. But they hadn't succeeded in getting a confession out of him, which was the thing that they'd most wanted.

Chris still wasn't free to leave. The detectives wanted to get writing samples from him. They wanted to get hair samples. While this was being arranged, Bivens chatted with him about his stint with the Marines. He chatted with him about the boys and the things that they'd enjoyed doing. He still hoped that he might somehow get through to the guy. He might just as well have saved his breath.

Chris asked about his dad. Was he still at the station? He asked whether he could gain access to his house. Not once did he bring up the subject of his slain family.

"I can't believe any of this is happening," he said at one point.

There was nothing suggestive of grief in his tone. He simply sounded incredulous, like somebody forced into a last-minute change of travel plans by freakish weather.

Somebody popped into the room and handed Bivens another soda. He pulled the tab and took a drink. He got up and walked slowly toward the door, then swung around and sat down again. He seemed exhausted.

Chris turned in his chair and looked at the clock on the wall behind him.

"Is that clock right?" he asked.

"I don't know," Bivens said.

Barlow returned to the room with Abby Keller, the CSI investigator who'd videotaped the house on Robert Drive several hours before. She was young and pretty and chipper. She told Chris that she wanted to take some pictures of him.

He broke into a half smile when she began to photograph him, as if posing for a high school yearbook picture. He took off his sweatshirt at her request, revealing a hairless, bulked-up torso with a touch of flab around the middle. Then he took off his size nine sneakers and his shorts. Abby photographed these various items of clothing, then bagged them.

Chris seemed unperturbed while all of this was going on. He showed not the least indication of emotional stress. He chatted about some kind of electronic gadget that he planned on purchasing, as calmly and carefree as if were sitting in a donut shop with a couple of buddies.

Abby shot him from various angles and took close-ups of his hands and arms. She collected hair samples from him and also writing samples.

And then Chris was free to go.

He left with his father, Ron, who'd gone to the trouble of picking up some new clothes for him. They drove down to Ron and Connie's house in Chester, which was where Chris planned on staying for the time being.

Major Jeff Connor had watched the entire interview on a monitor in an adjoining room. So had several other members of the Major Case Squad. The six-hour marathon had given Connor ample opportunity to take Chris's measure. He'd found the guy to be shallow and vain. He'd found him to be cowardly. And he believed that he had guilt written all over his face.

Joyce Meyer sent a press release to the local St. Louis media that same afternoon. "Chris Coleman is a very dear friend," it read. "Dave and I are grieving with him over this unexpected and devastating tragedy. Words are not enough. He knows that our love and our sincerest prayers are with him. Chris has a long journey ahead of him, but we know that his faith is strong."

CHAPTER TWENTY-FIVE

Karla Heine and Major Connor had called Sheri's mom, Angela, with the terrible news at 9:00 a.m. Angela had then called Mario in a state of hysterics. Mario was in the Chicago suburb of Tinley Park at the time, doing some work in his cousin Joe Miglio's father's garage. He phoned Joe, and the two of them raced over to see Angela to offer her whatever comfort they could.

Mario spent much of the rest of Tuesday, May 5, on the phone. He called friends and family members. And all day long he tried to call Chris and Ron Coleman. He left messages on Chris's BlackBerry and Ron's home phone, but neither of them got back to him.

He finally succeeded in getting through to Ron Coleman at 8:00 p.m. Mario didn't try to disguise his anger and frustration.

"I need to speak with your son, Chris, right now," he said. "Where is he?"

"He can't come to the phone. He's sleeping," Ron said. "I'll have him call you back."

Mario thought that Ron was trying to stonewall him. He lost his temper and started to yell over the phone.

"I want to know what happened," he said.

"You have to calm down," Ron said. "You're overreacting."

"Overreacting?" Mario said. "My younger sister and her two sons have just been murdered."

"I'll have Chris call you," Ron said. And then he added: "We're having funeral services for Sheri, Garett, and Gavin at Grace Church in Chester this Friday and Saturday. You can come if you want."

Mario couldn't believe the guy's nerve. He'd made these arrangements without consulting Angela? He'd made them without consulting a single member of Sheri's family? *Take it or leave it,* he was telling them. *This is the way it's going to be.*

You can come if you want.

What about flowers? Open or closed caskets? The dozens of details that went into a funeral? It didn't matter. Ron had apparently already decided all of this. Ron was large and in charge.

You can come if you want.

Why the big hurry? It seemed to Mario that Ron simply wanted to dispose of Sheri and the boys. *Good riddance.* He saw their murders not so much as a tragedy but rather a problem that needed to be dealt with as efficiently as possible.

You can come if you want.

The disrespect was staggering. No one in Sheri's family counted. Mario himself didn't count. Ron Coleman was treating him as if he were a subordinate, as if he were doing him a big favor simply telling him about the funeral.

Mario was a big-city guy. He knew that something wasn't right here. He wasn't going to let Ron Coleman simply shrug him off. He'd heard through the grapevine that Sheri and Chris had been going for marriage counseling. Now he wanted to know more about it.

"Tell me something," he said. "What's the name of the person who was giving Sheri and Chris marriage counseling?"

"That I don't know," Ron said. "But I do know they were having some marital problems."

"And what kind of problems were they having?" Mario asked.

"The kind of problems that every married man has," Ron said.

"Really?" Mario said. "And what kind of problems does every married man have? I've never been married myself, so please tell me."

"Well, you know, just problems," Ron said.

"Just problems?" Mario said.

"Listen, I've gotta go," Ron said. "But you're more than welcome to attend the funeral."

And then he hung up.

Mario was flabbergasted. Not once during the conversation had Ron asked about Angela. Not once had he asked how she was holding up. And this guy was supposed to be a man of God? The *Reverend* Ron Coleman?

Quite a few of Mario's friends and relatives were at the house when he got off the phone. He told them about the conversation, and everybody was understandably upset. The nerve of this Ron Coleman guy, thinking that he could ride roughshod over Sheri's entire family.

Mario and Sheri's cousin, Enrico Mirabelli, was one of the people at the house just then. Enrico was a divorce attorney, and now he came up with an idea. Why not file an application for a temporary restraining order? That way they could perhaps hold off the burial of Sheri and the boys and bring their bodies up to Chicago for a family funeral service.

It would be a terrific expense, but money meant nothing. The only thing that mattered was doing the right thing for Sheri, Garett, and Gavin.

Enrico Mirabelli had a lawyer buddy, Jack Carey, whose practice was based out of Belleville, Illinois, an old city scarcely a thirty-minute drive from Columbia Lakes. Enrico got in touch with Jack Carey later that evening, and the two men began to plot out the particulars.

Don Weiss hadn't tried to contact his daughter since February, when she'd deactivated her Facebook account. He'd assumed at the time that she'd done so because of him. That she hadn't wanted him pestering her. Ever since then he'd been trying to think of some other way that he could reach out to her.

In the early afternoon of May 5, Don received a phone call from Mario. He had trouble at first making out exactly what Mario was saying. He could tell, however, that his son was distressed.

"Calm down," he said. "What's going on?"

"It's Sheri and the boys," Mario said.

"What about them?" Don said.

"They're dead."

"What do you mean, 'They're dead'?"

"They've been murdered," Mario said. "Their bodies were found early this morning."

Don went into a sort of catatonic state. He couldn't talk. He couldn't move. He couldn't think.

A couple of hours later he went online and read a news report.

It was true. Sheri and the boys had indeed been murdered.

Tuesday, May 5, was Vanessa's son Brandon's birthday. His class at school was having a party for him, so at six o'clock that morning she went to the Market Place off Illinois Route 3 and bought some cupcakes. She made certain to buy enough so that nobody in the class would be left out.

She planned on dropping Brandon and a neighborhood boy off at school, and upon returning home from the Market Place she told both boys to go outside and wait for her in the car. While she was arranging the cupcakes on a platter, the neighborhood boy came running back inside.

"Vanessa," he said. "There's an ambulance and lots of police down the street."

Vanessa saw no reason for alarm. Nothing bad ever happened in Columbia Lakes. It was the perfect suburb.

"Just go get in the car," she told the kid. "I'll be there in a minute."

A moment later Vanessa went out to the car and noticed

that the police and the ambulance were at Sheri and Chris's house.

My goodness, she thought. *Hopefully everything's okay.*

She brought the kids to school, then raced back home and text-messaged Sheri.

"Hey, Girl," she wrote. "Is everything all right?"

Several minutes passed, and Vanessa grew more concerned. Sheri would normally respond to her text messages right away. But not now . . . now, nothing.

She went outside to her driveway, and just then Detective James Newcombe of the Major Case Squad approached her. Newcombe had been doing the canvass of the neighborhood, and several people had indicated to him that Vanessa was an especially good friend of Sheri's.

"Hi," he said. "Are you Vanessa?"

"Yes," she said. "What's going on?"

"There's been a triple homicide," Detective Newcombe said.

"Oh, no," Vanessa said. "Who was it?"

She hated to ask. She worried that she already knew the answer.

Newcombe told her that it was Sheri and the boys, whereupon Vanessa collapsed to the ground in the driveway.

Newcombe and a second detective helped her up and took her inside her house. They asked her if she needed medical attention, and Vanessa said no. She thought that she'd be okay.

The detectives asked her a lot of questions. They seemed especially curious about the three bales of hay that were in the backyard of the Coleman residence. Vanessa found this puzzling. What could it possibly have to do with the murders?

She explained that she and her fiancé had sown their front lawn with grass seed the previous fall, then covered the new seed with hay to protect it from birds and the winter cold. After the job was done, they'd had three bales of hay left over, which they'd given to Sheri and Chris.

She went on to explain that for quite some time Sheri and

Chris had thrown a Halloween bonfire in their backyard. They'd liked having bales of hay on hand for their guests to sit on. This past Halloween, however, they'd canceled the bonfire.

There was a good reason why the detectives were so interested in the bales of hay, which they couldn't go into with Vanessa. Just ten minutes earlier, an investigator with the Major Case Squad had found a piece of baling twine in the vicinity of the Jefferson Barracks Bridge. One end of the twine was fashioned into a noose. Might this be the ligature that had been used to strangle Sheri, Garett, and Gavin?

The bales of hay in Sheri and Chris's backyard were packed tightly with precisely the same sort of twine.

Vanessa wandered through the rest of the day in a fog. She couldn't accept that Sheri and the boys were really dead, though she knew that it was true. She couldn't imagine who might've done this to them. It didn't occur to her that Chris might've done it. She knew that he and Sheri had been having problems, but she still thought of him as a fundamentally decent husband. There was no way in the world that he would've murdered Sheri. And the boys? Chris loved Garett and Gavin with all of his heart. He wouldn't have harmed a hair on their heads.

And how would Vanessa break the news to her son, Brandon? How would she tell him that his two best friends and their mom had just been murdered? That they'd been strangled to death on his birthday?

Kathy LaPlante started work early at Joyce Meyer Ministries on May 5. She soon began to suspect that something was amiss.

Shortly past 7:00 a.m., her immediate boss, David L. Meyer, received an urgent phone call. Then David's wife, Shelly, showed up, and he and she conferred privately in his office. When they came back out, David told Kathy to clear his schedule for the day.

Not long afterward, management called an all-staff meeting in the chapel. Kathy wondered if something negative about Joyce Meyer Ministries had just appeared in the media. This had generally been the reason for all-staff meetings in the past.

Her curiosity piqued, Kathy went online and checked out the *St. Louis Post-Dispatch* Web site. Almost at once, she saw a picture of Sheri and Chris's house on Robert Drive. The house was surrounded by crime scene tape. The accompanying caption read: "Mother and two children murdered."

Kathy began to tremble. She was speechless. She left the office and drove home. Her husband, Bob, was sitting on the couch when she went inside the house.

"Sheri and the boys are dead," she said.

"What?" Bob said.

"They're dead," she said. "And Chris did it."

"What?" Bob said again.

"They've been murdered," Kathy said. "It's already in the news. And I know Chris did it."

Bob told her not to accuse Chris of so horrible a crime. He said that he knew the guy. Chris couldn't have done it.

"He did it," Kathy repeated.

"But that's unfathomable," Bob said.

Kathy held her ground. She reminded Bob of what Sheri had once told her. *If anything happens to me, Chris did it.*

Bob insisted that she was jumping to conclusions. What was her evidence for saying that Chris did it? And wasn't he innocent until proven guilty?

Kathy began to waver. She wanted to believe Bob. She wanted to believe that Chris couldn't possibly have killed his own family. But deep down she knew that he'd done it. She knew that he'd murdered Sheri, Garett, and Gavin.

David Meyer text-messaged Kathy, asking where she was. She responded, saying she'd gone home because of what had happened to Sheri and the boys. He text-messaged her again, saying there was a chapel meeting at 11:00 a.m., which she was expected to attend. Kathy was fearful of antagonizing David, so after a couple of hours she somehow managed to pull herself together and go back to work.

After returning home, Kathy sat down with her four children and told them the news. She told them that the beautiful young woman whom they'd grown to love over the past several years was now dead, and that the two little boys whom they'd come to think of as being part of their own family were also dead. She told them that they'd been murdered.

She didn't say anything to them about her suspicions concerning Chris. She'd wait for a better time before doing that.

Later that evening, Kathy phoned a couple of friends in California. She told them that she was haunted by something that Sheri had confided to her just before Christmas.

Sheri and Chris had just had a terrible argument, and she'd reportedly said to him: "Chris, I'm never going to divorce you. I will not leave. What are you going to do? Kill me?"

Meegan Turnbeaugh was now a senior project manager with an information technology company, having left Joyce Meyer Ministries some time before. She spent most of Tuesday morning, May 5, sequestered in her office, preparing for an important conference call, which was scheduled for 11:00 a.m.

Just as the conference call was about to get started, her personal cell phone rang. She knew that it was her husband, Lonnie, but she didn't bother to answer. But then Lonnie called again, and she had no choice but to respond. If he called twice, it meant that there was some sort of an emergency.

Meegan put the conference call on hold and picked up her cell phone. Lonnie told her that Sheri and the boys had been murdered.

"Where's Chris?" she said. "They have to find him. He's responsible."

Meegan hung up her cell phone. She gasped and sobbed, then she began to hyperventilate. A couple of women ushered her into a nearby office and closed the door. Once she'd calmed down a bit, she called Chris and left him a voice mail: "Chris, this is Meegan. Call me back now." She also sent him a text message saying essentially the same thing.

Meegan left the office and drove home. She'd completely forgotten about the conference call. She kept thinking about Sheri and the boys. She kept thinking about Chris. She wondered if he'd respond to her messages. Somehow she knew that he never would.

CHAPTER TWENTY-SIX

Joseph and Jenna Miglio didn't hear about the murders right away.

Both of them were full-time students at Eastern Illinois University, and on Tuesday, May 5, they had their hands full with end-of-semester matters. Joseph was done with final exams but still faced the daunting task of moving out of his dorm for the summer. Jenna had one more exam to go, which she was determined to ace.

That last remaining exam was the biggest reason why they didn't hear about the murders right away. Joe Miglio knew that his daughter was studying hard for it. He knew that her concentration would be shattered if she were to find out about Sheri and the boys. Jenna had always regarded Sheri as more of a big sister than a second cousin. And she'd loved Garett and Gavin as much as if they were her own little boys. So Joe Miglio had decided to keep the murders a secret from both her and her older brother, Joseph, until that last remaining exam was completed.

Joseph phoned his dad during the late afternoon on May 5. He asked him if he was planning on watching the Chicago Blackhawks–Vancouver Canucks NHL playoff game that evening. Joe Miglio sounded noncommittal. He said that he wasn't sure if he'd watch it. This surprised Joseph. His dad was a huge Blackhawks fan. Joseph then asked him if he and

Mario were coming to the campus the following day to help him move out of his dorm.

"Your mom and I will be there for sure," Joe Miglio said. "But I don't think Mario can make it."

The next morning Joseph went to the lobby of his dorm to greet his mom and dad, who'd just arrived from Chicago. Just inside the front door, there were stacks of both the *Chicago Tribune* and the *St. Louis Post-Dispatch*. Joe Miglio flipped the newspapers over, so that their banner headlines were out of view.

"Why'd you turn the papers over, Dad?" Joseph asked.

"I just wanted to tidy them up," Joe Miglio said. "They looked uneven."

They spent the day packing up Joseph's belongings, and afterward the entire family enjoyed a nice dinner at an off-campus restaurant. Joseph told his parents that they could drive back to Chicago without him. He said that he'd spend the night in Jenna's dorm, then return home with her after she'd finished writing her last final.

Joe Miglio, of course, was fighting a losing battle. In this new age of social media, he stood little chance of keeping the murders a secret from his kids for much longer.

Later that evening, while hanging out in the common room of Jenna's dorm and watching ESPN's *SportsCenter* on his laptop, Joseph got a Facebook message from his cousin, Aly.

"So sorry," the message read. "A horrible tragedy. Hope you're holding up."

Joseph had no idea what his cousin was talking about. He wondered if she'd perhaps sent the message to the wrong person. He called Jenna out of her room and said, "Look at this message." Then he phoned his cousin, Dino, who was good friends with Aly.

"Dino, what's going on?" he said. "Why'd I get this message from Aly?"

Dino realized that Joseph and Jenna weren't supposed to know about the murders just yet, and so he resorted to a little subterfuge.

"Listen, Joseph," he said. "Aly is new to Facebook. I'm pretty sure she meant to send that to some other Joseph."

A couple of minutes later, Aly sent Joseph a second message. "So sorry, Joseph," it said. "I meant that for somebody else."

When Jenna read this, she said, "Okay, good, family crisis averted," and went back into her room to continue studying.

But then Joseph received yet another Facebook message, this one from his cousin Natalie.

"I can't believe this happened," it read. "I'm shocked. How horrible."

Joseph called Jenna from her room once again and showed her the message. She suggested that he text-message Natalie and ask her what was going on. Joseph proceeded to do so, and Jenna returned to her studies.

Natalie responded, saying: "I don't know, Joseph. It's something with Sheri and the boys. Can't talk now. Catch you later."

Joseph decided that he'd try to text-message Sheri. He hadn't yet responded to a message that she'd sent him several days earlier.

"Hey, Sheri," he wrote. "Sorry I've been out of touch."

Joseph could see on his BlackBerry that the message had been delivered and read. When Sheri didn't respond, he sent her another one: "Please phone or text me whenever you can."

Joseph could tell that this second message hadn't been received. There was a red *X* next to the message on his BlackBerry, which meant that Sheri's BlackBerry was off-line. Now he really began to worry. Had something happened to the boys? Was one of them in the hospital? Had something happened to Sheri?

Just then Joseph received a text message from his cousin Phyllis. "Hey, Cuz," it read. "I'm so sorry. If you need to talk, I'm here."

This was the last straw. Joseph decided that he'd text-message Phyllis and demand some clarity.

"Phyllis," he wrote. "Tell me what the heck is going on. I have no idea what you're talking about."

Phyllis responded immediately.

"Are you sitting down right now?" she wrote.

"Yeah," Joseph said.

Phyllis then told him everything that she knew. Sheri and the boys had been murdered. They'd been found dead in their bedrooms early the previous morning.

Joseph read what she'd written, then he read it again. He began to tremble. He felt the blood drain from his face.

Jenna came out of her room and saw him sitting there clutching his BlackBerry.

"Joseph," she said. "What's wrong?"

"Sheri and the boys were murdered yesterday," he said.

Jenna refused to believe it.

"No way," she kept saying. "No way."

Joseph wanted to go online to see if it was really true, but he was too distraught to do so. Jenna's roommate came in at that point, and she went onto the Internet and found a news item about the murders.

"Yes," she said. "It's true."

Jenna collapsed to the floor, sobbing. The roommate phoned Joe Miglio. She told him that his kids had just found out about the murders and that they were in pretty rough shape.

Joe phoned back a couple of minutes later and spoke with them. There was nobody they needed to hear from more.

PART FIVE

Investigation

CHAPTER TWENTY-SEVEN

The criminal investigators strongly suspected Chris Coleman. They felt almost certain that he'd murdered his own wife and children.

Major Jeff Connor suspected him.

Detective Justin Barlow suspected him.

So did Chief Joe Edwards.

Chris had so many things going against him that it was a challenge simply keeping count.

He'd called Justin Barlow at 6:43 a.m., saying that he was on the Jefferson Barracks Bridge and heading straight home. But then he hadn't actually arrived home until 6:56 a.m. Why should it have taken him thirteen minutes to drive home from the bridge? Anybody who lived in the area knew that it was a seven- or eight-minute drive at most. Had he wanted to make sure that the police found the bodies of his wife and kids prior to his arrival?

Chris had shown little emotion upon being informed that Sheri, Garett, and Gavin were dead. He'd seemed remarkably incurious about what had happened to them. Was this because he already knew what had happened to them?

He'd pounded his right arm against the gurney in the ambulance, claiming afterward that this was how he'd gotten scratch marks on his right arm. But Captain Jerry Paul and Chaplain Jonathan Peters had noticed the scratch marks prior to his striking the gurney. Was it not possible that the marks had been inflicted while he was in the process of killing his family?

He'd gone through a lengthy interview at the Columbia police station without once asking about his wife and children. He'd fiddled with his BlackBerry when the detectives were out of the room. He'd stolen a peek at Detective Bivens's notes. And throughout the entire ordeal, he'd fed Barlow and Bivens a steady diet of half-truths and outright lies.

He'd initially denied that he and Tara Lintz were having an affair, insisting that they were merely friends. He'd changed his tune only when Barlow and Bivens informed him that Tara was already talking with the St. Petersburg police. And even then he'd tried to downplay the extent of their involvement. Had he mentioned their plans to get married? Or that he'd promised Tara that he'd serve Sheri with divorce papers that very day? Of course he hadn't.

He'd made only passing reference to the security cameras that he'd recently installed in the house on Robert Drive. If he was innocent, wouldn't this be one of the first things that he'd want the detectives to know about? One of these cameras might very well have caught the person who'd broken into his house and murdered his family.

He'd told Barlow and Bivens that he'd locked the doors and windows of the house before going to bed the previous evening. Why, then, was there no indication of forced entry? Why were there no pry marks on the open window at the rear of the house? If it was somebody other than Chris himself who'd killed Sheri and the boys, how had he gotten inside?

And then, of course, there was this: Chris had told the detectives that he'd left the house for the gym at 5:43 a.m. He'd told them that Sheri was alive when he left, which meant that the boys were presumably alive also. But then why were their bodies so cold and stiff when Justin Barlow, Jason Donjon, and Steve Patton discovered them just a little more than an hour later? Why was their skin so horribly discolored? It seemed obvious that they'd been dead for quite some time, certainly much longer than a mere hour.

It seemed obvious that they'd been murdered prior to Chris leaving the house for the gym. And didn't this suggest that Chris himself was responsible?

Though they strongly suspected Chris, the investigators knew better than to focus exclusively on him. They realized that they might be proven wrong, and that somebody else might eventually emerge as the culprit. In a sense, they actually hoped to be proven wrong. The idea of a guy murdering his wife and two little boys—strangling them to death in their beds—was almost too horrible to contemplate.

And so they kept their options open. They assumed nothing. They turned over every stone.

Twenty-five investigators from the Major Case Squad were assigned to the case on a full-time basis. They conducted a thorough canvas of the Columbia Lakes subdivision. They conducted intensive interviews with people at both Joyce Meyer Ministries and Destiny Church. They interviewed members of Chris's and Sheri's respective families.

They undertook an exhaustive search of the house on Robert Drive, and they obtained warrants for the search and seizure of all electronic equipment belonging to Chris, Sheri, and Tara Lintz. They searched the route that Chris had taken to the gym that fateful morning, on the chance that he'd disposed of some critical piece of evidence along the way.

They worked the phones day and night, fielding calls from concerned citizens. They developed a secondary list of suspects and compiled thick dossiers on each one of them. They pursued every new lead as if their very lives depended on it.

Then there were the threatening messages that Chris had reported to the police. The investigators could ill afford to disregard these. Perhaps the messages were legitimate and the person who'd sent them had really meant business. Perhaps this person did indeed hate Joyce Meyer and had thought that harming Chris's family was tantamount to harming her.

With this in mind, they identified a number of people across the country who might have harbored grievances against Joyce Meyer and her ministry. Then they enlisted the help of the FBI in tracking down these people and interviewing them.

The investigators also had a remarkable resource at their disposal. This was the video surveillance camera that Justin Barlow had installed in the window of his three-year-old son's second-floor bedroom a week before the murders. He'd installed it, of course, precisely for the purpose of capturing anyone attempting to leave yet another threatening letter in Chris and Sheri's mailbox.

The camera was fully operational on the morning of May 5, videotaping all activity in the immediate vicinity of the Coleman house. Major Jeff Connor and several members of his team sat down and studied the videotape at the earliest opportunity. This is what they saw:

At 5:43 a.m., Chris pulled out of his driveway in his green Ford Explorer.

At 6:00 a.m., a man walked his dog along the sidewalk, and then returned from the opposite direction a minute or two later.

At 6:24 a.m., a man walked two small dogs along the sidewalk.

At 6:33 a.m., first one vehicle and then another drove along the road. A pedestrian crossed the street and disappeared from view.

At 6:44 a.m., a white Jeep drove along the road.

At 6:51 a.m., eight minutes after having spoken with Chris on the phone, Justin Barlow crossed the street and went to the front door of the house.

At 6:53 a.m., Jason Donjon arrived in his patrol car and also went to the front door.

At 6:56 a.m., thirteen minutes after having phoned Barlow, Chris pulled back into his driveway. Seconds later,

Steve Patton arrived in his patrol car and parked at the curb.

And that was it. There was nothing else.

The videotape left no room for doubt. Chris pulled out of his driveway at 5:43 a.m. Sixty-eight minutes later, at 6:51 a.m., Justin Barlow showed up. *Sixty-eight minutes.* If somebody other than Chris himself had committed the murders, this was the time frame during which he must've done so. And had the videotape captured anybody breaking into the house during this time frame? Had it captured any suspicious activity whatsoever? Of course it hadn't.

What it captured was a couple of guys walking their dogs, a few vehicles driving past, and a lone pedestrian crossing the street. And this lone pedestrian was crossing the street at a diagonal, neither approaching nor leaving the Coleman house.

Might somebody have possibly gained access to the house through the backyard during this time frame? This seemed highly doubtful. The grass in the backyard was freshly mown and dewy. Nobody could've gained access to the rear door or window without leaving footprints or some sort of a trail. And the investigators had already determined that there were no telltale footprints on the grass. There was no trail of any kind.

After studying the videotape, Major Connor and his team were that much more convinced that Chris was the murderer. Still, they were determined to leave nothing to chance. Over the next several days they'd track down the drivers of those vehicles. They'd track down those guys walking their dogs, and that lone pedestrian crossing the street. They'd interview them all.

The investigation would prove to be a collaborative effort in the fullest sense. Jeff Connor and the Major Case Squad would play a critical role, of course. But so would Chief Joe Edwards and the Columbia Police Department.

Chief Edwards was a slim, gray-haired man with a lively intellect and a sharp eye for detail. He could be a demanding boss, but he was also fair and considerate. He treated everyone who worked under him with respect. He gave them the latitude to do their jobs. Those who knew him best liked to describe him as a cop's cop.

Edwards became chief of the Columbia PD in 2004, when he was just thirty-five years old. The department had never had a separate detective division, and one of Edwards's first moves as chief was to start one up. He made promising young patrol officer Justin Barlow the very first full-time detective in the history of the department, and shortly afterward he brought in Karla Heine from the nearby Cahokia PD to work as Barlow's partner.

Over the next several years, Barlow and Heine would distinguish themselves as a formidable duo. They were bright, resourceful, and tenacious. And they were terrific interviewers. They got a father to admit to the chronic sexual abuse of his own kids. They got a woman to admit to trying to drown her baby in the toilet. As testimony to their talents, they were both eventually selected for membership in the Major Case Squad. In the world of local law enforcement, this was the equivalent of making the dean's list.

So now, in this most important of investigations, both Justin Barlow and Karla Heine wore two hats. They were members of the Major Case Squad and also veteran detectives with the Columbia PD. And Barlow had an added responsibility, since Jeff Connor had named him report officer for the investigation. This meant that he was in charge of coordinating assignments and ensuring that all field reports were properly filed.

Another person of critical importance was Detective Kelly Cullen, a twenty-four-year veteran of the Illinois State Police who also belonged to the Major Case Squad. Besides being smart and sweet, Cullen was utterly relentless. She'd work late into the night at the command post, sifting through reports, sorting out leads, and brainstorming. Solving the case and bringing the killer to justice wasn't merely a job to Kelly Cullen. It was a personal crusade.

Perhaps the person responsible for murdering Sheri and

the boys had thought that he could outsmart Chief Joe Edwards, Justin Barlow, Karla Heine, and Kelly Cullen.

Perhaps he'd thought that he could outsmart Jeff Connor and the Major Case Squad.

If this was so, he was in for a rude awakening.

CHAPTER TWENTY-EIGHT

Investigators with the Major Case Squad interviewed dozens of people on Wednesday, May 6. They interviewed people who knew Chris, and also people who'd known Sheri and the boys. They interviewed friends, neighbors, and coworkers. They covered all of the bases.

Karla Heine and a couple of other investigators spent much of that afternoon at Joyce Meyer Ministries in Fenton, Missouri. They interviewed Joyce Meyer herself and quite a few members of her family. They also made a special point of interviewing Kathy LaPlante, since they'd heard through the grapevine that Kathy and Sheri had been the best of friends.

Kathy's boss, David Meyer, phoned her just as the interview was about to get started. He asked her what she was doing.

"I'm talking with the Major Case Squad," Kathy said.

"Why do they want to talk to you?" he asked.

"Because I was very good friends with Sheri," Kathy said.

David Meyer seemed to grow agitated upon hearing this.

"Listen to me, and you listen to me closely," he reportedly said. "You only tell them the facts and not your opinion. Do you understand?"

"Yes, sir," Kathy said.

And then Meyer hung up.

Kathy felt intimidated. She thought that her boss was displeased that she was talking with the Major Case Squad. She thought that perhaps he didn't want her to say anything negative about Chris. She went ahead with the interview but was careful not to say everything that was on her mind. She was fearful of jeopardizing her job.

David Meyer's wife, Shelly, spoke with Kathy after the investigators had left and advised her to take the next day off work.

Investigators with the Major Case Squad also continued to search for physical evidence. They'd already scoured the house on Robert Drive. They'd scoured the immediate neighborhood and also the route that Chris had taken to and from the gym the previous morning. They'd found the piece of baling twine that had been fashioned into a noose, and now they found two additional items of potential significance.

The first of these was a latex glove stained with red paint that they found along the median on the Illinois side of the Jefferson Barracks Bridge.

The second was the faceplate for a digital video recorder, or DVR. They found it on the lower deck of the bridge, next to a catwalk. It seemed likely that somebody had tossed it off the bridge while traveling westbound into Missouri.

The investigators knew that Chris had recently installed three security cameras in the house on Robert Drive. They knew that the cameras were supposed to have been recording straight to a DVR. They'd found the DVR in the basement of the house the day before, sitting atop a computer monitor. Somebody had torn off the faceplate and removed the recorder that was designed to store the video images. Whoever had done it seemed not to have been in any particular hurry. The wires that fed into the recorder hadn't been stripped but rather carefully unscrewed and left perfectly intact.

Was it Chris who'd done this? If he was the murderer, the last thing that he'd want was for the security cameras actually to be recording. That way the police would know for certain that there had been no intruder. They'd know that the only person who possibly could've killed Sheri and the boys was Chris himself.

Had he disabled the DVR of his own security system, then tossed the faceplate over the side of the Jefferson Barracks Bridge while driving to the gym the morning of the murders?

It seemed likely that this was the case. Shortly after finding the faceplate, investigators were able to determine that its make and model perfectly matched the DVR to Chris's security system.

On a different front, investigators also found that Chris had boasted a fan club of sorts over the past several years. Certain followers of Joyce Meyer had started an Internet site that was dedicated to him, but the site was removed the day of the murders.

Forensic pathologist Raj Nanduri conducted the autopsies in mid-afternoon on May 6. She did so in a basement room of a funeral parlor in downtown Columbia. The small room was crowded. Six people were on hand, including a couple of investigators with the Major Case Squad.

Sheri's autopsy was first. Those in attendance saw the double ligature marks around her neck. They saw her blackened eye and the contusions on her head. Besides being strangled, she'd obviously been badly beaten.

Garett's autopsy was next, and then Gavin's. Both boys had ligature marks around their necks, and nine-year-old Gavin also had scratch marks on his throat, a contusion on his head, and an ugly bruise on his left biceps.

And that wasn't all.

At the actual crime scene, the people from the coroner's office had noticed strands of hair in the crook of Gavin's left arm at the elbow. They'd thought at the time that it resembled Sheri's hair.

The autopsy showed that it was indeed probably Sheri's hair. And it showed something else besides: strands of Sheri's hair were also matted against young Gavin's neck.

All of which suggested the following scenario:

The killer went after Sheri first. He wrapped the ligature around her neck and tried to strangle her in her sleep. But she woke up and fought for her life. The killer pummeled her into submission, then wrapped the ligature around her neck a second time and finished the job.

In the process, some of Sheri's hair became attached to the ligature.

He went into Gavin's room next and tried to strangle him. But Gavin also woke up, and during the ensuing struggle Sheri's hair was transferred from the ligature to the young boy's left arm and neck. After finally succeeding in strangling Gavin, the killer went into Garett's room and strangled him as well.

This meant that nine-year-old Gavin actually saw his assailant, and fought desperately hard against him. Might the assailant have been his very own dad?

On Wednesday afternoon, May 6, Mario visited a diner in Chicago with a couple of good friends. They'd just sat down at a table when Mario's cell phone rang. It was Chris Coleman, finally responding to his incessant calls and messages. Mario went outside so that he could talk with the guy in private.

"What's going on?" Mario said. "Why didn't you get back to me yesterday?"

"I didn't have a chance to," Chris said. "I was being interrogated for about eight hours."

Mario asked him for details. What had happened to Sheri and the boys? How exactly had they been murdered?

"I don't know," Chris said. "I just came home and they were gone."

He seemed calm, in control.

"What do you mean, you 'just came home and they were gone'?" Mario said, fighting back frustration. "I don't understand."

Chris told Mario exactly what he'd already told the police. That Sheri and the boys had seemed perfectly fine when he'd left for the gym at 5:43 a.m. That he'd returned home a little more than an hour later to discover that they were dead. And that he had no idea who'd killed them.

Mario's heart went out to Chris. He began to sob in empathy for him. Imagine the poor guy's suffering. Imagine his torment. He'd just lost his wife and two little boys under the most horrific of circumstances.

"I'm so sorry, buddy," Mario said. "I'm so sorry. Are you okay? Is there anything I can do?"

"I'm okay," Chris said.

Mario said that he realized that Chris's father had arranged funeral services for Sheri and the boys at Grace Church in Chester that Saturday, with plans to bury them immediately afterward. He said that Sheri's family wanted to have a separate funeral service in the Chicago area early the next week. He asked Chris if the burial could be put off so that this could be accommodated.

Chris said that he didn't think this should pose a problem.

Mario emphasized that Sheri's family were more than willing to pay all costs for transporting the bodies.

"Sure," Chris said. "Listen. I gotta go."

Then he hung up.

And that was that. Never again would Chris bother to contact Mario. Never again would he bother to contact a single member of Sheri's family. Nor would his parents, the Reverend Ron and Connie Coleman.

CHAPTER TWENTY-NINE

Detective James Newcombe of the Troy, Illinois, Police Department flew to Florida that same afternoon. Detective Dan Reed of the Illinois State Police accompanied him. Both men also belonged to the Major Case Squad. The purpose of the trip was to find out more about Tara Lintz and her affair with Chris.

James Newcombe, a husky, good-looking guy in his mid-thirties, was a terrific choice for the assignment. He was smart, personable, and adaptable. He had a talent for making people talk. He had an added advantage in this particular instance, since he'd already had a chance to develop some rapport with Tara. He'd spoken with her over the phone on the morning of May 5.

Once their plane had landed, the two men rented a car and drove straight to the St. Petersburg PD, where they met up with Detective Shannon Douglas. And then the hunt for Tara began.

With Detective Douglas serving as guide, they went to Tara's condominium apartment, which she'd reportedly bought with her ex-husband in 2006. Though her late-model black Cadillac was there, Tara herself was nowhere to be found.

They next went to Derby Lane dog track in St. Petersburg, where Tara worked as a cocktail waitress. But she wasn't there, either. They tried some of her known haunts and spoke with some of her acquaintances. Nobody seemed to have any idea where she might be.

They had better luck the following day, Thursday, May 7. First they managed to track down a good friend of Tara's, who knew all about her affair with the preacher's son from Chester. The friend told them that Tara was infatuated with Chris, that her entire world revolved around him. She told them that Tara had been documenting the relationship through cell phone pictures and messages.

Next they spoke with a guy who'd known Tara for five or six years. He, too, told them that she was crazy about Chris, adding that she'd talked endlessly about their plans to get married. He alerted the detectives to a YouTube video in which Tara was singing karaoke at a local club and all the while text-messaging Chris.

Finally they succeeded in tracking down Tara herself. They found her at her mother's house. It was a nicely kept ranch-style home in Clearwater, with pictures of Tara and her brother on one of the living room walls.

Tara was wearing shorts and a T-shirt. She told the detectives that she was getting ready for work and didn't want to be late. They advised her to call her boss and let him know that she wouldn't likely make it on time that afternoon.

This was the first time that Detective Newcombe had actually laid eyes on Tara, and he couldn't help but notice that there was a striking resemblance between her and Sheri. Though Tara was rather the bigger of the two, they were both very pretty, with long dark hair and brown eyes.

The detectives wanted to take her to the St. Petersburg PD for questioning. However, they soon realized that this might not be the best idea. Tara's mother seemed frantic with worry, and she asked them if they could question her daughter right there in her home. Tara also seemed nervous, and the detectives didn't want to risk having her shut down on them before they'd even gotten started.

They agreed to do the interview in the kitchen. Tara sat down at the table with her Chihuahua, Gizmo. The detectives set up their videotaping equipment so that they'd be sure to capture every word, every nuance.

They were just about to start the interview when Tara's BlackBerry rang. It was lying on the table in front of her, and she glanced down at it.

"It's him," she said.

Newcombe understood this to mean that it was Chris.

"Answer it," he said.

She picked up the BlackBerry and said hi.

"Hey, baby," Chris said.

"I'm talking to the police right now," Tara said.

"That's interesting," Chris said.

"Well, it's detectives from St. Louis," Tara said.

"Yeah?" Chris said. "They're looking for motive."

James Newcombe could hear this exchange as clear as a bell, and right then he was convinced that Chris was guilty. Newcombe wasn't known for rushing to judgment. He tended to go about his business with a scrupulously open mind, much like a scientist testing hypotheses. He believed that criminal investigators should make no assumption about the guilt or innocence of a given individual until all of the relevant facts had been gathered and sorted through.

But this was something else. Chris might've said, *Glad they're looking into it*. He might've said, *I wonder what they want*. He might've said a hundred different things other than what he did in fact say: *They're looking for motive*. The comment reeked of guilt.

Tara cut the conversation short. She leaned back in her chair, and the detectives could tell from the look in her eye that she was now open to cooperating with them.

They'd already gotten access to her credit card account via a search warrant, so they knew about the Caribbean cruise that she'd booked. They asked her if she'd planned on taking the cruise with Chris, and she told them that this was so. She also told them how she'd posed as Sheri and succeeded in canceling the Coleman family vacation to Disney World. She described herself as a "Disney World freak" and admitted that she couldn't stand the prospect of Chris going there with Sheri. *We'll take the boys to Disney World,* she'd told him. *Forget about Sheri.*

"Look," she told the detectives. "I know what I did was wrong, but I'm in love with Chris."

She said that she'd often referred to Sheri in her text messages to Chris as "Coolio," after the well-known hip-hop artist. She said that she'd done so because she felt a twinge of guilt whenever using Sheri's real name.

She admitted that she and Chris had planned on getting married, hopefully no later than January 2010. She said that she'd already signed up for a bridal registry, and that she'd been looking for houses and jobs in the St. Louis area. She said that she and Chris had talked about getting his vasectomy reversed, and that they'd picked out a name for the daughter they hoped to have together.

She said that Chris had planned on divorcing Sheri and that he'd seen a divorce lawyer and gotten papers drawn up. She said that he was supposed to have served her with the papers on May 4 but had noticed a misspelling of Sheri's name and so had delayed it until the next day. She said that she'd often spoken about the terms of the divorce with Chris. "We'll give Sheri anything she wants," she'd tell him. "Full custody of the boys, partial custody—anything. So long as we get her out of the picture."

She talked about Chris's job with Joyce Meyer Ministries. The detectives could tell that she was impressed with the travel and the swanky hotels. She seemed to think that the job lent Chris a certain stature. She specifically mentioned the flag football game that he'd participated in a couple of months previously in Arizona. Imagine her boyfriend actually catching touchdown passes from Kurt Warner!

She said that Chris had text-messaged her on May 5 from the interview room at the Columbia police station. And that he'd e-mailed her the following day, using a new account that he'd just created. He'd assured her in the e-mail that he was innocent and that he had an alibi.

Newcombe decided that he'd disabuse her of at least one illusion. He told her that there was no evidence whatsoever that Chris had ever seen a divorce lawyer. She sat there with a dumbfounded look upon hearing this. Newcombe couldn't tell for sure if she believed him.

With Tara's consent, the detectives looked through her BlackBerry. They noticed that it contained pictures of Garett and Gavin.

"I've got to tell you, Tara," Newcombe said. "The last pictures I saw of these boys sure look a lot different from the ones you've got here on your phone."

She began to cry. Newcombe thought that the full gravity of the situation was perhaps just now hitting home. He also thought that she still wanted to believe in Chris's innocence. That she couldn't abide the possibility that he might actually have murdered his family.

The detectives wrapped up the interview shortly thereafter, and Tara consented to Newcombe and Reed taking her BlackBerry and laptop back to Illinois with them.

"I'll be your contact person," Newcombe told her. "You'll be hearing from me a lot."

Newcombe and Reed spent another two days in the sweltering heat of Florida tracking down yet more friends and acquaintances of Tara, trying to get as complete a picture as possible. They were there so long that Newcombe eventually ran out of clothes and had to stop off at a mall for reinforcements.

It was almost midnight when they finally got back to St. Louis. Nevertheless, they jumped into their squad car at the airport and drove straight to the command post at the Columbia police station. They knew that Major Connor, Chief Edwards, Justin Barlow, Karla Heine, and Kelly Cullen would still be there. They knew that none of them would be going anywhere until the case was solved. They could hardly wait to report on what they'd found out in Florida.

CHAPTER THIRTY

Ron Coleman thought that he had the plans for Sheri and the boys' final farewell nicely mapped out. Visitation or viewing was scheduled for Friday, May 8, at Grace Church in Chester, starting at four o'clock in the afternoon. The funeral was scheduled for the following day, Saturday, May 9, and the burial at Evergreen Cemetery on the outskirts of town immediately afterward.

Mario and his cousin, Enrico, had something rather different in mind, however. They were still committed to bringing the bodies to Chicago for a family wake. And they were determined, if need be, to get a court order permitting them to do so. Chris had assured Mario over the phone that this shouldn't pose a problem, but they somehow knew better than to count on his word.

On Thursday afternoon, May 7, Mario and Enrico flew to St. Louis. Enrico's lawyer buddy, Jack Carey, picked them up at the airport and brought them to his office in Belleville. Once there, Enrico came up with an idea:

Mario would telephone Chris. He'd tell him once again what they wanted to do and ask if he or his father had any objections. Only this time they'd tape-record the conversation. If the Colemans insisted on going ahead with the burial immediately after the funeral on Saturday, May 9, Enrico and Jack Carey could use this as ammunition to help them get a court order. It would show the court that the Coleman family was being totally uncooperative.

Mario called the Coleman house in Chester and got Chris on the line. He told him that Sheri's family still wanted to bring the bodies to Chicago for a wake and that they'd happily cover all expenses that this might involve.

"Is that okay with you?" he asked.

Chris said that he'd check with his dad, who was apparently in the same room. Mario could hear Chris asking him about it and then Ron responding with an emphatic "No."

Chris came back on the phone with the answer.

"No," he told Mario. "I can't do that."

"Okay," Mario said.

The next day, Friday, May 8, Mario, Enrico, and Jack Carey went to the Monroe County Courthouse in Waterloo. They filed an application for a court order that would permit them to bring the bodies of Sheri and the boys to Chicago for a family wake. There was a hearing on the matter at the courthouse later the same day, and the judge granted them the order.

Mario phoned Joe Miglio with the good news and asked him exactly where in the Chicago area they should have the services. Joe suggested Hursen Funeral Home in the suburban community of Hillside-Westchester. Mario then contacted the funeral director at Hursen and made the necessary arrangements.

Visitation took place later that same day, at Grace Church in Chester. It began with a thirty-minute open-casket service for family members and close friends. Then the caskets were closed and the general public was admitted.

Don Weiss was there, along with his brother, Ron. No one from Sheri's mom's side of the family was on hand for the occasion.

Don thought that the proceedings were dignified for the most part, if not always easy to endure. There was a receiving line, and at one point he inadvertently wandered to the front of it. Almost at once, people began coming up to him and offering their condolences. Some of them quoted scripture. Others prayed and said, "Praise the Lord."

Don found this offensive. His impression was that most of these people were members of the Grace Church congregation. How many of them had truly known Sheri, Garett, and Gavin? And why should they assume that he shared their religious beliefs?

Don saw Chris, who was standing alongside the caskets with his brother, Brad. He went over and embraced him, and told him how sorry he was about the murders. He wondered aloud who could've done so monstrous a thing, but Chris had nothing to say on the subject.

Ron Weiss had never previously met Chris. But now he, too, went over and commiserated with him. He shook his hand and gave him a big hug. Chris said scarcely a word in return. Ron thought that he seemed emotionally vacant, almost catatonic.

Vanessa Riegerix had driven down from Columbia Lakes for the viewing. Since the morning of May 5, she'd revised her opinion of Chris. She'd initially refused even to consider the possibility that he might've been responsible for the murders. But then she'd thought about the bruises that she and her fiancé had noticed on Sheri. She'd thought about Chris's belligerent attitude during that awkward evening in late April. And she'd thought long and hard about how he'd forbidden Garett and Gavin to sleep over with her son, Brandon, on Monday, May 4.

Tonight's not a good night, he'd said.

Perhaps she'd been wrong about the guy. Perhaps he had in fact murdered Sheri and the boys.

She saw him now and she realized that he'd also seen her. So she went up and offered her condolences, trying her best to play it cool.

Chris wrapped her in an embrace. It lasted so long that Vanessa began to feel sick to her stomach. She felt immensely relieved when he finally let her go.

"Sorry you lost your friend," he said.

Vanessa said nothing. She merely looked at him.

"How's Brandon handling this?" he asked.

Vanessa took her time answering. She wanted to keep her emotions under control.

"How do you *think* he's handling it?" she said. "His two best friends were just murdered. And also the woman he regarded as his second mom."

Kathy and Bob LaPlante had come with their youngest son, Alex, who'd been like a brother to Garett and Gavin. Kathy was a bundle of nerves. She'd barely been able to function over the past several days.

Meegan Turnbeaugh was there, too, and she and Kathy went to the front of the church, where Chris was standing next to his father.

Chris collapsed into Meegan's arms and began to bawl. He laid his head on her shoulder and cried his eyes out. Meegan was repulsed. She felt certain that Chris had murdered Sheri and the boys. She'd have bet her life on it.

After two or three agonizing minutes, he regained his composure.

"Meegan," he said. "This is my dad, Ron."

Ron Coleman patted Meegan's wrist.

"Sheri talked about you all the time," he said. "But don't worry. She had broken bones in her face and bruises all over. She fought to the very end."

He patted her wrist again and smiled.

Meegan couldn't believe her ears. Had the guy actually just said this? Had he thought that she'd somehow find it consoling? And he was supposed to be a pastor? She stood there with her mouth open. She felt her body going limp. Her husband, Lonnie, came over and put an arm around her shoulders.

Ron Coleman then approached Kathy LaPlante and repeated almost exactly the same words to her.

Realizing that they needed a breath of fresh air, Meegan and Kathy went outside and sat together on the curb.

Meegan asked Kathy if the Major Case Squad had interviewed her yet. Kathy said yes but that she hadn't told them everything she knew. She said that David Meyer had called her at the start of the interview and effectively intimidated her into silence. Meegan encouraged her to contact the squad and arrange another interview. She told her not to worry about any possible repercussions from Joyce Meyer Ministries.

At this point Karla Heine approached the two women. She and several other investigators had been monitoring the proceedings inside the church. She said hello and sat beside them on the curb.

"I'm pretty sure you've got more to share with us," she said to Kathy. "I sensed that you kind of shut down on us the other day."

"It's true," Kathy said.

"You and Sheri were good friends," Karla said. "Sheri can't speak for herself right now, so maybe this is a chance for you to serve as her voice."

"Yes," Kathy said.

"Will you come to the police station later this evening, then?" Karla asked. "And tell us everything you know?"

"Yes, I will," Kathy said.

And so she did. She told the investigators that she'd initially felt intimidated but now wanted to tell the whole story. She said that Sheri had consistently refused Chris's demands for a divorce. That Sheri had once reportedly asked him: *What are you going to do? Kill me?* That she'd called Kathy in a panic one day and said: *If anything happens to me, Chris did it.*

Kathy told them everything that she knew.

The next morning, Saturday, May 9, there was a bit of a ruckus at Grace Church. Somebody, it was rumored, had phoned in a bomb threat. The local police undertook a thorough search but found nothing suspicious, so the funeral went ahead as planned.

The church was jam-packed for the event, which lasted scarcely half an hour. Phil Stern of Destiny Church spoke, and so did the Joyce Meyer pastor Mike Shepherd, but absolutely nobody else.

Chris text-messaged Tara from the church. "You wouldn't believe it down here," he wrote. "There's more than a thousand people."

Afterward there was a short graveyard ceremony at Evergreen Cemetery. Chris stood on the damp ground and gazed teary-eyed at the caskets. He exchanged hugs with his mom and dad.

Then he stepped aside and text-messaged Tara Lintz, saying he loved her and missed her. He text-messaged her on his company phone, since the police still hadn't returned his BlackBerry.

While walking from the grave site after the ceremony had ended, Meegan and Lonnie Turnbeaugh came upon a cream-colored Chevy Malibu. Ron and Connie Coleman were sitting up front, and Chris was alone in the backseat.

He rolled down his window, reached out, and grabbed Meegan's arm. He pulled her closer to the window and stuck his face right up against hers.

"Thanks for coming," he said.

"Nothing could've prevented me from being here," Meegan said.

She thought of the messages that she'd left him on May 5, right after she'd learned of the murders.

"I sent you some messages," she said. "Did you get them?'

"No," Chris said, smirking. "The police took my phone."

An hour or so later, the caskets were reloaded into a waiting hearse for the trip to Chicago.

The hearse arrived at Hursen Funeral Home in Hillside early on Sunday, May 10. The undertaker contacted Mario and advised him that the bodies weren't in good enough condition for an open-casket service. Mario went to the funeral home and took a look, and he agreed. The bruising on Sheri's face was still clearly visible, and so, too, were the ligature marks on her and the young boys' necks.

"You gotta fix them up as best as you can," Mario said. "My mom can't see them like that."

The undertaker did what he could, and the service for

Sheri's mom's relatives took place on Monday, May 11. Don Weiss also attended, having made the lonely drive to Chicago in a rental car for the occasion.

The caskets were then loaded once again into the hearse and shipped back down to Chester for burial at Evergreen Cemetery.

A candlelight vigil was held for Sheri and the boys in Columbia, Illinois, on Sunday evening, May 10. It was held at Bolm-Schuhkraft Memorial City Park, a beautiful green space immediately adjacent to Garett and Gavin's school and the field where they'd played football. Several hundred people attended the event.

Quite a few of Garett and Gavin's classmates were on hand, and also boys with whom they'd played baseball and football. None of them could understand how such a monstrous thing could have happened. Neither could their parents.

CHAPTER THIRTY-ONE

On Monday morning, May 11, Chris went to the Columbia police station again so that investigators could take his finger and palm prints. By this point the Coleman family had hired a pair of first-rate St. Louis–based attorneys to represent them: the father-and-son team of Arthur and William Margulis. William Margulis accompanied Chris on the trip to the station.

After the fingerprinting was done, Chris walked out to the parking lot with his attorney. He was wearing designer jeans and a long-sleeved white shirt. He was also wearing a smirk. Perhaps he thought that he'd won. That he'd withstood the best shots that the police had in store for him. Perhaps he thought himself invincible.

Major Jeff Connor watched as Chris left the station. He couldn't help but notice the smirk, and he wouldn't soon forget it. He felt confident that eventually he'd have an opportunity to wipe it off the guy's face.

Chris and William Margulis drove from the police station to the house on Robert Drive. The investigators had finished searching the house for evidence, so Chris now had limited access to it.

Several members of his family pulled into the driveway in a Jeep that was towing a large trailer. Chris remained in Margulis's car for a full two hours while the family members carried furnishings, clothing, children's toys, and boxes from the house and loaded everything into the trailer. Then he got into the Jeep with them and they towed the trailer away.

Sometime later, perhaps the very same day, Chris seems to have returned to the house on Robert Drive in order to retrieve some more belongings.

Over the previous week, friends and neighbors had erected a curbside memorial to Sheri and the boys at the front of the house. It consisted of Mother's Day balloons, teddy bears, pictures of Garett and Gavin, and flowers. There were also Lego models of a mom and two little boys, and a football that all of the local kids had signed.

Vanessa Riegerix was standing in her own backyard with her mom when Chris arrived. This afforded her a direct line of vision onto the front of the Coleman house. She saw him pull up and get out of his vehicle. And she watched as he bent over and gathered up all the items from the memorial. He gathered everything into his arms and tossed the works into a big trash bin.

Right then Vanessa knew for sure. She was astonished that he'd tossed out this tender tribute to his slain wife and sons, and that he'd done so with such apparent nonchalance. It was the most heartless thing that she'd ever seen.

Right then she'd have bet anything that he was the murderer.

The command post on the second floor of the Columbia police station buzzed with activity. Investigators with the Major Case Squad nailed down new leads and filed away old ones. They sorted through evidence and reviewed field reports. They kibitzed and they brainstormed. They drank coffee by the barrelful.

However, in a room off to the side, there was one investigator who generally worked alone. This was Detective Ken Wojtowicz, a slim, affable guy in his mid-thirties who belonged to the Granite City PD. Detective Wojtowicz was an expert in computer forensics, and his assignment was to search through Chris and Tara Lintz's laptops, and also their cell phones, with a fine-tooth comb.

It was a painstaking assignment, but one for which Wojtowicz seemed perfectly suited. Besides being smart and patient, he was a student of human nature. He thought that people often revealed more about themselves though their habitual computer usage than they did through more traditional activities. In face-to-face interactions, they'd try to project a certain image. They'd try to sell some idealized version of themselves. While on their computers, however, they'd feel a false sense of privacy and anonymity. They'd become bold and do things that they mightn't otherwise do.

Imagine, then, the potential advantages of computer forensics for criminal investigation. In searching his browsing history, for example, investigators might be able to develop a psychological profile of a particular suspect. If they got lucky, they might even find evidence incriminating him.

Wojtowicz had gone through Chris's and Tara's BlackBerrys first, and he'd been amazed at the number of images that he'd found, many of them sexually explicit. They'd quite clearly wanted to document every single aspect of their affair. They'd seemed determined to leave nothing to the imagination.

Chris had tried to delete most of the compromising images on his personal BlackBerry. He might actually have been trying to delete some of them while he was in the interrogation room at the Columbia police station. But Wojtowicz had been able to retrieve all of these images from the phone's microSD card, which is the functional equivalent of a computer hard drive. Tara's BlackBerry had been much easier to search. She hadn't tried to delete anything, probably because she had no one to fear. Her conduct might've been unsavory, but she hadn't committed a crime. Chris, on the other hand, had the police to fear.

More recently, Wojtowicz had been searching through their laptops. He'd found various sex videos that they'd exchanged, and still more pictures.

And now, on Monday afternoon, May 11, he was sitting

in his second-floor office at the police station, giving Chris's Dell laptop yet another thorough going-over. His three forensic computers—silent assassins, he called them—were fired up and running, and he was working on his third Mountain Dew of the day.

Major Jeff Connor and Detective Justin Barlow had asked him to focus on the typewritten threat letters that Chris claimed to have retrieved from his mailbox on January 2 and April 27 and that he'd subsequently reported to the police. Connor and Barlow believed that Chris himself had written these letters, as well as the threatening e-mails that had preceded them. They believed that Chris had been planning on murdering his family for months, and that the e-mails and letters were intended to cast suspicion in advance on some mysterious enemy of Joyce Meyer Ministries. They hoped that Wojtowicz might be able to find the threat letters on Chris's laptop.

Wojtowicz couldn't find the actual threat letters on Chris's laptop that Monday afternoon, but he did succeed in finding something almost as valuable. He'd noticed that the word *opportunities* was misspelled in the letter from January 2. "No more oppurtunities," it had read. "Time is running out for you and your family!" And so he searched the laptop for documents in which the word might be similarly misspelled.

Almost at once, he got seven positive hits. In seven different documents, Chris had misspelled *opportunities* as *oppurtunities.* One of these was a memorandum about a discussion that he was planning on having with Joyce Meyer. Another was an e-mail draft to Daniel Meyer. In seven separate instances, Chris had misspelled *opportunities* precisely as the word was misspelled in the threatening letter of January 2. This didn't necessarily prove that Chris had written the letter, but it strongly suggested that he had.

Wojtowicz was excited. He told Major Jeff Connor and Justin Barlow what he'd found, and they agreed that it was pretty damning evidence. They suggested that he now shift his focus to the threatening e-mails that had shown up at

Joyce Meyer Ministries on November 14 and 15. Perhaps he'd find something even more damning.

And indeed he did.

The e-mails had been sent via a Google account called "destroychris." Wojtowicz had subpoenaed Google for information on this account, and the Internet giant had just now gotten back to him with the Internet protocol (IP) address that had originated it. Armed with this new information, he searched through Chris's laptop yet again, where he found the very same IP address. This meant that Chris had created the "destroychris" account on his own laptop. It meant that he—and no one else—had authored the e-mails that had shown up at Joyce Meyer Ministries.

Searching still further, Wojtowicz was able to determine precisely when Chris had created the account. He was able to determine precisely when he'd written the seven threatening e-mails, five of which he'd sent out on November 14, and two on November 15. Was it possible that somebody else had written them? That somebody had remotely accessed his computer? No, it wasn't—not unless this particular somebody had actually sat down in front of Chris's computer and turned it on. Not even a magician could remotely access a computer without it already being turned on.

So there seemed no question about it. Chris had written and sent the e-mails from his own Dell laptop. He'd done so because he'd been planning on murdering his family and he'd wanted to divert suspicion from himself in advance. He'd wanted to create the impression that some enemy of Joyce Meyer Ministries was intent on killing Sheri and the boys.

Another investigator with the Major Case Squad, Detective David Vucich, was with Wojtowicz when all of this came to light. The two men immediately reported the new findings to Jeff Connor and Justin Barlow.

Connor and Barlow weren't surprised. They'd suspected that Chris had written those threat e-mails himself. Now they had indisputable proof of it.

* * *

Chris was losing the battle of public opinion. Most of his neighbors in Columbia Lakes thought that he was guilty. Just about everybody chiming in on the Internet thought so too. Only within the upper echelons of Joyce Meyer Ministries, it seemed, was he still accorded the benefit of the doubt.

On Monday, May 11, Joyce's son David asked Kathy LaPlante to make some copies of a document and deliver them to his office. When she did so, he asked her where she stood on the whole Chris Coleman business.

"He's guilty," Kathy said. "He killed them."

According to Kathy, David seemed displeased with this response. He reminded her that not all of the evidence was yet in.

"Sheri told me that if anything ever happened to her, Chris did it," Kathy said.

David suggested that this was mere hearsay and ultimately didn't count for much.

"Please just promise me one thing," Kathy said. "Never let Chris be around Joyce again, and never let him back on the property."

David turned away from her and went back to his work.

"That'll be all," he said.

Joyce Meyer herself, however, was apparently having second thoughts about Chris. The very next day, Tuesday, May 12, she contacted the Major Case Squad and said that several things had occurred to her since being interviewed the previous week.

She said that Chris had seemed distracted in recent months. He'd seemed less than fully engaged with his job.

She said that she'd noticed a personal cell phone charging up in his car one day. She'd found this curious, since she'd never known him to use anything other than a company phone. She'd considered asking him about it before deciding that it was probably none of her business.

She said that he'd called her on Monday morning, May 4, asking if he could take the day off work. She'd also found this curious. She couldn't recall Chris ever phoning and asking for a day off.

She also said that he'd approached her following the Tampa conference in November requesting permission to stay behind in Florida to visit with some longtime friends of his and Sheri's.

"Chris has a long journey ahead of him," Meyer had written in her May 5 press release, "but we know that his faith is strong."

She now seemed to have altered her opinion about Chris. Perhaps his faith wasn't quite so strong after all.

CHAPTER THIRTY-TWO

It was more than a week now since the murders, and investigators with the Major Case Squad still had just one serious suspect. So far, nobody other than Chris Coleman had really grabbed their attention.

However, there was somebody else whom they'd not yet entirely ruled out. This was Chris's younger brother, Keith. Though they weren't quite ready to pronounce Keith an actual suspect in the case, he definitely qualified as a "person of interest."

Several things worried the investigators about Keith. In November 2008, Sheri's name had been removed from the deed of the house on Robert Drive in some sort of a refinancing maneuver. According to several people, Keith had played a pivotal role in this.

Moreover, they'd heard from various sources that Sheri had been uncomfortable with Keith and quite possibly afraid of him. Had she picked up some threatening vibe? Was this perhaps why she'd declined his offer to stay over at the house in late April?

The investigators had also heard troubling things about Keith from current and former members of Grace Church in Chester. They'd heard that he was arrogant and abrasive. That he oozed danger and menace. Several people had suggested that he was a far more likely candidate to have committed the murders than Chris himself was.

The Major Case Squad decided that they should give Keith a closer look. They knew that he'd recently moved from the Chester area to Rogers, Arkansas, an upscale community located just several miles outside of Fayetteville. So early on Wednesday morning, May 13, four investigators—James Newcombe, Karla Heine, Dave Bivens, and Dan Reed—made the eight-hour drive to Rogers.

They tracked Keith down at a nice town house where he was living with his girlfriend and her young daughter. They told him that they wanted to interview him and that they'd prefer doing so at the Rogers police station. Keith seemed less than thrilled with the idea, but he agreed to follow them to the station in his souped-up Jeep Wrangler.

Karla Heine and Dave Bivens conducted the interview while Detectives Newcombe and Reed watched the proceedings on a monitor in an adjoining room. Keith was cocky and belligerent. He was totally uncooperative. Heine and Bivens couldn't get anything more than a yes or no response out of him.

Heine finally decided that she'd had enough.

"You got a problem?" she said.

"A problem?" Keith said.

"You got a problem with us coming down here to talk with you?"

He sat there smirking.

"Because we're here investigating a triple homicide," Heine said.

"Yeah?" Keith said.

"That's right. I'm treating you with respect. Your brother's wife and two little boys were just murdered. You got a problem with us investigating that?"

Just then a detective with the Rogers PD walked past the room where Newcombe and Reed were sitting. She did a double take when she saw Keith on the monitor.

"Hey, is that Keith Coleman?" she said.

"Yeah," Newcombe said. "You know him?"

The detective said that Keith had applied for a job as a public information officer with the local fire department, and that she was right then in the process of doing a background check on him.

"Is it true what I just heard?" she said. "You're down here interviewing him about a triple homicide?"

"Yeah, it's true," Newcombe said.

The detective furrowed her brow and walked away. Newcombe and Reed somehow didn't like Keith's chances of landing that job with the fire department.

Heine and Bivens kept plugging away. They asked Keith where he was on Monday evening, May 4, and Tuesday morning, May 5.

"I don't know," he said.

"You don't know?"

"That's right. I can't remember."

He said that his girlfriend might remember, and so they put in a call and asked her to join them at the police station.

"Hey, where were we last Monday evening?" he asked her when she arrived. "I can't remember."

She said that they were at the Walmart store on Pleasant Crossing Boulevard in Rogers. They'd bought baking supplies and then gone home and made cookies.

"Oh, yeah," Keith said.

The girlfriend also said that they'd spent the rest of the evening at home, and that Keith had taken her daughter to school the following morning.

The investigators went to the Walmart on Pleasant Crossing and inspected the surveillance video. They saw Keith, his girlfriend, and her daughter come into the store at 8:10 p.m. on Monday, May 4. They then confirmed that Keith had indeed taken his girlfriend's daughter to school on the morning of May 5.

The guy's alibi checked out. It would've been physically impossible for him to drive all the way to Columbia Lakes after 8:10 p.m. on May 4, commit the murders, and return to Rogers, Arkansas, in time to take the little girl to school.

The investigators drove back to Illinois in a persistent rain. Newcombe was especially anxious to get home. His wife's grandfather had just passed away, and he'd promised her that he'd attend the funeral.

Earlier that same day, Wednesday, May 13, Chris visited Evergreen Cemetery in Chester with his parents. The caskets had just returned from Chicago, and the three Colemans stood arm in arm and gazed at them for several minutes. Major Case Squad investigators in unmarked cars watched their every move.

Chris resigned his position at Joyce Meyer Ministries the following day. He seemed to have been pressured into doing so. Joyce Meyer spokesman Roby Walker told the news media that an internal inquiry found that Chris had "failed to follow a ministry policy." Walker wouldn't say precisely what that policy was.

On Thursday, May 14, Mario and his cousin Jimmy drove to Columbia Lakes from Chicago. They arrived in mid-afternoon and met Justin Barlow at the front door of the house on Robert Drive. Barlow let them inside and then stood guard on the porch.

Several days earlier, Mario had seen a news clip of the Coleman family emptying the house of furnishings and so forth. He'd watched as one family member carried Sheri's winter coat outside and loaded it onto a trailer. He'd immediately called his cousin Enrico.

"You won't believe it," he'd said. "It looks like they're ransacking the place."

Enrico and Jack Carey had then gotten a court order permitting Sheri's family access to the house with police protection. The family was primarily interested in recovering one item. This was Sheri's wedding ring, which had previously been her mom's wedding ring, and before that her maternal grandmother's.

Once inside, Mario and Jimmy saw that the Colemans had indeed ransacked the place. They'd cleaned it out, leaving behind only a scattering of boxes and plastic bags. Most of these were stuffed with household detritus, although Mario did succeed in finding a box that contained his old baseball card collection. He'd given the collection to Garett three years earlier. There was a note on the side of the box, signed by Ron Coleman. "Mario," it read, "Christopher wanted you to have these."

Mario found another box in the basement that contained items of sentimental value, though not apparently to the Colemans. There were family photographs. There were little trinkets that the boys had made, along with homemade birthday cards and crayon drawings. There was an album with pictures from the surprise party that the DeCicco family had thrown for Mario and Sheri's maternal grandparents, Dominick and Josephine, on the occasion of their fiftieth wedding anniversary in January 1983.

A wave of raw grief washed over Mario. He grabbed Sheri's old softball bat and smashed up a collapsible card table. Then he loaded the box of family memorabilia into Jimmy's car.

He never did find Sheri's wedding ring.

CHAPTER THIRTY-THREE

It was now Friday, May 15, and the Major Case Squad had been going strong for eleven straight days. Detectives had conducted hundreds of interviews. They'd followed up on every imaginable lead. Forensic investigators had turned the house on Robert Drive upside down searching for evidence.

At Wednesday morning's briefing, Major Jeff Connor had asked his team if anyone other than Chris Coleman could be regarded as a serious suspect. Everybody had said no. There was nobody besides Chris even worth talking about.

Later that same day, Major Connor, Chief Joe Edwards, and Detective Justin Barlow had met with the Monroe County state's attorney, Kris Reitz, at the courthouse in Waterloo. They'd briefed him on the evidence that they'd collected. They'd advised him that everything pointed to one guy: Chris Coleman.

Kris Reitz had wanted to proceed cautiously, however. He'd told them that he wasn't prepared to file charges until all the results from the forensic evidence tests had come back.

So now, on Friday, May 15, Connor and his team gathered at the command post and did some brainstorming. They hated the idea of waiting until all the test results had come back, which could take six weeks or longer. They wanted to arrest Chris as soon as possible. They wanted to put him out of circulation. They were convinced that he was a public menace.

They knew that they had plenty of evidence against him. They also knew that the most potentially damning piece of evidence was the condition of the three victims' bodies on the morning of May 5. Chris had left the house at 5:43 a.m., and Justin Barlow, Jason Donjon, and Steve Patton had discovered the bodies scarcely seventy minutes later. What if some intruder had in fact miraculously slipped into the house during that seventy-minute time frame? So what? This still wouldn't account for the advanced deterioration of the bodies upon their discovery. It wouldn't account for the severe rigor mortis and livor mortis. There seemed no question about it. Sheri and the boys had been murdered before Chris left for the gym that morning. And this meant that the only person who could've murdered them was Chris himself.

Major Connor and his team needed just one thing then. They needed a medical expert to determine unequivocally that Sheri, Garett, and Gavin had indeed died prior to 5:43 a.m. on May 5. This would clinch the case against Chris. If they could get such an expert opinion and bring it to State's Attorney Kris Reitz, he'd almost certainly arrange for an arrest warrant to be issued.

Connor and his team were facing a problem, though. Dr. Raj Nanduri, the pathologist who'd performed the autopsies, seemed reluctant to hazard an opinion on the matter. She'd told the investigators that the bodies hadn't had much food in their stomachs, which had prevented the undertaking of certain tests. She'd also told them that determining time of death was hardly an exact science.

So, where to go from there? Major Connor had an idea. Two or three years previously, he'd taken a weeklong course with Dr. Michael Baden, a former chief medical examiner of New York City who'd once had his own HBO series. Dr. Baden was the most famous forensic pathologist in the country. He was also indisputably top-notch.

Major Connor had chatted with Dr. Baden during breaks and told him about the Major Case Squad. At the end of the course, Baden had given Connor his card and said: "Any time you need help, feel free to call me."

Which is precisely what Connor now did. He left a message on Baden's phone providing some background on the triple homicide. He asked the pathologist to get back to him at his earliest convenience.

The Major Case Squad deactivated that same afternoon with the idea of reactivating when it came time for making an arrest. The investigators hoped that this would be soon.

Major Connor stayed home the next day, Saturday, May 16. This was his first break from the investigation since the previous Saturday, when he'd slipped away for a few hours to attend his older son's college graduation.

He was mowing the grass when Dr. Michael Baden returned his phone call. The pathologist said that he was just then on his way to the airport and so couldn't talk long. Connor gave him some more background details on the case, and the two men agreed to touch base again on Monday morning.

When they spoke on Monday, Dr. Baden suggested that Connor send him all relevant materials from the case, including crime scene photos, autopsy photos, and the actual autopsy reports. He promised that he'd review these materials right away and get back to Connor the following afternoon.

Dr. Baden was as good as his word. The next day he contacted Major Connor with a clear-cut verdict. He said that the materials that he'd reviewed left no room for doubt. There was no way in the world that the victims had died *after* Chris had left for the gym at 5:43 a.m. on May 5. The most conservative estimate was that they'd died at roughly 3:00 a.m. The pooling of the blood, or lividity, in the lower parts of the bodies suggested that they might actually have died a good three or four hours earlier than this.

He added that they'd all likely been strangled with the same ligature, and that it would've taken four or five minutes for each of them to die.

At four o'clock that afternoon, Tuesday, May 19, Dr. Baden spoke with State's Attorney Kris Reitz on a conference call.

Major Connor, Chief Joe Edwards, Detective Justin Barlow, and Detective Dave Bivens also participated in the call.

Baden told Reitz exactly what he'd already told Major Connor. Sheri and the boys had died no later than 3:00 a.m. on May 5 and quite possibly as early as 11:00 p.m. the previous evening. They'd died while Chris was still in the house. There was no question about it.

This was all that the state's attorney needed to hear. A warrant for the arrest of Chris Coleman was issued within the hour.

CHAPTER THIRTY-FOUR

The Major Case Squad was reactivated at lightning speed. Detectives in unmarked cars watched Ron and Connie Coleman's house in Chester. Other detectives waited in the wings, ready to pounce on any new leads that might crop up in the course of the arrest.

Major Connor assigned Detectives Karla Heine, Kelly Cullen, and Dave Bivens the job of actually taking Chris into custody. He knew that they'd handle it deftly, and he also wanted to reward them for their diligent efforts over the previous two weeks.

Dave Bivens rang the doorbell at Ron and Connie's house, and Chris answered. He was barefoot and wearing gym shorts and a T-shirt. His head was freshly shaved. Bivens thought of an idea for getting him out of the house without incident.

"We have some mail for you," he said.

Chris took the bait and stepped out onto the porch.

"You're under arrest," Bivens said.

Kelly Cullen slapped handcuffs on him, and the three detectives escorted him to a waiting squad car.

Before heading off, Karla Heine returned to the house. The front door was open, and Ron Coleman was standing in the doorway. As a courtesy, Karla wanted to let him know what the immediate game plan was.

"We'll be taking Chris to the Columbia police station for processing," she said. "Then he'll be held at the Monroe County Jail in Waterloo."

She tried to give him her card, but he stuck an arm out and pushed her away. Then he slammed the door shut.

Chris's brother, Brad, came running down the street just as the detectives were about to drive away.

"How dare you!" he shouted to them. "How dare you! You don't know what you're doing."

"We're finished here," Dave Bivens said to him. "If you want to see you're brother tomorrow, you'll find him at the Monroe County Jail."

Karla and Jason Donjon transported Chris back to Columbia. He didn't say a single word during the hour-long drive.

Chris had last visited the Columbia PD on May 11, so that the police could obtain fingerprints and other physical samples from him. He'd left the police station that day wearing a nice shirt and jeans, and a smug smile.

This time it was a different story. After criminal processing was completed, he was brought out of the station in shackles and an orange prison jumpsuit. Media photographers snapped his picture as he was put into the backseat of a squad car for the drive down to the Monroe County Jail. He certainly wasn't smiling now.

This was exactly what Major Jeff Connor had wanted. He'd wanted to send a very specific message to the general public: *We have this monster.*

A rambunctious crowd of about thirty people awaited Chris as he arrived at the Monroe County Courthouse for his arraignment the following morning. Some of them taunted him with cries of "Murderer!" and "Baby killer!"

Chris pleaded not guilty to three counts of first-degree murder, and the court ordered that he be held without bond until his trial. Attorney William Margulis cautioned reporters against drawing premature conclusions.

"My client maintains his innocence, and we're going to play this out in the judicial process," he said.

* * *

Sheri's family members had kept up with developments in the case, and so the news of Chris's arrest wasn't entirely shocking to them. Still, the idea of him being the murderer was hard to digest. How could any man possibly do such a thing? How could he strangle his own wife and children?

Mario felt even guiltier now than before. He thought that he'd somehow failed to protect Sheri and the boys from Chris. That he'd let them down in their hour of need. Was there something that he could've done to prevent this atrocity? Were there warning signals that he'd missed? Chris was hardly a stranger, after all. He was a guy whom Mario had known and trusted.

Don Weiss's deep sadness over the deaths of his daughter and grandsons was now mixed with revulsion. He remembered how he'd tried to console Chris at the funeral in Chester. How he'd embraced him and whispered words of encouragement. The very thought of it was enough to turn his stomach.

Sheri's friends were pleased simply to know that Chris was being held accountable. Meegan Turnbeaugh had believed all along that he'd committed the murders. Vanessa Riegerix had resisted believing it at first, but she was now fully convinced. But how could she break the news to her son? Brandon had liked and admired Chris. And why shouldn't he have? Chris was his best friends' dad.

Kathy LaPlante had sat down with her four children on May 5 and told them about the murders. Now she sat down with them again and told them about Chris's arrest. Her son Austin stared at her in disbelief. He thought that the arrest must be a mistake. He couldn't accept that Chris was capable of so horrendous a crime.

"It was Chris," Kathy told him. "Chris did it."

Austin saw the look in his mom's eyes. He knew that she was telling him the truth.

Chris's preliminary hearing took place at the Monroe County Courthouse on Wednesday morning, June 10. It was a hot and humid day, with a threat of rain in the western sky.

The small gallery at the rear of the second-floor courtroom filled up half an hour before the hearing was scheduled to begin. Chris's parents were on hand, along with about a dozen friends and supporters. They were clustered in the first two rows of the gallery, next to the main entrance. Ron Coleman seemed quite jovial, as if this were all a lark. He laughed and smiled and chatted with his friends. The friends laughed and smiled too. A casual observer would never have guessed that they were there to hear evidence on a brutal triple homicide.

Mario, Angela, and Joe Miglio sat at the opposite end of the gallery. They stared straight ahead. Their faces were ashen, somber.

Two sheriff's deputies escorted Chris into the courtroom. He was shackled at the hands and the feet and was wearing an orange jailhouse jumpsuit. One of the deputies uncuffed his hands and he sat at the defense table alongside his attorneys, Arthur and William Margulis. He didn't so much as glance at his coterie of supporters.

The hearing got under way at 10:00 a.m., whereupon Chief Joe Edwards took the stand. At State's Attorney Kris Reitz's skillful prompting, the chief described the reams of evidence that the police had uncovered in their investigation of the triple homicide. He told the court that all of it implicated Chris Coleman, who also had a motive for committing the crime. He'd wanted to divorce Sheri so that he could marry Tara Lintz, but he was fearful of jeopardizing his high-profile job with Joyce Meyer Ministries. The ministry frowned on employees getting divorced, especially under morally dubious circumstances.

Ron and Connie exchanged glances. They smiled and shook their heads, as if all of this were patently ridiculous. Chris scribbled notes on a yellow legal pad.

Chief Edwards told the court that Chris had left home for the gym at exactly 5:43 a.m. on May 5 and that the three victims had most certainly not been alive when he'd done so.

The inescapable conclusion was that Chris himself had murdered them.

Ron and Connie made a quick departure when the hearing ended. Mario spoke briefly with reporters on the courthouse lawn. He said that he'd come close to vomiting while listening to all of the evidence against his brother-in-law.

Two days later, while checking her e-mail, Meegan Turnbeaugh noticed that somebody had logged onto Sheri's profile in a Yahoo! Messenger chat room.

"Who is online here?" Meagan wrote. "Chris, is this you?"

It was Ron Coleman, who'd somehow managed to gain access to Sheri's account.

"No, this is his dad, Ron," he wrote. "Are you doing okay?"

"Hi, Ron," Meegan wrote. "I am doing okay. Just freaked out that Sheri's name came up. How are you doing?"

Ron didn't respond, and so several minutes later Meegan tried again.

"You still there?" she wrote.

"We are doing okay, I guess," Ron wrote. "We're chasing a lead. Do you know if Sheri was trying to get anyone out of another country? A source thinks her husband may have been the killer."

"No, I am sorry, Ron," Meegan wrote. "I was not aware of anything like this . . . I can ask around if you want me to."

Again Ron didn't respond.

Ron sent Meegan an e-mail the following evening. He wrote that a missionary from the Netherlands had suggested to him that the real killer was the husband of a woman whom Sheri had been trying to bring into the United States. All of this had apparently been revealed to the missionary in a dream.

"The Lord will help us find the truth," he wrote.

Meegan responded two days later, saying she'd asked around but that nobody had heard anything about Sheri trying to bring a woman from another country into the United States. "But if you think this is a solid lead, you may want to contact the police," she wrote.

Ron got back to her later that day. He thanked her for her trouble and said that Sheri had valued her friendship. "We sure miss them," he wrote. "God will help us through all of this."

We sure miss them. Ron Coleman deserves some credit here for suggesting that he even cared about Sheri and the boys. As often as not over subsequent months, he'd convey the impression that he cared only about Chris. That the murders of his daughter-in-law and grandsons had scarcely registered with him.

CHAPTER THIRTY-FIVE

The Major Case Squad deactivated once again following Chris's arrest. However, this didn't mean that the investigation was finished. There were still plenty of angles to explore and loose ends to tie up. Major Jeff Connor would stay with the investigation, as would several other members of the squad. And Chief Joe Edwards, Detective Justin Barlow, and Detective Karla Heine of the Columbia PD would continue to make it their highest priority. They wanted to be certain that the case against Chris Coleman was as convincing as possible when it came time for it to go to trial.

James Newcombe traveled to Florida again in mid-June, this time with Karla Heine. They made contact with Shannon Douglas of the St. Petersburg PD upon their arrival, then spent a couple of days interviewing various acquaintances of Tara Lintz. Before heading back to Illinois, they also had a lengthy interview with Tara herself.

Nothing earthshaking came of the trip, although the detectives were able to confirm just how obsessed with each other Chris and Tara really were. The marvel was that the obsession had set in so quickly. They'd resolved to make a new life together almost immediately upon becoming romantically involved.

Forensic scientists with the Illinois State Police had been going strong since May 5, examining potential items of evidence from the crime scene, and the results of their tests were just now beginning to trickle in.

Melody Levault specialized in the microscopic analysis of hair and fiber samples. She'd examined the loose strands of hair that were recovered from Gavin's body and had determined that they were indeed consistent with Sheri's hair. The strands were fourteen inches long and artificially colored.

Michael Brown specialized in the analysis of biological samples. He'd examined fingernail clippings from all three victims and also articles of bedding, and had found absolutely no genetic markers that could be attributed to anyone from outside the family. Suzanne Kidd, who specialized in DNA analysis, had examined the same items and come to the same conclusion. In other words, neither Brown nor Kidd had found the slightest evidence indicating that an unknown intruder might have committed the murders.

Thomas Gamboe specialized in the analysis of both tire tread and footwear impressions. He'd examined the footprints that were found in the house on Robert Drive after the murders and had determined that they matched the shoes of investigating officers. Again, there was no evidence of some intruder having entered the house.

The toxicology test results were made available to investigators in early July. No trace of alcohol or drugs had been found in the bodies of the victims. This meant that Sheri, Garett, and Gavin hadn't been rendered artificially submissive at the time of the killings. It likely also meant that they'd endured horrific suffering.

And there was still much more.

Chris had told the investigators that he'd locked all the doors and windows to the house on Robert Drive just before going to bed on the eve of the murders. Yet, on the morning of May 5, Justin Barlow and Jason Donjon had found an open window at the rear of the house. Was it possible that some intruder had broken in through this window after Chris had left for the gym that morning? And that it was this same intruder who had committed the murders?

The very idea, of course, was outlandish. There was no

physical evidence whatsoever of any such intruder. And Dr. Michael Baden had already determined that the murders had been committed long before Chris had left home for the gym.

In the interests of thoroughness, however, the investigators thought it prudent to consider even outlandish possibilities. So they arranged for the test-lab manager of the company that had manufactured the window to give it a rigorous examination. The test-lab manager did so and found no indication of forced entry. The window was in perfect working condition. There wasn't a chance in the world that someone had broken into the house through it.

Chris had called Justin Barlow at 6:43 a.m. on May 5 saying he was just then crossing the Jefferson Barracks Bridge on his way home. He'd then called Sheri's cell phone at 6:53 a.m. before finally arriving home at 6:56 a.m. Barlow had thought this odd right from the start. Why should it have taken Chris thirteen minutes to drive home from the Jefferson Barracks Bridge? It was an eight-minute trip at most, especially with the light traffic conditions that prevailed at so early an hour.

The investigators suspected that Chris had delayed his return home by taking a roundabout route. That he'd wanted to give the police every opportunity to find the bodies before his arrival.

To see if this was so, they enlisted the help of James Kientzy, a veteran network director at AT&T. By consulting a map of cell towers in the area, Kientzy was able to determine that Chris had been near the town of Dupo when he'd called Sheri's cell phone at 6:53 a.m. This meant that he had indeed taken a roundabout route. He'd gone north after crossing the Jefferson Barracks Bridge rather than turning south and driving directly to Columbia Lakes.

This was strange behavior indeed for a guy who was ostensibly frantic with worry about the welfare of his family.

The investigators also enlisted the help of Lindell Moore and Richard Johnson, both of whom were handwriting analysts with the Illinois State Police. They asked them to compare the spray-painted messages that were found at the house on Robert Drive with samples of Chris's known handwriting. This was a tricky comparison, since writing on a wall with spray paint is much more physically awkward than writing on paper with a pen or pencil. Still, Moore and Johnson were able to find some striking similarities.

The letter *I* in Chris's known handwriting was made with a continuous stroke, and so was the same letter in the spray-painted messages. The letter *P* in both the known handwriting and the spray-painted messages was made with a distinctive back slant. And there were additional matches or correspondences: the shrunken upper loop in the letter *B*, for example; the single stroke formation of the letter *K*; the hook at the bottom of the stem in the letter *D*.

All of this strongly suggested that it was Chris himself who'd spray-painted the obscenity-laced messages on the walls of his house.

The investigators sent some scrapings of the spray paint to Adrienne Bickel, a forensic chemist with the Illinois State Police. They also sent her a paint-stained picture frame that had been hanging on the kitchen wall. Through chemical analysis, Bickel was able to narrow down the particular brand of the spray paint. It was either American Accents or Painter's Touch, both of which were manufactured by Rust-Oleum.

Richard Osterman, a paint analyst at Rust-Oleum, confirmed that this was indeed the case. He told the investigators that the American Accents and Painter's Touch brands had a very distinctive resin, which matched that found in the spray paint samples from the house on Robert Drive. And the color chemist at Rust-Oleum, Michael Harloff, was able to identify the precise color of the spray paint samples. It was apple red.

The investigators hadn't yet found the actual aerosol can that had been used to spray-paint the obscenities at the Coleman house. But they now knew that the spray paint was a Rust-Oleum product—either American Accents or Painter's Touch—and that its color was apple red.

* * *

Shortly after the murders, the investigators had found the faceplate to Chris's DVR on a lower platform of the Jefferson Barracks Bridge. They'd assumed that he'd tossed it over the side of the bridge while en route to the gym the morning of May 5. They'd thought it quite possible that he'd tossed other items of evidentiary value off the bridge that same morning, which might've landed in the murky waters of the Mississippi River. However, the river had been too high for them to undertake a thorough search.

The river finally subsided during the first week of August, and so Karla Heine and several other officers, including Shawn Westfall of the Columbia PD, went out on johnboats and searched beneath the bridge. At one point Karla climbed atop a dike that was piled with rocks, thinking that maybe a piece of physical evidence had washed up onto it. Almost at once, the dike caved in and a big rock smashed against her left ankle, fracturing it in three places.

A week and a half later, Karla hobbled into the Columbia PD on crutches. She felt guilty for having missed time on the case because of the injury. She felt frustrated by her impaired mobility. She asked Justin Barlow if there was anything that she could do to help out. Barlow suggested that she comb through a passel of credit card statements. Who could tell: perhaps she'd find something of interest.

Karla got right down to it, and after a while she did indeed find something of interest. It was a purchase for $3.77 that Chris Coleman had made on February 9, 2009, at a hardware store on Telegraph Road in St. Louis.

Karla drove to the store and asked the clerk for more specific information. What exactly had Chris purchased for $3.77?

The clerk punched up the information on her computer.

"It was a can of Rust-Oleum spray paint," she said. "Painter's Touch. Apple Red."

At Karla's request, the clerk retrieved the credit card receipt for the purchase. The electronic signature on the receipt read, "Christopher E. Coleman."

CHAPTER THIRTY-SIX

The Reverend Ron Coleman was accustomed to calling the shots at Grace Church in Chester. He'd tell his flock what to believe and expect them to fall into line. Now he was telling them in no uncertain terms that his oldest son was being railroaded, that the charges against him were an outright disgrace.

After Chris's arrest, Ron reportedly stood before his congregation and issued an ultimatum: "Anybody who believes my son did this, leave my church right now."

As the months passed, he pounded away at the subject. He proclaimed Chris's innocence at almost every church service. He insisted that Chris had had nothing to do with the murders. He said that anyone who thought otherwise was guilty of sinning against a righteous man, and therefore also against God.

"How dare any of you think that Chris isn't innocent," he reportedly said. "Shame on you. How dare you."

He forbid his flock to follow the case in the news media. He accused the beat reporters of lying. He accused the police of lying. The affair with Tara Lintz? The sex videotapes? Nothing but lies, he'd insist. Lies and distortions for the sake of portraying Chris in an unflattering light.

He reportedly said that Chris was born-again, that he was a member of the holy elect. And that once the case came to trial, the judge would be cursed if he permitted him to be found guilty. Everybody involved in such a miscarriage of justice would be cursed.

Most churchgoers apparently bought into all of this. They were convinced that Chris was innocent. That it was preposterous to think that he might've been involved in such a horrible crime. They believed that crooked cops and an ungodly media were conspiring against him.

"Most of the congregation was with Ron all the way," one ex-church member said. "He had them brainwashed. If the media reported something negative about Chris, they were convinced that it was a total lie. Tara Lintz could've waltzed into Grace Church herself and told them about the affair, and they wouldn't have believed her."

And so it went. During church services most Wednesdays and Sundays, the Reverend Ron would stand up and proclaim his golden boy's innocence. He'd rail against the police and the media. He'd rail against anyone who so much as hinted that Chris might actually be guilty.

However, very rarely would he mention Sheri, Garett, and Gavin. He'd go on and on about Chris, but his daughter-in-law and two grandsons? It was almost as if they'd never even existed.

On August 14, 2009, Monroe County state's attorney Kris Reitz filed paperwork signaling his intention to seek the death penalty against Chris Coleman in the upcoming trial. This posed an immediate problem for the defense team, since Arthur and William Margulis were based out of St. Louis, Missouri, and therefore not certified to handle death penalty cases in Illinois.

The judge who was scheduled to preside over the trial, the Honorable Milton Wharton, wasted little time settling the problem. In September 2009, Judge Wharton appointed attorneys John O'Gara and James Stern to the case. Both men were highly respected defense attorneys, and both were certified to handle death penalty cases in the state of Illinois. William Margulis became similarly certified not long afterward, which meant that the defense team was now all set. With John

O'Gara serving as lead attorney, and Stern and Margulis assisting, no one could reasonably suggest that Chris Coleman was heading to trial with anything less than first-rate legal representation.

There was a certain advantage for Chris in having his case designated a "death penalty case." This gave him access to the Illinois Capital Litigation Trust Fund, providing he could convince Judge Milton Wharton that he was indigent. Which is exactly what happened. Judge Wharton examined Chris's finances and determined that he was essentially broke. This meant that the taxpayers would be footing the bill for the bulk of his legal expenses.*

The investigation into the triple homicide received a major boost in November 2009 when Kelly Cullen rejoined it full-time. As a detective with the Illinois State Police and a member of the Major Case Squad, Kelly had played a critical role during the first three months of the investigation. Then in August, having just turned fifty, she'd retired from law enforcement with plans of finally leading a more sedate life. Twenty-four years of endless murder and mayhem had been quite enough.

Chief Joe Edwards of the Columbia PD had different plans in store for her, however. In early November, he contacted Kelly and asked her if she'd come out of retirement and help once again with the Coleman case. Kelly agreed to do so. Chief Edwards wasn't the easiest man to turn down, and she was grateful in any event for the opportunity to see the case through to its conclusion.

The investigators still had plenty of work to do: sifting through evidence, conducting follow-up interviews, making sure that every detail was in order. They wanted to make sure that Chris Coleman didn't wriggle off the hook.

---

* In paperwork filed with the court, Chris claimed that his liabilities and debts amounted to $243,000. In the same paperwork, he said that he was single with no children.

They'd already produced evidence that Chris had written the threatening e-mails and the threatening letters, and that he'd also written the spray-painted messages that were found on the walls of his house. They realized, however, that there was no such thing in criminal proceedings as *too* much evidence. So now they contacted Robert Leonard, a professor at Hofstra University, who was an expert in so-called forensic linguistics. They asked him to examine and compare two distinct sets of writing:

1. a large sample of Chris's known writing, consisting mostly of documents gleaned from his computer, and
2. the threat e-mails, the typewritten threat letters, and the spray-painted messages.

Were there striking similarities in style, syntax, and spelling between these two sets of writing? Was it likely that the same person had written them?

Professor Leonard responded in the affirmative. He said that both sets of writing featured similar contraction patterns (*Im'* instead of *I'm*, for example). Both featured similar fused spellings (*goodtime* instead of *good time*, for example) and similar apostrophe reversals (*dont'* instead of *don't*, for example). Both also featured similar misspellings, including the misspelling of *opportunities* that Detective Ken Wojtowicz had duly noted a week or so after the murders.

And this, Professor Leonard said, was just the tip of the iceberg. There were also striking similarities in style and syntax between the two sets of writing. All of which strongly suggested that it was Chris himself who'd written the threatening e-mails and letters. And Chris himself who'd spray-painted the lurid messages on the walls of the house on Robert Drive.

The investigators also reached out to renowned FBI criminal profiler, Mark Safarik. They asked Safarik to review all of the evidence that they'd gathered and to offer his own assessment. Did he likewise think that Chris Coleman was the murderer?

Mark Safarik seemed not to have much doubt about it.

* * *

It was almost the holiday season now, and Major Connor, Chief Edwards, Justin Barlow, Karla Heine, and Kelly Cullen—indeed, all of the investigators—were anxious for the case to go to trial. They'd worked hard on it for eight full months, burning the midnight oil at the Columbia PD, sacrificing time with their families. The case had gotten under their skins. It had become intensely personal to them. They couldn't put those crime scene images of Sheri, Garett, and Gavin out of their minds.

From the evidence that they'd gathered over the course of the investigation, they'd developed a clear narrative of the crime. It was far more chilling than anything that they could've dreamed up on their own.

Chris became thoroughly obsessed with Tara Lintz, and she with him, in early November of 2008. They wanted to start a new life together, but Chris was already married to Sheri. He couldn't divorce Sheri without putting his coveted job with Joyce Meyer Ministries at risk, and so he decided to kill her instead. And for good measure, he also decided to kill his two young sons, Garett and Gavin.

The challenge was to pull this off without getting caught. And so he devised a plan. He'd cast suspicion in advance on some mysterious enemy of Joyce Meyer. He began to implement the plan in mid-November, when he sat down at his laptop and wrote the threatening e-mails. Then in early January, he reported having received a threatening letter—which he'd also written himself—in the mailbox at his home. In early February he purchased the can of apple red spray paint, and in late April he reported having received a second threatening letter in his mailbox.

He might not have known at first exactly when he'd commit the murders, but his hand was forced when Tara gave him a deadline for serving Sheri with divorce papers. So on May 4, 2009, he helped tuck the boys into bed and waited until Sheri had also retired for the night. Then early the next morning he sneaked into Sheri's room and strangled her with a ligature. When she struggled for her life, he beat her into submission and completed the job. He next went into Gavin's room and strangled him with the same ligature. The nine-year-old boy awoke and fought for his life too. Finally he went into Garett's room and strangled him.

After killing his wife and two sons, he spray-painted the obscene messages on the walls of the house. He scrawled FUCK YOU on Gavin's bedsheets and was in the process of scrawling something similarly lurid on Garett's when he apparently ran out of paint.

Somewhere along the line—either before or after having committed the murders—he removed the rear basement window from its encasement and disabled the DVR to his home security system.

He left for the gym in south St. Louis County at 5:43 a.m., and over the next hour or so he went through the charade of calling and text-messaging Sheri. He phoned Justin Barlow from the Jefferson Barracks Bridge at 6:43 a.m. but then took a roundabout way home so that the police would have every opportunity to find the bodies prior to his arrival.

The investigators had no doubt that Chris was the murderer. The principal difficulty in winning a conviction at trial was that their evidence was entirely of the circumstantial variety. They hadn't been able to get a confession or admission of guilt out of Chris. They hadn't been able to find any traces of paint on his body or clothing, or any DNA unequivocally linking him to the killings.

Very early on in the investigation, they'd found a couple of items of potential evidentiary significance along the route that Chris had taken to the gym: a piece of baling twine fashioned into a noose, and a latex glove stained with red paint. But here, too, it was the same story: they hadn't yet succeeded in linking these items directly to Chris.

Nevertheless, their circumstantial evidence was thoroughly convincing. The condition of the bodies upon being discovered by Justin Barlow, Jason Donjon, and Steve Patton seemed enough in itself to win a conviction. There was no chance in the world that Sheri and the boys had been alive when Chris left for the gym at 5:43 a.m. and no chance that anyone other than he himself had killed them.

The investigators had irrefutable evidence that he'd written the threatening e-mails on his own laptop in November of 2009. That he'd become romantically involved with Tara Lintz just a short time previously. That he'd purchased a brand and color of spray paint that was identical to what was found on the walls of his house.

Consider also his odd demeanor upon finally arriving home from the gym at 6:56 a.m. on May 5. Consider his evasiveness while being interviewed at the Columbia PD later that same day. And the nonchalance that he displayed over the next week or so, as if the deaths of Sheri, Garett, and Gavin counted for nothing.

Consider also the following:

Chris was hardly in the habit of visiting the gym in south St. Louis County. He went for the very first time on Saturday, November 15, the day after he sent the threatening e-mails. Already then, it would seem, he was setting up his fake alibi. He went again in mid-February, quite possibly for the purpose of timing the drive home. And that was it: he wouldn't go again until the morning of May 5.

Chris text-messaged and phoned Tara almost incessantly on Friday, November 14. He took just a single block of time off from doing so, between the hours of eight and nine in the evening. This was exactly the time frame during which the "destroychris" account was created and the threatening e-mails were sent.

There was nothing sudden or spontaneous about the murders. Chris had planned them for six full months. He'd planned precisely how he'd go about killing his family and how he'd try to get away with it. And then on Monday, May 4, he decided that the time was right.

"Tonight's not a good night," Chris said when Garett asked him about sleeping over at Brandon's house.

No, it wasn't a good night for a sleepover. It was the night that he intended to kill Garett, Gavin, and their mom.

PART SIX

Reckoning

CHAPTER THIRTY-SEVEN

Waterloo, Monroe County, Illinois

It was a sparkling day in late March 2010, with the temperature in the low forties and the skies blue and cloudless. Several of the shops on the town square had their doors propped open, letting in a breath of fresh air after the long winter. The deli at the corner advertised a spring special—veggie sub with sixteen-ounce soda—on its front window. The tall, leafless oaks on the courthouse lawn crackled in the breeze.

Half a dozen reporters stood in a cluster on the sidewalk outside the redbrick courthouse, marking time until Chris Coleman's hearing was due to start. They were young and lean and casually dressed in jackets and jeans.

"So, where's the lynch mob?" one of them said, drawing bemused shrugs from his colleagues.

The reporters hadn't really expected anything approaching a lynch mob, not in a town as well behaved as this one. They were surprised, however, that the town seemed so quiet. Traffic was sparse, pedestrians few and far between, and the parking lot of the small motel on Market Street very nearly empty. The reporters had assumed that the hearing would attract a great deal more attention.

At one o'clock they went into the courthouse's spotless lobby, where an elderly woman at the information desk was knitting a sweater. They took a flight of stairs to the second floor and passed through a security checkpoint that was manned by two burly guards with metal detectors. Then they filed into a dimly lit courtroom and sat in the spectators' gallery at the rear.

They waited, pencils poised, notepads on knees, while the bailiff and the court reporter busied themselves up front. The minutes ticked by and about a dozen more people filtered through the security checkpoint and found seats in the gallery.

Mario and Joe Miglio came in and sat at the far end of the front row, directly across from the defense table. They crossed their arms and lowered their heads.

A middle-aged man with thin, graying hair was turned back for having a cell phone with him. He returned shortly afterward, having jettisoned the phone, and this time got through without any trouble.

A reporter nudged a colleague.

"Chris Coleman's father?" he whispered.

"Yeah," the colleague said. "That's the Reverend Ron."

A hush fell over the courtroom when a door opened off to the side. Might this be Chris himself, on the verge of making his entrance? It proved a false alarm, however—just somebody wanting to confer with the bailiff. A reporter wondered aloud if perhaps the hearing had been canceled. It was almost two o'clock now, half an hour past the scheduled starting time.

Defense attorney John O'Gara entered the room carrying a thick stack of folders. He was a rotund guy in his forties, wearing glasses and a rumpled suit. He plopped the folders onto a table and then exchanged greetings with the Reverend Ron, who was seated in the front row of the gallery next to the main entrance.

And then, without a whisper of warning, the door off to the side—the same one as before—opened and two sheriff's deputies escorted Chris Coleman into the courtroom. He was shackled at the ankles and wrists, with a restraining belt around his waist. He wore a bright orange jumpsuit and prison-issue flip-flops with white socks. He glanced toward the gallery and spotted his father, who gave him a jaunty salute. Chris smiled faintly in response before taking a seat alongside John O'Gara at the defense table. Then he shifted in his chair so that he was facing away from Mario and Joe Miglio.

He looked very different from the photographs of him that had appeared in the media over the previous year, all of which depicted a strapping guy in his early thirties with a buzz cut and a confident smile. He looked worn and thin, almost frail, and startlingly pale in the gloom of the courtroom. And with his blond hair grown out now and combed straight back, he looked scarcely old enough to walk into a bar and buy a beer.

After almost a year in the Monroe County Jail awaiting trial, he looked like a younger, more fragile version of himself.

State's Attorney Kris Reitz, tall and austere in a gray suit, entered the courtroom from a side door toward the front. The Honorable Milton Wharton entered from the opposite side and took his place behind the bench. Judge Wharton was a trim man in his early sixties, with glasses and a silver mustache. He was also black—hardly an incidental detail in a community that seemed otherwise as white as a fifties sitcom.

The purpose of the hearing was to decide whether the trial, scheduled for late October, should be moved elsewhere. Defense attorney O'Gara insisted that it should indeed be moved, saying that public sentiment in Monroe County was already heavily stacked against his client and that finding impartial jurors there would be next to impossible. Kris Reitz disagreed, arguing that Chris Coleman stood as decent a chance of receiving a fair trial in Monroe County as he would anywhere else.

As the lawyers wrangled, Coleman slipped a foot out of his flip-flop and tapped it nervously on the carpeted floor. Otherwise he sat perfectly still at the defense table, with his head tilted slightly forward. The two deputies, forearms crossed, expressions blank, stood behind him.

Saying that he wasn't quite yet ready to decide on the matter, Judge Wharton scheduled another hearing for early May. He then flicked a hand toward Coleman and told him to approach the bench.

Coleman got up and shuffled over, the chain connecting his leg manacles clinking ever so slightly. He stood erect before the judge, the two deputies stationed by his shoulders.

"Good afternoon, Mr. Coleman," the judge said. "Have they been treating you all right in jail?"

The tone was kindly, the voice a rich tenor.

"Yes," Coleman said.

Compared to the judge, he sounded tinny, insubstantial.

"And your lawyers?" the judge said. "You're pleased with them so far?"

"Yes, sir," Coleman said.

"They're doing everything you expect them to do?"

"Yes."

"Okay, then, Mr. Coleman, we'll see you again in May."

And with that, the two deputies escorted Coleman out of the courtroom, and the hearing was over.

The reporters hurried down the stairs, through the rear exit, and around to the side of the courthouse, where there was a sally port with a big metal door on the lower level. They knew that this would be Coleman's point of departure on his way back to the county jail, and they wanted to be sure to catch a glimpse of him.

A couple of camera crews were on hand now, too, and everybody stood in a loose circle on the sidewalk and the edge of the lawn and chatted about the hearing. Some of the reporters expressed surprise at how thin, pale, and boyish Coleman had looked. "Like some poor, lost waif," one of them said.

The day was still bright and cool, and the area surrounding the courthouse still strangely quiet. It was almost as if the local citizenry were taking special pains to stay away. Several women who worked at the courthouse appeared at a large window on the second floor and waved to a reporter from a St. Louis–based television station. "We're practically old friends by now," he said, waving back.

The big metal door clanked open and a sheriff's car emerged from the bowels of the courthouse and crept up a paved ramp toward the curb. Coleman sat in back, cuffed hands on lap, staring straight ahead. The car reached the curb and hesitated for a moment before swinging onto the road.

Just then Coleman turned toward the side window and made fleeting eye contact with a reporter. The corners of his mouth curled into a sneer. His eyes were flat and lifeless.

CHAPTER THIRTY-EIGHT

There were quite a few more hearings over the ensuing months, most of which played out in similar fashion. Mario and Joe Miglio would attend, sometimes with Angela. Ron Coleman would sit at the opposite end of the spectators' gallery, usually with Connie or Brad and a handful of supporters from Grace Church. Reporters would settle into the second and third rows of the gallery and wonder why so few people were in attendance. Had the citizens of Monroe County already lost interest in the case?

Chris would be brought into the courtroom in shackles and an orange jumpsuit. He'd exchange glances with his father before taking his place at the defense table. He'd never so much as cast a sideways glance at Mario or Joe Miglio. Then the lawyers would argue a point of evidence or some other matter of importance for the forthcoming trial. And afterward the reporters would race outside in the hope of catching a glimpse of the accused murderer on his way back to the county jail.

As might be expected, most of the hearings dealt with motions that were filed by the defense team. Besides seeking a change of venue, John O'Gara, William Margulis, and Jim Stern sought to restrict the evidence that the prosecution could present at trial. They wanted the Chris-Tara sex pictures and sex videos disallowed. Wouldn't material of this sort almost certainly prejudice the jury against their client? They wanted to prevent Sheri's friends—Meegan Turnbeaugh, Kathy LaPlante, and so forth—from testifying about things that Sheri had ostensibly told them about Chris. Wouldn't this constitute flagrant hearsay? They wanted to prevent handwriting analysts and forensic linguists from testifying that the spray-painted messages were *absolutely* the handiwork of Chris. Wouldn't this foster the mistaken impression among jurors that handwriting analysis and forensic linguistics were precise scientific disciplines?

In ruling on these various matters, Judge Wharton proved a master of the reasonable compromise. He ruled that the trial would remain in Monroe County but that jurors would be selected from elsewhere. That a sampling of the sex pictures and the sex videos could be presented to the jury but certainly not the entire lot. That several of Sheri's friends could testify about things that she'd ostensibly told them, providing that such testimony was duly presented to the jurors as hearsay. And that the defense would have every opportunity at trial to hold the prosecution's expert witnesses accountable.

The judge also granted a request that the trial be pushed back so that the defense attorneys could more properly prepare for it. Originally scheduled for late October of 2010, it now seemed unlikely to get under way until April of 2011.

Throughout all of this legal maneuvering, Chris remained confined in the Monroe County Jail. The jail was a low-strung structure located just several blocks from the courthouse in Waterloo. It consisted of twenty individual cells—each with its own toilet and shower—arranged around a circular security pod.

Chris was held in protective custody, which meant that he had limited opportunity for interaction with other prisoners. He took his meals and recreation alone. He made no special dietary requests—indeed, no special requests of any kind. He rarely spoke with the guards, including those who were charged with escorting him to and from the courthouse for hearings. He caused no problems. By all accounts, he was a model prisoner.

This hardly surprised Sheriff Dan Kelley, the person ultimately entrusted with Chris's confinement. Throughout his long tenure as sheriff, the delightfully frank and witty Kelley had observed that accused murderers very rarely caused problems. It was rather the jailhouse riffraff—thieves, druggies, wife beaters—who made the most noise and created the most grief for correctional officers.

Chris lost a good twenty pounds during his time in jail. This was likely a consequence of his not having access to steroids. However, he did have access to a laptop (sans Internet) so that he could more readily review his discovery and other legal materials. He was the first prisoner in the history of the county jail to have such access.

He also had quite a few visitors. A Joyce Meyer minister visited him fairly regularly at first but then stopped coming. A couple of youngish ministers from Grace Church—Neal Adams and Derek Doiron—would come once a week. Adams was the music director at the church and a near-constant presence at pretrial hearings. Doiron was an associate pastor and a friend of Chris's since childhood. He'd actually lived with the Colemans for a while after graduating high school.

Other people—friends, family members, church supporters—would drop by occasionally. And his parents would visit for about an hour every Sunday after church services.

Ron and Connie would also talk with him over the phone almost daily. They'd discuss the case, though not in much depth. Ron was convinced that highly sophisticated "international killers" were responsible for the murders. "They'll catch those turkeys," he'd say. "They'll catch them." Chris could never quite bring himself to respond to this.

Ron would ask Chris about his jailhouse diet. He seemed concerned that his oldest son wasn't getting his daily requirement of vitamins. Only very rarely would Ron or Connie say anything about Garett and Gavin. Chris would never mention the boys at all. None of them would ever say a word about Sheri.

As it turned out, Chris stood a good chance of avoiding execution even if convicted of the murders. On January 11, 2011, the state legislature passed a historic bill to abolish the death penalty in Illinois. All that was required for the bill to become law was the endorsement of Democratic governor Pat Quinn.

At a hearing later that same week at the Monroe County Courthouse, Judge Wharton denied a defense request to stay proceedings in Chris's case until the governor had decided whether to sign or to veto the new bill. "It's in the best interests of everyone that the court move toward active resolution of this case," Wharton said.

On March 9, 2011, Governor Quinn did indeed sign the bill, and he also commuted the sentences of Illinois's fifteen death row prisoners to life imprisonment. The only catch was that the new law wouldn't take effect until July 1. And Chris's trial was scheduled to start in late April. Which left open the possibility that he still might be sentenced to death if he was convicted of the triple homicide. Might Chris Coleman be the very last person to suffer execution in the state of Illinois?

The prosecution wanted Joyce Meyer to testify at trial, mainly to bolster its claim that Chris might very well have lost his coveted job with the ministry if he'd divorced Sheri. But the famous evangelist apparently pleaded inconvenience, saying she'd be holding a conference in Hampton, Virginia, at the time of the trial. And so the court afforded her a special dispensation, permitting her to testify instead at a closed-door, videotaped deposition on Wednesday, April 6.

Meyer arrived at the courthouse in Waterloo at 2:00 p.m. on April 6. She wore a floral-patterned jacket over a black top, dangling earrings, and a necklace. Several ministry lawyers accompanied her, as did her son Daniel, who was also scheduled to give a videotaped deposition. Her new personal bodyguard—a young, lean guy in a gray suit—escorted her from her black Chrysler 300 sedan into the courthouse.

She emerged an hour and a half later and spoke briefly with a scrum of reporters, none of whom were thrilled at having been barred from the courtroom for the deposition. She said that she'd testified "honestly and truthfully" but that she wasn't at liberty just then to go into specifics. A reporter asked her if she was praying for Chris Coleman.

"Certainly," she said.

CHAPTER THIRTY-NINE

Jury selection got underway on April 12, 2011, in the town of Pinckneyville, Illinois. Located in coal-mining country, a good two-hour drive from the scene of the triple homicide, Pinckneyville was the seat of Perry County. This was the county from which Judge Milton Wharton had decided that jurors would be picked, in the interests of ensuring as impartial a panel as possible. Media coverage of the case hadn't been nearly as intensive here as it had been in the St. Louis area.

Judge Wharton presided over the proceedings, which took place in a modest courtroom on the first floor of the county courthouse. The judge was trim and dapper, with a courteous demeanor and a reflective cast of mind. As the days stretched on, he'd often enliven things with some philosophical or cultural aside. The asides were always welcome and always instructive.

Most of the other key players were also on hand. State's Attorney Kris Reitz would drive daily to Pinckneyville from his home in Waterloo for the proceedings. Reitz was sharp, confident, and single-minded. He wanted a conviction in the case and seemed certain that he'd get one.

Sitting adjacent to Reitz at a long table toward the front of the room was Ed Parkinson, a special prosecutor with the office of the State's Attorneys Appellate Prosecutor in

Springfield. Reitz had called Parkinson shortly after the murders asking for his help. It was a shrewd move. The sixty-five-year-old Parkinson had worked on almost seventy murder cases during his two-decade tenure as a special prosecutor, helping to secure convictions in all but three of them. He had an incisive legal mind, and he was personable, literary, and mordantly funny.

Lead defense attorney John O'Gara sat at the opposite end of the table. O'Gara was the sort of lawyer to whom you'd want to entrust your kids if ever they should run into trouble. He was warm, expansive, and considerate. He positively oozed compassion and humanity. He also had a slightly shambling look about him that nicely understated his sharpness of intellect. William Margulis and Jim Stern, the other defense attorneys, would prove somewhat less vocal than O'Gara throughout the week of jury selection but no less impressive. They, too, seemed not only smart and capable but also eminently trustworthy. Under most circumstances, they'd have been easy guys to root for.

Bailiff Forrest Bevineau was also on hand, as were court reporter Kathleen Brunsmann; Judge Wharton's personal clerk, Maddie Ponder; Monroe County circuit clerk Sandra Sauget; and Perry County circuit clerk Kim Kellerman. It was Kim Kellerman who'd gone to the trouble of summoning all of the prospective jurors to the courthouse.

And then, of course, there was Chris Coleman himself. Each morning he'd enter the courtroom wearing dress slacks and a button-down shirt with a striped tied. He'd sit at the table up front, immediately to the left of John O'Gara and directly across from Judge Wharton, with three sheriff's deputies ranged behind him.

A prospective juror would come into the room and sit on a chair next to the door, practically within arm's reach of Chris. Everyone around the table would introduce themselves, and when it came his turn, Chris would make eye contact with the person and say, "Chris Coleman," in a small voice.

Some of the prospective jurors would look at him and say hello. Others would simply avert their eyes.

The proceedings proved unusual in at least one critical respect. Just a month previously, Governor Pat Quinn had signed into law the bill banning the death penalty in the state of Illinois. More recently, the governor had suggested that he'd commute any death sentence that was handed down before the new law was due to take effect on July 1. This meant that Chris's chances of actually being executed sometime down the road were exceedingly slim. Nevertheless, the death penalty was still technically an option in his case, and so both the prosecution and the defense comported themselves accordingly.

Kris Reitz and Ed Parkinson sought to rule out any prospective juror who might have qualms about sentencing Chris to death in the event of a conviction. John O'Gara, William Margulis, and Jim Stern, on the other hand, sought to rule out anyone who might feel *compelled* to sentence him to death.

With rare exceptions, the prospective jurors seemed good and decent folk. They came to the courthouse—men and women alike—in blue jeans and plaid shirts. They sometimes agonized over the questions that the lawyers asked them.

A skinny, middle-aged guy told O'Gara that he'd have no choice but to vote for death if Chris was found guilty.

"Why?" O'Gara asked.

"Because of the children," the guy said. "I mean, what did they do? What did anybody do? It's a terrible thing."

A gray-haired woman told O'Gara that young Garett and Gavin were "a sticking point" for her.

"I don't know if this man did it," she said, looking directly at Chris. "I hope to God he didn't."

Kris Reitz asked her if she'd be equally open to voting for either the death penalty or life imprisonment if Chris was convicted.

"Yes, either way," she said. "Because either way, he'd have to face what he's done. If the death penalty, he'd have to face his God. If life imprisonment, he'd have to face himself every day for the rest of his natural life."

Just before leaving the courtroom, she turned and gave John O'Gara a warm smile.

"And I expect you fellows to do your best," she said. "Anybody in his shoes wants—needs—the very best lawyers doing their very best job."

The courtroom's spectators' gallery, which consisted of nothing more than a scattering of chairs, was never full during the week of jury selection. Several reporters attended the proceedings, but no one from Sheri's family and hardly anyone from the local community.

However, Ron Coleman was there every day, and sometimes Connie would join him. Connie was battling lupus by this point, and she'd also recently experienced leg problems, so she'd usually enter the courtroom in a wheelchair. They'd sit next to one another in the gallery and shake their heads in dismay whenever a prospective juror said something not to their liking.

On the fifth day Ron got up from his chair at lunch recess and gave the reporters who'd been sitting behind him a little wave.

"All right, see you guys," he said.

The reporters' hearts went out to the guy. They could only imagine what he had to be going through.

The proceedings in Pinckneyville concluded on Tuesday, April 20. The Coleman jury would consist of ten women and two men, with four additional men serving as alternates. The plan was that they'd travel by bus to and from the Monroe County Courthouse in Waterloo every single day of the trial, which most observers expected would last two weeks or longer. Perry County circuit clerk Kim Kellerman would accompany them and see to their every need.

There was a heightened sense of expectancy in Waterloo, with the trial now finally about to get under way. Just about everybody in town had been following the case in the news.

Most people already seemed to have decided that Chris was guilty.

Waterloo was located a scant ten-minute drive down Illinois Route 3 from Columbia. It boasted a historic downtown of tidy brick buildings and spotless streets. The redbrick courthouse, with its green lawns and tree-lined paths, might easily have passed for a building on a small college campus.

The town prided itself on its German cultural heritage and its well-deserved reputation for civility and peacefulness. It was the kind of place that conjured up memories of simpler, more trusting times. If you needed a prescription filled after hours, the proprietor of the local pharmacy would arrange to meet you at his shop so that he could take care of it. If you wanted to return a bulky mail-order package, you could simply leave it on top of the mailbox on Main Street without fear of anybody stealing it. The town's biggest crime one recent summer was when a couple of drunks stole a pork truck from the high school homecoming celebration and took it for a joyride. The police tracked them down by following the trail of grease.

Now the town was on the verge of hosting the trial that would decide the fate of Chris Coleman. And just then all of southwestern Illinois was experiencing its worst hurricane season in recent memory. For several straight nights before the trial began, tornado alert sirens in Waterloo wailed almost constantly.

CHAPTER FORTY

The trial began on Monday, April 25, 2011, almost two full years after the triple homicide. It was a rainy day, with temperatures hovering in the high sixties. The spectators' gallery of the second-floor courtroom was jam-packed.

Mario and Angela were there, along with Joe Miglio, his son, Joseph, and several other relatives on Sheri's mom's side of the family. They sat in the front row of the gallery, near the main entrance to the courtroom. Don Weiss, his brother, Ron, and their mom, Dortha, sat directly behind them in the second row.

Ron and Connie, along with Chris's brother Brad and three other Coleman relatives sat at the opposite end of the front row. A couple of reporters who were seated in the very middle of the row served as a buffer of sorts between the two families.

Sheriff's deputies escorted Chris into the courtroom. He was wearing black slacks and a gray shirt with a striped tie. He glanced at his father before sitting down at the defense table with his attorneys.

Prosecutors Kris Reitz and Ed Parkinson came in, and then Judge Wharton. The twelve jurors and four alternates filed into the jury box. Monroe County circuit clerk Sandra Sauget swore them in, and the proceedings began.

Kris Reitz handled the opening statement for the prosecution. He spoke deftly for twenty-five minutes, summarizing the state's evidence against Chris Coleman. William Margulis countered for the defense, suggesting that the evidence was circumstantial and not enough to prove beyond a reasonable doubt that Chris was indeed guilty.

Chris sat calmly throughout all of this, hands clasped and resting on the edge of the table. Apart from a slight quiver to his jaw, he seemed entirely impassive.

Reitz called Angela to the stand and showed her a framed photograph of Sheri, Garett, and Gavin. He asked her to identify the people in the photograph.

"My daughter," Angela said in a faltering voice. "My grandsons."

Jason Donjon testified next, and then Steve Patton. The two police officers described in turn exactly what they and Justin Barlow had found upon entering the house on Robert Drive that May morning two years earlier. They described the spray-painted grotesquerie on the walls and the terrible condition of the dead bodies in the upstairs bedrooms. They then described Chris's odd behavior upon finally returning home from the gym.

Donjon and Patton proved to be terrific witnesses. They were cool, precise, and articulate. They projected a sense of unimpeachable integrity.

So did emergency medical technicians Gary Hutchison and Jared Huch, who provided additional testimony on the condition of the bodies that same morning.

Kris Reitz called Deborah Von Nida to the stand. Von Nida was the coroner's investigator who'd taken Sheri and Garett's core body temperatures at the crime scene. Before she was sworn in, Judge Wharton warned the spectators that some "pretty rough" photographs were about to be entered into evidence. "If you feel you can't handle them, please take this opportunity to leave the courtroom," he said.

Angela, her older sister, Elvira, and their cousin, Debbie, got up and hurried out. All of the Coleman family members remained in their seats.

Crime scene photographs of Sheri and the boys were then

projected onto a large screen directly behind the defense table. The photos were startling in the dimmed lights of the courtroom. Von Nida carefully described the condition of each body and the procedure that she'd deployed in taking the core temperatures.

Mario crossed his arms and lowered his eyes. Joe Miglio gave him an encouraging tap on the shoulder. Chris sat at the defense table writing on a legal pad. At one point his eyes seemed to tear up. Never did he so much as glance backward at the images on the screen behind him.

The last witness of the day was Dr. Raj Nanduri, the pathologist who'd conducted the autopsies on Sheri, Garett, and Gavin. Photographs were once again projected onto the video screen, these ones taken from the autopsies. They depicted with brutal clarity Sheri's battered face and the ligature marks around her neck and the necks of her two sons.

Nanduri testified that all three victims had died from ligature strangulation. She said that the Major Case Squad had asked her to determine a precise time of death but that she'd been hesitant to do so. She added that she could only speculate that the deaths had occurred somewhere between 3:00 a.m. and 5:00 a.m. on May 5, 2009.

Nanduri seemed stiff and officious. Her responses to the lawyers—first Reitz and then Jim Stern in cross-examination—were clipped and charmless. She looked as if she'd prefer to be just about anywhere else.

Court recessed for the day at 3:05 p.m. After the jury was dismissed, Judge Wharton commended the courtroom spectators for "maintaining proper decorum" in the face of some difficult and disturbing evidence.

The prosecution's star witness, Dr. Michael Baden, took the stand first thing the next morning. Baden wore a dark gray suit with a blue tie. With his silver hair and rimless glasses, he looked like a kindly small-town physician. Some people in the courtroom knew him from his HBO series, *Autopsy.* Others recognized his name from his involvement in such celebrity cases as O.J. Simpson's and John Belushi's.

Angela and several other women on Sheri's side of the family had elected to skip Baden's testimony, realizing that it would feature yet again graphic crime scene and autopsy photographs. Ron and Connie were seated in their usual places at the far end of the front row.

The prosecutors had a great deal invested in Dr. Baden. They wanted him to testify that Sheri, Garett, and Gavin were already dead when Chris left home for the gym on May 5, 2009. They wanted him to be convincing.

Baden didn't disappoint. He was lucid and congenial on the witness stand. As photographs of the victims' bodies were projected onto the video screen, he carefully highlighted the indications of advanced rigor mortis and lividity. He paused occasionally for dramatic effect. Whenever he happened to use a technical term, he jotted it down on a slip of paper, which he then passed to court reporter Kathleen Brunsmann so that she'd be certain to have the correct spelling. Baden was obviously an old hand at giving expert testimony.

He said that the photographs left no room for doubt. The three victims had *absolutely* died before 5:00 a.m. on May 5, 2009, and quite probably before 3:00 a.m. There was no chance in the world that they'd died after Chris had left home for the gym at 5:43 that morning. He added that it would've taken four to five minutes for the killer to strangle the life out of each victim.

Jim Stern tried his best in cross-examination to rattle Baden, but to no avail. The veteran pathologist was unflappable. He had science and the evidence on his side. As a former chief medical examiner for New York City, he also had experience on his side. Sheri, Garett, and Gavin had died prior to Chris leaving for the gym. This wasn't idle speculation. It was indisputable fact. The science is the science, Baden said.

Chris took notes throughout much of Baden's testimony, never once glancing at the gruesome photographs that were projected onto the screen behind the defense table. At one point he put his pen down and closed his eyes.

Ron and Connie sat perfectly still, lips pursed, arms crossed. One couldn't help but wonder what was going through their minds. Was the grim truth finally beginning to dawn on them? Were they suffering terrible inner agony?

While waiting for proceedings to resume after lunch recess, however, they seemed in fine fettle. They chatted with friends and family members in the far left-hand aisle of the courtroom. They laughed and joked. They might just as well have been at a church picnic.

The state's next witness was Justin Barlow, who'd played a critical role in the investigation right from the start. Barlow was now a deputy U.S. marshal based out of Iowa, having left the Columbia PD just a short time previously. He looked sharp in a dark suit with a crisp white shirt and a red tie. His voice was clear and confident.

He testified about the threatening e-mails and letters that Chris had ostensibly received, and about the video surveillance camera that he'd installed in the window of his three-year-old son's second-floor bedroom a week before the murders. Then the surveillance tape from those early morning hours on May 5, 2009, was played for the jury.

The jury saw Chris departing the driveway in his green Ford Explorer at 5:43 a.m. They saw Barlow arriving for a welfare check at 6:51 a.m., and Jason Donjon and Steve Patton doing the same shortly afterward. Finally they saw Chris returning in his Explorer at 6:56 a.m. They most certainly did not see any intruder breaking into the house.

Barlow told the jurors about the spray-painted messages on the walls and the terrible condition of the three bodies in the upstairs bedrooms. He told them about Chris's troubling behavior not only at the crime scene but also during the subsequent interview with Dave Bivens and himself at the Columbia PD. Then the lights were dimmed and the videotaped interview was played on the screen behind the defense table.

Chris shifted sideways in his chair so that he had a good view of the screen. This was something that he apparently didn't want to miss.

* * *

There was time on Tuesday to watch only the first portions of the videotaped interview, which was a six-hour marathon. So the next day, Wednesday, April 27, everybody settled in for the remainder of it.

Ron and Connie were seated in their usual place at the far end of the front row. They seemed not to mind what was happening on the screen until Justin Barlow and Dave Bivens began to get a little rough with Chris. They told him that they didn't believe his story. They didn't believe that Sheri and the boys were alive when he left for the gym. They pleaded with him to come clean and tell them what had really happened.

Ron and Connie grimaced and squirmed and then finally decided that they'd had enough. Ron got up from his seat and pushed Connie in her wheelchair down the aisle and through the rear door of the courtroom. They took the elevator to the first floor and went outside.

It was a remarkable performance. For almost two full days, Ron and Connie had sat through horrific visual evidence depicting the lifeless, contorted bodies of their daughter-in-law and young grandsons. They'd listened as Justin Barlow, Jason Donjon, and Steve Patton testified in graphic detail about finding the bodies. They'd listened as expert witness after expert witness testified about rigor mortis, lividity, and ligature marks.

None of this had been enough to drive them from the courtroom. They'd sat through every second of it. But the videotape of Barlow and Bivens asking their firstborn son some tough questions? This was beyond their limits. This they could not stand.

The videotaped interview played on without Ron and Connie. Chris sat at the defense table with his chair at an angle, giving him a good view of the screen. He watched intently.

When the videotape was finished, State's Attorney Kris Reitz had some questions for Justin Barlow, who was still under oath from the day before.

"Did the defendant ever ask how his family had died?" Reitz asked.

"No, not specifically," Barlow said. "He never did ask."

"To your knowledge," Reitz said, "he did not ask and was not told how his family died?"

"That is correct," Barlow said.

From his vantage point on the witness stand, Barlow had a clear view of Chris's brother, Brad, who was sitting next to his wife in the front row of the spectators' gallery. He noticed that Brad was giving him a hard stare. Barlow returned the stare, locking eyes with the guy. Then he saw Brad mouth the words, *You're dead.* Barlow had no doubt whatsoever about it. *You're dead,* the guy had mouthed.

Court recessed for the day several minutes later, and Barlow pounced off the stand and confronted Brad on the courtroom floor.

"I saw what you mouthed to me," he said. "*You're dead.* I will not accept that. I want no repeat performance. And no threats to my family. Do you understand?"

Brad looked thuggish with his shaved head and trim beard. He insisted that Barlow had it all wrong, that he'd actually been talking to his wife at the time and had said to her, *I don't believe him.*

"I know what I saw," Barlow said. "There was no mistaking it."

Brad apologized for any misunderstanding and extended his hand. Barlow shook his hand but he was still obviously displeased.

"That's it, though," he said. "I don't want to see anything like that again."

Judge Wharton overheard the ruckus on the courtroom floor and returned to his bench. He advised Brad that he was at risk of contempt of court. He told him that he'd tolerate no inciting gestures or comments whatsoever.

After the judge's lecture, Barlow took Brad into a small witness room just outside the courtroom, where he once again warned him against making any more threats.

Brad repeated what he'd said before. He'd been talking to his wife and had said, *I don't believe him.*

"And I *don't* believe you," he told Barlow. "I'm looking at this from both directions. I'm a correctional officer at Menard and a part-time police officer in Chester, but I'm also Chris's brother. I don't believe what you said on the witness stand."

"Look, Brad," Barlow said. "I can't even imagine what you've been going through. Your sister-in-law was murdered, your two nephews."

Brad began to cry.

"Those boys were my little buddies," he said.

"But it is what it is, Brad," Barlow went on. "And no more threats or behavior of that sort will be tolerated. You understand?"

Brad nodded. He seemed to have gotten the message.

CHAPTER FORTY-ONE

Most of Thursday morning, the fourth day of the trial, was taken up with Jim Stern's cross-examination of Justin Barlow.

Stern suggested that the police had pursued the investigation with tunnel vision. They'd zeroed in on Chris right from the start and not taken anyone else seriously as a suspect.

Barlow denied that this was so. They'd kept an open mind and followed up on every lead. However, no one other than Chris had stood out to them.

Stern asked about Chris's brother, Keith. Wasn't it true that he had some dirty laundry? Had the police done an adequate job of investigating him?

Barlow said that they had indeed done an adequate job in this regard. They'd interviewed Keith in Arkansas and determined that he had a credible alibi.

Stern asked about a report that an older-model brown car had stopped on the Jefferson Barracks Bridge early in the morning on May 5, 2009, and that the driver had thrown something over the side. Mightn't this be linked to the murders?

Barlow said that they'd looked into this and found nothing that warranted further investigation.

Stern asked about Dr. Michael Baden. Hadn't he told the police precisely what they'd wanted to hear? Was this perhaps why they'd sought his help?

Barlow insisted that this wasn't so. They'd reached out to Baden simply because of his scientific expertise. They'd had no ulterior motive for doing so.

And so it went. Stern took some good shots, but Barlow held his ground. Both men comported themselves well.

Detective Ken Wojtowicz, the Major Case Squad's computer expert, took the stand after lunch recess. A sampling of the images that he'd retrieved from Chris and Tara's BlackBerrys and laptops were projected onto the courtroom screen. Sensitive body parts in the more provocative of these were blacked out.

Next a couple of sex videos were shown, though once again without revealing genitalia and so forth. The second of these was the video that Chris shot of himself masturbating in the shower at the house on Robert Drive. The screen was blacked out entirely once the actual masturbation began, though the sound of Chris moaning and groaning reverberated throughout the courtroom. It seemed to go on forever.

Ron and Connie Coleman were back in the courtroom for this. They somehow managed to sit through every second of it. Ron lowered his head at one point and covered his face with his hands. Chris stole a glance at the screen but otherwise sat perfectly still at the defense table with his heavy-lidded eyes half shut. The defense attorneys, especially William Margulis, seemed absolutely mortified.

The video that Chris shot of Tara and himself in the hotel suite in Hawaii was also played, though only the audio portion of it. The prosecution had wanted the pictures and videos admitted into evidence at trial as a way of showing the intensity and audacity of the affair, and thereby also establishing possible motive for the crime.

It would be difficult to argue that they'd failed to make their point.

Detective Wojtowicz also testified about the misspelling of *opportunities* in one of the threat letters, and how the word was similarly misspelled in documents retrieved from Chris's laptop.

* * *

Tara Lintz was the last witness of the day.

She hadn't wanted to come. She'd claimed that she couldn't bear the prospect of facing the media and that she couldn't afford to miss time at work. In the end, a judge in St. Petersburg had ordered her to testify.

Chief Joe Edwards and Karla Heine had flown to Florida to fetch her. They'd sat with her for five hours in the Tampa airport when their return flight was delayed. They'd gotten the impression that she wasn't quite as media-shy as she liked to make out. It seemed to them that she was actually relishing all of the attention.

The *click-click-click* of high heels in the hallway echoed throughout the courtroom. Then Tara came in and walked to the witness stand. She looked at Chris while sitting down and then tilted her chin slightly upward.

She wore a ruffled magenta blouse with a black pantsuit, a small gold cross on a necklace, and open-toe four-inch heels. She also wore the promise ring that Chris had given her more than two years before. Her lustrous brown hair hung in layers over her shoulders.

She looked at Chris again when Reitz asked her to point him out in the courtroom. Chris gave her a sheepish glance in return.

At Reitz's prompting, Tara testified about her relationship with Chris. She said that she "started talking with him" in November 2008 at the Joyce Meyer conference in Tampa. She added that Sheri had called her prior to the conference and encouraged her to attend. She said that they became "more than friends" the following month, when Chris brought Joyce Meyer to Orlando for a vacation. She said that Chris assured her at a New Kids on the Block concert in Orlando that he and Sheri were no longer sleeping together, and that Sheri had also confided the same thing to her. She said that Chris told her that he often slept on a couch in the basement, and that he subsequently sent her pictures attesting to the truth of this.

"Did he profess his love for you?" Reitz asked.

"Yes, he did," she replied, adding that he did so often, and she for him also.

Reitz asked how often they communicated.

"All the time," she replied. "Constantly."

She said that they made plans after Orlando to meet in early March at a Joyce Meyer–related function in Arizona.

Reitz asked if they'd had sex in Arizona.

"That's questionable, but probably," she replied.

She said that they'd hooked up again the next month in Hawaii, where they'd most definitely had sex.

Reitz asked her how she felt upon learning that Chris was planning a vacation to Disney World with Sheri and the boys.

"I'm sure I didn't care for it," she said. "I told him to cancel."

She went on to describe how she'd schemed to have the vacation canceled and subsequently booked a cruise with Chris for St. Thomas in the Virgin Islands.

Reitz asked if she and Chris had planned on getting married.

"Yes," she said. "The divorce had to happen first."

She said that they'd gotten "matching rings" and that she was still wearing hers. She showed the ring to Reitz.

She said that she and Chris talked over the phone and text-messaged back and forth constantly on May 4, 2009, even when he was at home with Sheri and the boys. She said that he promised her that he'd serve Sheri with divorce papers the next day.

And what was her response to this? Reitz asked.

"I'm sure I told him good luck," she said.

She said that Ron Coleman phoned her the next day with news of the killings, and that she and Chris exchanged text messages while he was in the interrogation room at the Columbia PD. She also said that they spoke over the phone shortly after he'd left the police station.

Tara seemed confident on the stand, if not entirely pleased at having to be there. She spoke in a rich voice, answering questions directly and without elaboration. Several of her responses had courtroom observers scratching their heads. Was it really true, for example, that she and Chris hadn't become sexually intimate ("more than friends") until December of 2008? But what about the document entitled "All About Tara" that Chris had created on his Dell laptop? Why had he specified November 5, 2008, as "the day Tara changed my life"? Might one not reasonably infer that this was the day when they first became intimate?

Chris sat at the defense table with his eyes averted. Occasionally he glanced up at her with a hangdog look on his face. Ron leaned forward with his chin in his hands. He seemed pensive. Perhaps he was wondering what he'd tell his congregation. It seemed that reports of the affair hadn't been baldfaced lies after all.

William Margulis handled the cross-examination, which proved mostly uneventful. He asked Tara if she'd ever received a sexually explicit picture or video from Chris's brother, Keith. Yes, she said, but she hadn't responded to it. He asked her if she'd had much contact with Chris after the murders. Yes, she said. They'd spoken over the phone "constantly." He asked her if the police had ever mentioned to her that they suspected Chris in the murders. Yes, she said. They'd mentioned this to her "lots of times, constantly."

And that was it. She shot Chris one last look upon leaving the stand and *click-click-click*ed out of the courtroom.

Her entire testimony had taken less than thirty minutes. Courtroom spectators were left feeling vaguely disappointed. They'd somehow hoped for more from the mystery woman. They'd hoped that she wouldn't prove quite so obvious.

CHAPTER FORTY-TWO

Quite apart from the daily parade of witnesses, several side dramas played out throughout the course of the trial.

First of all, it was hardly a secret that Sheri's mom's family was planning on filing a wrongful-death lawsuit against Joyce Meyer Ministries. The contention was that the ministry had reasonable grounds to suspect that Chris posed a threat to Sheri and yet had failed to give her appropriate warning. That the murders might never have happened if the ministry had exercised greater responsibility.

Perhaps in anticipation of the lawsuit, Joyce Meyer attorneys were present every day of the trial. They usually sat in the last row of the spectators' gallery, taking notes and calculating odds.

Then there was Sheri's dad, Don Weiss. Don was a tragic figure in the courtroom. For years he'd desperately hoped that he might become reconciled with his estranged daughter. He'd hoped that he might once again become a meaningful part of her life. But now his daughter was dead. His grandsons were dead. So were Don's hopes. He was left with guilt and sorrow, and a sense of unredeemed possibilities.

Moreover, the murders seemed not to have brought him any closer to his son, Mario. Don and Mario rarely interacted throughout the course of the trial. There was an icy distance between them. During court recesses, Mario would hang out with his mom, Angela, Joe Miglio, Joe's son, Joseph, and other relatives on Angela's side of the family. Don would sit with his mom, Dortha, and brother, Ron, in a windowed alcove at the end of a long corridor.

Don and Mario were fundamentally decent men. The trial was a terrible ordeal for both of them. Their unresolved differences couldn't have made it any easier.

Finally, there was the demeanor of Ron and Connie Coleman. On the whole, they seemed actually quite cheerful. While waiting for court to resume after recesses, they'd chat and joke with their coterie of friends, relatives, and church supporters. They behaved as if the trial were merely an interlude in their otherwise busy schedules.

Of course, this isn't to suggest that they weren't suffering inwardly. Perhaps their carefree demeanor was simply a way of showing support for their son. Perhaps it was meant as a testament to their faith. To quite a few courtroom observers, however, it was horribly inappropriate. It was rude and disrespectful. It defied common sense.

Sheri's side of the family, after all, was also there. Angela, Mario, Don Weiss, and Joe Miglio certainly weren't kibitzing in the courtroom. They were still in a state of shock and grief over the murders of Sheri, Garett, and Gavin. And it was Ron and Connie's very own son who was on trial for murdering them.

The occasion called for an attitude of solemnity—and humility—on Ron and Connie's part. They seem not to have realized that.

The fifth day of the trial, Friday, April 29, was one of the busiest. Sergeant Michael Grist of the Illinois State Police testified about the spray-painted messages that were scrawled on the walls of the Coleman house. And state police crime scene technician Abby Keller played the actual video that she'd shot of the house just hours after the bodies were found.

Six of Sheri's friends—Kathy LaPlante, Meegan Turnbeaugh, Vanessa Riegerix, Christine Cincotta, Jessica Wade, and Stephanie Jones—testified about her mounting fears and concerns during the months preceding the murders. All of these women were strong and articulate on the witness stand. Chris studiously avoided making eye contact with any of them.

Officer Shawn Westfall of the Columbia Police Department testified about the threat letters that Chris had ostensibly retrieved from his mailbox, and Captain Jerry Paul and Chaplain Jonathan Peters testified about his odd behavior in the ambulance prior to being taken to the police station for questioning.

The highlight of the day was Joyce Meyer's videotaped deposition, which was played on the courtroom screen. Chris shifted sideways in his chair for a better view. Ron and Connie seemed positively aglow. Joyce Meyer was one of their heroes.

The famous evangelist sounded hoarse, as if she'd just given a three-hour sermon. She said that Chris had seemed distracted during the months preceding the murders, and oddly indifferent to his work. She said that he might very well have been fired if she'd realized at the time that he was having an affair.

She insisted that her ministry didn't have a blanket policy on divorce. She said that only those employees who got divorced for ungodly or immoral reasons were at definite risk of losing their jobs.

Her son Daniel's videotaped deposition was played next. Daniel testified about the marriage counseling that the ministry had arranged for Chris and Sheri. He also testified about the threatening e-mails and letters, saying he'd invited Chris to take time off work until the matter was resolved.

Saturday, April 30, was Garett's birthday. He would've been thirteen years old.

Justin Barlow, Karla Heine, Kelly Cullen, Jason Donjon, and Steve Patton were devout Catholics. They went to Mass at Immaculate Conception Church in Columbia the next day and said a special prayer for Garett. They also prayed for Sheri and Gavin. For almost two full years now, they'd prayed for Sheri and the boys every single Sunday at Mass.

Mario, Angela, and Joe Miglio visited the grave site at the cemetery in Chester that same weekend. Afterward Mario reminisced with a reporter.

He said that when Garett was just three years old, he and several friends took him to a Chicago White Sox game at U.S. Cellular Field, where they sat in the 500 level. Mario bought a beer from a vendor for one of his friends and asked Garett to pass it along to the guy. Before doing so, however, Garett stuck a finger into the plastic cup and gave the beer a little taste. "Tastes like apple juice," he said. Mario and his buddies roared with laughter. "Next time we better card this kid," somebody said.

During the summer of 2009, a month or so after the murders, one of Mario's cousins pulled some strings and got him an ushering job at U.S. Cellular Field. He was stationed in the 500 level, in the same section where he'd sat with Garett eight years before. Mario couldn't hack it. The tragedy was still too fresh. He had to give up the job.

"One thing I can't understand," Mario said, his thoughts drifting to Chris. "If he doesn't want his family, why not just say, 'I'm going out for a beer,' and then never come back? It would be a bad thing to do, but so much better than what he actually did. In the long run, they'd have been better off without him anyway. He had no genuine love or affection for Sheri and the boys, just a sham of affection. He wanted Tara Lintz and he also wanted to keep his job. He wanted everything, except his family."

Monday, May 2, was mostly taken up with testimony concerning physical evidence at the crime scene. Four forensic scientists with the Illinois State Police led the way. Melody Levault testified about hair samples, Michael Brown and Suzanne Kidd about DNA analysis, and Thomas Gamboe about footprints. Then a manager from the company that had manufactured the rear window at the house on Robert Drive testified that it showed no signs whatsoever of having been tampered with.

James Kientzy of AT&T testified that an analysis of Chris's cell phone records indicated that he had indeed taken a detour on the way home from the gym on May 5, 2009. The inference seemed clear. It wouldn't have done Chris much good to arrive home before the police had found the bodies. This would have thrown his whole plan out of kilter.

Detective Ken Wojtowicz of the Major Case Squad, testifying for the second time, took the stand next. Wojtowicz said that Chris had sent the threatening e-mails from his own laptop. He said that there was no question about this. The computer forensic evidence was indisputable.

John O'Gara went after Wojtowicz in cross-examination but wasn't able to deliver any telling blows. Was it not possible, he asked, that somebody else had remotely accessed Chris's laptop and sent the e-mails?

Wojtowicz answered that nobody could've remotely accessed the laptop unless it was already turned on. And the forensic evidence indicated that it was turned on shortly before the e-mails were sent, then turned off again.

The prosecution got off to a flying start on Tuesday, May 3. Marcus Rogers, a professor of computer forensics at Purdue University, testified that he was in complete agreement with Detective Wojtowicz. The threatening e-mails had indeed been sent from Chris's own laptop. And it would've been next to impossible for somebody else to access the laptop remotely.

However, momentum ground to a halt with the next witness: Professor Robert Leonard, the expert in forensic linguistics from Hofstra University. Leonard testified that there were striking similarities between Chris's known writings, on the one hand, and the threatening messages and spray-painted messages, on the other. This was fine insofar as it went. There were indeed close similarities in style, syntax, and so forth. The problem was that Leonard overplayed his hand. He tried to portray forensic linguistics as a precise science, something akin to chemistry or physics. He tried to make it into something that it wasn't. The longer he droned on, the more his credibility suffered.

John O'Gara was too sharp a lawyer not to take advantage of this. He lacerated Leonard in cross-examination. At one point, after establishing that the professor had once performed at Woodstock as a member of the group Sha Na Na, he even succeeded in eliciting a roar of laughter from the courtroom.

"That brown acid they had at Woodstock," O'Gara said. "Let me ask you about that. Do you know anything about that brown acid?"

Not even Judge Wharton could resist breaking into a smile.

Some observers thought that the prosecution had committed a strategic blunder in scheduling Leonard so late in the trial, or perhaps in scheduling him at all.

The prosecution fared better with its remaining witnesses. Lindell Moore, the handwriting analyst with the Illinois State Police, also testified that there were striking similarities between Chris's handwriting samples and the spray-painted graffiti that was found on the walls of his house. However, Moore readily admitted in cross-examination that he couldn't state with scientific certainty that Chris was the person responsible for the graffiti.

A succession of witnesses established that the actual spray paint was a Rust-Oleum product—either American Accents or Painter's Touch—and that its color was apple red. All of which set the stage for Detective Karla Heine.

Karla testified that Chris had purchased a can of precisely this make and color of paint at a hardware store in St. Louis on February 9, 2009. He'd purchased it not with cash but rather with a credit card. He'd signed the receipt "Christopher E. Coleman."

A chill fell over the courtroom. This seemed the coup de grâce. Could there possibly be any doubt now that Chris was indeed the killer?

William Margulis handled the cross-examination. He asked Karla about Chris's brother, Keith. Had investigators ruled him out as a suspect prematurely?

This was the third time in the trial that the defense had brought up Keith's name. They seemed to be trying to get Chris off the hook by casting suspicion on the younger of his two brothers. It was an interesting strategy. Ron and Connie appeared to have no problem with it.

Karla replied that they'd investigated Keith thoroughly and determined that he wasn't involved with the murders.

The prosecution rested its case. The defense would have its turn the next day, Wednesday, May 4.

The defense called only two witnesses the next day, a handwriting analyst and an expert in forensic linguistics. Neither was especially impressive on the stand, and neither stood up well to Kris Reitz's grilling in cross-examination.

John O'Gara advised the court that Chris had decided against taking the stand on his own behalf. Judge Wharton asked the jury to leave the courtroom for a moment. He then asked Chris to approach the bench.

"You have an unqualified right to take the stand," the judge said. "Do you understand that?"

"Yes, sir," Chris said. His voice quaked. His eyelids fluttered.

"Have you consulted with your defense attorneys about this?" the judge asked.

"Yes, sir," Chris said.

"Has anyone tried forcing you *not* to take the stand?"

"No, sir."

"Has anyone tried forcing you *to* take the stand?"

"No, sir."

"Mr. Coleman, do you want to take the stand on your own behalf?"

"No, sir."

Of course, Chris was under no obligation to testify on his own behalf. Judge Wharton had made this eminently clear to prospective jurors during jury selection. He'd told them that they mustn't hold it against him if he elected not to take the stand.

Still, there seemed something viscerally wrong with the decision. After all, here was a guy who was on trial for brutally murdering his wife and two young sons. If he hadn't in fact committed the murders, wouldn't he want to take the stand and proclaim his innocence? Wouldn't he want to shout it from the rooftops?

Yes, I was unfaithful to my wife. Yes, I was a poor father and a worse husband. But this? Actually murdering my wife and kids? This I could never do. This I could never even contemplate.

Instead Chris stood meekly at the front of the courtroom, saying, "No, sir," "No, sir," in a voice so small that it was scarcely audible.

Keith Coleman had been conspicuously absent from the trial till this point. His name had come up often enough, but Keith himself was nowhere to be seen. During lunch recess on Wednesday, May 4, however, he arrived at the courthouse in a white pickup with Arkansas plates. His head was shaved, and he wore jeans and a long-sleeved shirt. His new wife was with him. They went up to the courtroom and sat directly behind Ron and Connie in the second row of the spectators' gallery.

They were just in time for closing arguments.

Kris Reitz spoke for twenty minutes. He summarized the evidence against Chris and praised the police for their superb investigative work.

Jim Stern spoke for about the same length of time on behalf of the defense. He said that the case against Chris was purely circumstantial, that there wasn't a single piece of physical evidence definitively linking him to the murders. He accused the police—Justin Barlow in particular—of having tunnel vision. He said that they'd pegged Chris as the culprit right from the start and not seriously considered any other possibility. He said that Chris—clean-cut, ex-Marine, religiously devout—was a most unlikely candidate to have committed so heinous a crime. "People like that just don't wake up one morning and slaughter their families," he said.

In his rebuttal argument, Reitz insisted that the evidence proved otherwise. It proved that Chris had plotted the murders for almost six full months. That he'd carried them out with ruthless attention to detail. And that afterward he'd displayed not so much as a twinge of remorse.

Reitz's final words of rebuttal almost attained the level of tragic poetry. He said that Sheri was the first victim, after which the murderer turned his attention to Gavin and Garett.

"When [he] went to each of those little boys' rooms in turn, and sat down on their beds and reached for them to strangle them, they didn't get up and run," Reitz said. "They didn't scream. Of course they didn't. Why should they? It was just Dad."

The jury left the courtroom at 3:05 p.m. to begin deliberations. Judge Wharton asked the spectators to remain seated for several minutes. He warned them against any "unseemly displays of emotion" when the verdict came in.

"This is not a sporting event," he said.

CHAPTER FORTY-THREE

Most of the reporters who were covering the trial expected a quick verdict. They thought that Dr. Baden's testimony on time of death was enough in itself to secure a conviction. They thought that the prosecution had proven beyond a reasonable doubt that Chris had committed the murders. They thought that his guilt was transparently obvious.

The verdict proved anything but quick. The jury deliberated for five hours on Wednesday, May 4, then returned to their homes in Perry County. They started up again at 10:00 a.m. on Thursday, May 5, and deliberated throughout the course of the day. They took time off for lunch. They took smoke breaks. They asked to take a look at the rear window of the house on Robert Drive. Several times they had questions for Judge Wharton. They asked him for a definition of "reasonable doubt." They asked him about other points of law.

The defense attorneys left the courthouse at 2:00 p.m. on Thursday and walked over to JV's bar and grill on North Main Street for lunch. They gave several reporters a friendly nod but didn't stop to chat.

The wait was agonizing for both Sheri's and Chris's relatives. At 4:00 p.m., Don Weiss told a reporter that he wasn't discouraged by the lengthy deliberations. "I don't take it as a bad sign," he said. "I'm still confident they'll convict him." His gaunt face and hollow eyes suggested otherwise.

The media speculated endlessly. Was the jury hung? Was there some issue of reasonable doubt holding them up? But what could this be? Hadn't the prosecution's case been practically airtight?

The wait was also agonizing for the criminal investigators who'd worked so long and hard on the case. At 6:45 p.m., Major Jeff Connor, Chief Joe Edwards, and Detectives Karla Heine, Kelly Cullen, and Jason Donjon left the courthouse and drove to the Applebee's restaurant on Illinois Route 3. It wasn't so much that they were hungry. They simply needed a break from the tension.

By 7:00 p.m., the temperature outside the courthouse had plunged a good ten degrees. Gusty winds kicked up and a cold drizzle began to fall. The sky was a turquoise green. Then somebody opened the rear door and told the reporters who were lingering on the sidewalk that the jury had just reached a verdict.

Major Connor, Chief Edwards, and the others were just about ready to order dinner at Applebee's when a woman from the State's Attorney Office phoned them. "Better come back," she said. "We've got a verdict." They hurried to their cars and sped to the courthouse. "Please, God, please, God," Kelly Cullen prayed as she drove. "Let him be found guilty."

Spectators, family members, and reporters filed into the gallery at 7:25 p.m. Several of Sheri's friends stood in a cluster in the foyer outside the courtroom. There was no room for them inside.

Three sheriff's deputies escorted Chris to the defense table. He wore gray dress slacks with a blue shirt and a tie. His face was ghostly white. His lips were quivering. William Margulis and Jim Stern sat on either side of him. John O'Gara walked over to Ron Coleman, who had his head bent in prayer. O'Gara shook his hand and whispered something into his ear. Ron nodded.

Kris Reitz and Ed Parkinson entered the courtroom from a door toward the front. Parkinson caught the eye of a reporter and winked. Then he went over to Mario, who was wearing a shirt with a Chicago White Sox emblem. He leaned over the railing of the spectators' gallery and smiled.

"Do you think this will end the Sox's losing streak?" he said.

"I hope so," Mario said.

The bailiff called court to order, and Judge Wharton came in and took his place behind the bench. Once again he admonished everyone to maintain proper decorum when the verdict was announced.

The jurors filed in and took their seats. Judge Wharton asked them if they'd reached a verdict.

"Yes," they said in unison.

Judge Wharton asked for the verdict forms. Then he asked the jury forewoman to read the verdict aloud.

"We, the jury, find Christopher Coleman guilty of the first-degree murder of Sheri Coleman," she read.

Chris shot his father a confused look and slumped into his chair. His attorneys folded their arms and lowered their eyes.

"We, the jury, find Christopher Coleman guilty of the first-degree murder of Garett Coleman," the forewoman read.

Angela wept softly, clutching a Kleenex. Mario, staring straight ahead, reached over and squeezed her hand.

"We, the jury, find Christopher Coleman guilty of the first-degree murder of Gavin Coleman," the forewoman read.

Jenna Miglio had missed most of the trial, partly because of final exams at college and partly because her dad hadn't wanted her to see the gruesome crime scene and autopsy photos. But she was there now, convulsing in sobs.

Judge Wharton next polled the jurors individually. Each one said that he or she "agreed with the verdict on all three counts." The judge thanked them for their service and excused them.*

---

* One of the jurors would subsequently speak with the news media about the lengthy deliberations. She said that all twelve members of the panel thought that Chris was guilty but that several were initially reluctant to

The deputies led Chris from the courtroom. He glanced back at his parents on his way through the door.

Sheri's family members lingered in the foyer outside the courtroom for several minutes. They were jubilant, but quietly, almost shyly so. They didn't celebrate. They didn't make a scene. They'd comported themselves with class and dignity throughout the entire trial, and they continued to do so now.

Don Weiss hugged his mother, who was fighting back tears. Don's brother, Ron, shook hands with a reporter. "They got it right," he said softly. "They made the right decision."

Sheriff Dan Kelley approached Joe Miglio. He told him that Sheri's family should exit the courthouse through the side door. The sheriff wanted to make certain that there was no chance run-in with members of the Coleman family.

Kathy LaPlante was at the courthouse with Meegan Turnbeaugh. Kathy was so fraught with emotion that she lost her balance while leaving and fell down the back staircase. She'd later be taken to the hospital in an ambulance, where it was determined that she'd escaped serious injury.

Ron and Connie went outside into the sputtering rain. Brad and Keith were with them, and also about a dozen supporters. Several of the supporters used open umbrellas to shield Connie from the media. They started down the sidewalk toward the curb, where Ron's late-model Oldsmobile sedan was parked.

Fox 2 St. Louis's talented investigative reporter Chris Hayes and ace cameraman Dave Sharp were stationed on the courthouse lawn. They'd covered the case from the very beginning and certainly weren't about to stop now.

convict him because of the circumstantial nature of the state's evidence. She said that the panel reached a consensus only after reviewing time stamps on romantic photographs retrieved from Chris's and Tara's cell phones. Tara had testified that she and Chris first become romantically involved in December 2009. However, some of the photographs were dated a good month or so earlier than this, which suggested deception on Tara's part. It seems odd that the verdict should hinge on so seemingly trivial a detail, but such are the vicissitudes of jury deliberation.

Brad walked up and confronted them. "We need the sidewalk," he snarled.

"We're not *on* the sidewalk," Sharp replied.

Brad and Keith led the way to the curb. They seemed angry, belligerent. When still more media people crowded in, matters threatened to get ugly. Ron loaded Connie's wheelchair into the trunk of his car and then stepped back and appraised the situation.

"Let them have their pictures," he called out to Brad and Keith. "Let them have their pictures."

His sons did as they were told. They turned away and walked to their vehicles. It was a strong moment for Ron Coleman. With the guilty verdict still ringing in his ears, he was somehow able to rise above the fray.

About a hundred townsfolk gathered on the opposite side of the courthouse in the hope of catching a glimpse of Chris on his way back to the county jail. The crowd didn't seem angry or vindictive. The prevailing mood was one rather of relief that the ordeal was finally over. The conviction had come exactly two years to the day since Sheri, Garett, and Gavin's murders.

The door to the sally port cranked open and a squad car backed up the ramp to the street. Chris was sitting in the rear seat, with his head tilted toward the window. His eyes were listless, his face a frozen mask.

The crowd erupted in cheers as the squad car reached the curb and turned onto the street. Patrons of a bar across the street surged outside and joined in the cheering.

The squad car sped off toward the jail. Two other squad cars, blue lights flashing, served as escorts.

Sheri's mom's side of the family gave an impromptu press conference on the courthouse lawn. Mario and Joe Miglio did most of the talking. They thanked the police and the prosecutors for their efforts on Sheri and the boys' behalf. They seemed emotionally spent.

Chief Joe Edwards, Major Jeff Connor, and special prosecutor Ed Parkinson spoke with several reporters in the cold drizzle. Kris Reitz, for his part, refused to answer any questions. "I did my talking in court," he said.

Major Connor and Detectives Karla Heine, Kelly Cullen, and Jason Donjon went to Applebee's for a victory dinner. They called Justin Barlow, who'd flown back to Iowa after his testimony several days before. "Hey, Justin," they said. "Have you heard?"

Chief Edwards took a pass on the victory dinner. Instead he stopped off at the local Walmart with his wife and bought a box of candy and a twelve-pack of Diet Dr Thunder. Then he went home and gave his twin daughters a big hug. For the first time in two years, he slept the whole night through.

The next morning, Friday, May 6, Karla, Kelly, and Jason visited the cemetery in Chester with fresh flowers for the graves. Mario and Joe Miglio were there when they arrived.

It occurred to everyone that Mother's Day was on Sunday, two days later.

Mario remarked that the murders had occurred just a few days prior to Mother's Day in 2009. He said that Sheri had sent Angela a Mother's Day card that year. However, by the time it showed up in the mail, she and the boys were already dead.

Karla and Kelly said they were glad that the verdict had also been handed down just several days prior to Mother's Day.

Now maybe Sheri could rest in peace, they suggested.

CHAPTER FORTY-FOUR

There was a hearing at the courthouse on Friday, May 6, to determine if Chris was eligible for the death penalty. For him to be determined eligible, the prosecution had to prove to the jury at least one of three aggravating circumstances.

1. that he'd murdered two or more people
2. that he'd murdered a child or children under the age of twelve
3. that he'd committed the murders in a cold, calculated, and premeditated manner.

The hearing seemed a mere formality. The prosecution had already proven all of these aggravating circumstances to the jury during the first stage of the trial. And in any event, there seemed no chance of Chris actually being executed. Governor Pat Quinn had promised that he'd commute any death sentence that might be handed down prior to Illinois's new anti–capital punishment law taking effect on July 1.

The death penalty was still technically a possibility, however, so special prosecutor Ed Parkinson stood up and addressed the jury.

The hearing might've been a mere formality, but Parkinson certainly didn't treat it as such. He spoke passionately and incisively for twenty minutes, reminding the jury of just how cold, calculated, and premeditated the murders really were.

"This weakling, this Marine—are you kidding?" he said, summoning up a tone of utter scorn. "He slaughtered his own family."

Chris sat at the defense table with his head lowered. His parents, brothers, and a small coterie of supporters stared straight ahead from their seats in the gallery.

"He thought he was so smart," Parkinson went on. "He thought that he could easily outsmart the tiny Columbia Police Department. Well, he found out differently, didn't he?"

John O'Gara, speaking on behalf of the defense, encouraged the jurors to vote on the matter according to their individual consciences. "This is the stage of the trial where we have a heavy heart," he said.

Parkinson had the last word. "Yes, this is the stage where we have a heavy heart," he said. "But that evening [two years ago], there were four hearts throbbing, four hearts beating." He gestured toward Chris. "Now the only one left is his."

It took the jury only fifteen minutes to decide that Chris was indeed eligible for the death penalty. The only question remaining was whether they'd vote to sentence him to death when court reconvened on Monday, May 9.

There were a couple of mild surprises on Monday, May 9.

First, Chris waved his right to a mitigation hearing, whereby friends and relatives would've taken the stand and attested to his positive qualities and so forth. He informed the court through his attorneys that his decision was based on wanting to spare his family any further anguish and to "speed the process along."

The defense attorneys had rounded up quite a few character witnesses for the hearing. Not everybody whom they'd contacted, however, had agreed to testify on Chris's behalf. Most of Chris's old friends from high school had bailed on him after the conviction, and so, too, had his former cronies from the Marines. Screw him, they'd essentially said. If he killed his wife and kids in cold blood, then he deserved to die.

Second, Chris waived his right to have the jury decide his sentence, opting instead to put this entirely in the hands of Judge Wharton. He'd apparently decided to do so on the strength of some "spiritual revelation" that he'd received.

"Has anyone tried to talk you into this?" Judge Wharton now asked him.

"Absolutely not, sir," Chris replied, sounding far more self-assured than at any point thus far during either jury selection or the actual trial.

And with that, proceedings went directly to closing arguments. State's Attorney Reitz spoke first, emphasizing the premeditated and vicious nature of the crimes.

"He strangled them," Reitz said. "He felt his own children die in his own hands. He's not like us. He doesn't value life the same way we do. He killed his wife and children."

None of Sheri's relatives were in the courtroom. They'd decided to stay away for the sentencing. Ron and Connie were on hand, though. They sat with their heads slightly bent as the state's attorney excoriated their oldest son.

John O'Gara spoke for the defense. O'Gara was a longtime foe of the death penalty. He was also a devout Catholic who'd always try to find a spark of humanity—an intimation of Christ—in every person whom he defended, even those charged with the vilest of crimes. It wasn't clear if he'd succeeded in finding such a spark in Chris, but he delivered an impassioned speech nonetheless.

He implored Judge Wharton to give Chris a sentence of life imprisonment rather than death. He asked him to focus not simply on the crime (conceding that "the crime is horrible, unimaginable") but rather on mercy and "the possibility of some sort of redemption." He insisted that life imprisonment was in certain respects a fate even worse than execution. "[Chris] would spend his days locked away in a dungeon, locked away with other criminals, locked away to die."

He said that he realized that the present proceedings were rather an academic exercise, since the governor almost certainly wouldn't permit Chris to be executed even if a death sentence was handed down. Nevertheless, O'Gara suggested, the proceedings had tremendous symbolic importance. They afforded the court an opportunity to affirm the value of mercy over strict retribution.

Judge Wharton called for a recess. He returned to the bench ninety minutes later to issue his decision.

"The horrible nature of the crime cannot be diminished," he said. "Look at the pictures of the wife and two kids, particularly the ones in their beds. That should be a place of safety."

He spoke of visiting the maximum-security Menard Correctional Center years before as a young lawyer.

"I saw a lot of young men, age nineteen and twenty, but I came away with something else that shocked me," he said. "I saw old men in wheelchairs, with canes and with long beards. Those were the 'lifers.'"

He suggested that a life sentence ("dying an old man in a cell") qualified as a "most potent retribution."

Chris sat impassively at the defense table throughout all of this. Occasionally he'd frown and close his eyes.

"Mr. Coleman, would you please come forward?" Judge Wharton finally said.

Chris got up and walked to the bench. He stood there flanked by John O'Gara and William Margulis.

Judge Wharton sentenced him to life in prison without the possibility of parole. He advised him that he had the right to appeal.

The deputies escorted him from the courtroom. Just before leaving, he cast a forlorn glance at his parents.

PART SEVEN

Conclusion

CHAPTER FORTY-FIVE

The day after his sentencing, Chris was sent to Pontiac Correctional Center, a maximum-security prison located about a hundred miles south of Chicago.

His prison mug shot made quite a splash on the Internet. He scarcely resembled the clean-cut young man who'd seemed intent on passing himself off as a choirboy at the trial. Instead he looked hardened, bitter. He looked like a murderer whose mask of innocence had finally been yanked off.

The guilty verdict and sentencing seemed not to have made the slightest difference to Ron and Connie. They remained stubbornly convinced that Chris hadn't committed the murders. They seemed to regard him as a victim.

A week or so after the trial, investigative reporter Ryan Dean of KSDK-TV in St. Louis scored an exclusive interview with Ron and Connie at their home in Chester. Brad was also present for the occasion.

The Colemans told Dean that they'd just recently received their very first prison letter from Chris.

"Dad and Mom," it read in part. "I love you and miss everyone. God is good. And though the changes have been huge, His grace, peace and favor have been obvious."

Dean asked them about the prison mug shot, which

depicted Chris as a remorseless killer. What did they themselves see when they looked at it?

"A tired, disappointing, hurting young man, because that is not his character at all," Ron said. "[He] loved his kids, loved his wife. [He] had the affair but he did not kill, did not kill his family."

The Colemans said that Chris had repeatedly assured them of his innocence and that they had no reason to doubt him.

"I just flat out asked him and said to him," Brad said. " 'Hey, if you lost your marbles and did this, don't put me, Mom, Dad, and Keith through this. It's too much on top of losing family. We are going to have to deal with this.' He started to break down crying and say, 'No, I didn't do it.' He's my brother and I'm going to believe him until he tells me different."

Dean brought up Chris's affair with Tara Lintz. If he'd deceived them about this, how could they be certain that he wasn't also deceiving them about the murders?

"No, it's a whole different [situation]," Ron said, his voice betraying frustration. "He can't go there. He couldn't go there to the murders. He couldn't go there with the boys. He could not go there."

The Colemans suggested that the guilty verdict was a travesty of justice. They said that there were no solid evidentiary grounds for convicting Chris.

"This man was convicted on his character," Ron said.

They also raised the specter of conspiracy. They claimed that some people had lied on the witness stand. That Chris's own defense attorneys had sat on critical evidence that might very well have turned the tide in his favor. That Chris had wanted to take the stand but "was advised not to." That Sheri herself might have created the threatening e-mails that were sent to Joyce Meyer Ministries.

They said that they were hopeful of the truth coming out on appeal and that in the meantime they'd continue to give Chris their full love and support.

Dean asked Ron how he'd respond if Chris were someday to admit to having committed the murders.

"He would be forgiven by me and we would move on," Ron said. "That's the way it's supposed to be . . . I would never turn my back."

Ron Coleman's most strident rhetoric after the trial was reserved for the pulpit. At Grace Church in Chester, according to informants, he positively raged against Chris's conviction and sentencing.

He reportedly told his congregation that the guilty verdict was nothing less than the devil's handiwork. That it was all part of a diabolical plan to persecute the church and sow doubt among the faithful.

He told them that the entire trial was a tissue of lies and deception. That all of the police officers who'd taken the stand had lied, and most other witnesses had also. That the reporters who'd covered the trial had lied right from the outset. He told them that the devil had simply been using all of these people.

Most members of his congregation seem to have believed him. Most believed that the trial was indeed a conspiracy meant to bring down Grace Church.

"You won't find better people anywhere in the world than a lot of those churchgoers," an ex-church member recently said. "But now they're blinded to the truth. They're totally under Ron's sway. He had two full years to condition them to this belief in Chris's innocence. Remember, we're talking about people who wouldn't even think of changing jobs or residences without first seeking Ron's approval. So now how are they supposed to doubt him on this? The guilty verdict doesn't matter in the least. Most of these people still believe that Chris didn't commit the murders. You'd have a hard time getting any of them to admit otherwise."

"A lot of the people in the church would stake their lives on Chris's innocence," another former church member said. "They'll believe anything Pastor Ron tells them. They're totally under his control. Ron rules through fear, anger, and intimidation."

However, Pastor Ron hasn't quite succeeded in convincing his entire flock of Chris's innocence. Several high-ranking members left the church before the trial, and others have left since the guilty verdict.

"I just decided that I was leaving," one of these defectors said. "I can't be going to church listening about Chris Coleman every single Sunday and Wednesday, being told by Ron how to think and what to do. Ron lives by a different standard. He's a master of twisting words, which is exactly what he accuses the media of doing. Finally I'd had enough."

"My best friend and I refused to 'drink the Kool-Aid,'" another said. "And after we left, other people did too. It wasn't an easy decision for some of these people. They felt loyalty to Ron. They knew he was hurting, and they didn't want to put extra strain on the Coleman family. But there's only so much you can take."

Still another described driving away from Grace Church for the last time as "one of the happiest moments" of her life.

"It was like a thousand-pound weight being lifted from my shoulders," she said. "And I know others have left since I did. You'd never know it, though, from just listening to Ron. He'll tell the media that the church has actually grown since Chris was arrested for the murders. He'll say that it's never been stronger. And you know how he and Connie try to convince people that this is true? They move the chairs farther apart, so the church seems fuller than it really is. They make sure everybody parks up front, and nobody in back, so the parking lot looks full. For Ron and Connie, it's all about the power of suggestion."

Still, many more people have stayed than have left, and there seems little question that most of them continue to see things Ron Coleman's way.

"Ron was unhappy about that crowd cheering outside the courthouse after the conviction," an ex–church member said. "But if Chris had been found not guilty, hundreds of people at Grace Church would've been hooting and hollering. And if it ever happens that he gets off on appeal, he'll be given a hero's welcome down there. Because Ron still has them under his thumb. They'll believe whatever he tells them to believe."

Several weeks after the trial, Ron and Connie spoke with journalist Jeannette Cooperman of *St. Louis Magazine*. Among other things, they talked about Chris's mental state since his arrest and imprisonment.

Ron and Connie suggested that he was doing quite well and that his spirituality had actually deepened of late. They said that he'd been reading lots of Christian literature and ministering to fellow prisoners. And that he'd answered hundreds of letters from people seeking his spiritual advice.

But could this really be true? Why on earth would anyone want to solicit spiritual advice from Chris Coleman? Except, of course, members of Grace Church who might perversely regard him as some sort of a martyr.

"He always loved the Lord," Ron told Cooperman, "but he didn't have a relationship with Him until now."

He always loved the Lord. Could any sentiment be more grotesque than this? How about when he was plotting the murders of his wife and two young children, or strangling them to death in their beds with a ligature? Was Chris loving the Lord then? But Ron, of course, doesn't believe that Chris committed the murders. And he continues to insist that much of the trial evidence was sheer fabrication.

Captain Jerry Paul, for example, testified that Chris asked Ron to phone Tara Lintz on the morning of May 5, 2009. However, according to Ron, this simply didn't happen. He told Cooperman that it was his idea, not Chris's, to give Tara a call. "I said to Chris, 'I need to call Tara,' and he kind of nodded and handed me the phone." The outside observer might be forgiven for trusting Captain Paul's version of events over that of Pastor Ron Coleman.

Ron clings to the belief that highly trained mercenaries hired by some enemy of Joyce Meyer were responsible for the killings. He told Cooperman that they "could have done the murders cleanly, inside an hour."

Of course, this is preposterous. Sheri and the boys were already dead when Chris left for the gym that morning. And there is absolutely no evidence of anyone having broken into the house before then. So the highly trained mercenaries of Ron's imagination must've been ghosts or aliens. They must've entered the house out of thin air while Chris was still there. Then they must've killed Sheri and the boys and spray-painted graffiti on the walls before vanishing into the ether. And they must've done all of this with Chris being none the wiser.

And why, in any event, should some lethal enemy of Joyce Meyer want to murder the family of her bodyguard? Why not murder Joyce herself instead?

Sometime before the murders, Chris took a personality test for Joyce Meyer Ministries in which he described his flaws as being "withdrawn," "moody," and "unaffectionate." Cooperman asked Ron and Connie about this. Might it not suggest that Chris wasn't quite as perfect as they believed him to be?

Ron was quick to dismiss the idea, insisting that it was Sheri who'd convinced Chris that he possessed flaws such as these.

"She told Chris all the time that he was moody and he wasn't affectionate enough," Ron said. "She never did compliment him. That's why he was so attracted to this Tara."

But of course: the affair was all Sheri's fault. Everything was Sheri's fault. Golden boy Chris was simply a poor, hapless victim.

Elsewhere in the interview, Ron spoke almost fondly of Tara, certainly more so than he did of Sheri. He told Cooperman that Tara "got born-again after it all happened."

"She called me and said, 'Pastor Ron, this is Tara.' My thought was, 'Tara, you shouldn't be calling me.' She asked for our forgiveness, said she recognizes now that [the affair] was wrong."

Cooperman asked them about their puzzling behavior

during the trial. They sat through the grisly crime scene and autopsy photos. They sat through the sex tapes. But as soon as Detectives Justin Barlow and Dave Bivens began to get more aggressive with Chris during the videotaped interview at the Columbia PD, they stalked out of the courtroom. Why? What were they thinking?

"It was like they were abusive to him, and he was just like a lamb led to slaughter," Connie said.

But what about the terrible photos of Sheri and the boys? What about the videotape of Chris masturbating in the shower? Why hadn't any of this seemed to bother them?

"Most people don't understand Christianity," Ron said. "Most people don't live as Christians."

"What would Christ have done?" Connie added. "Would He have made a scene? No. He might have cried, which we did, but most of that was done in the back room. Actually, we were asking the Lord to help us for Chris's sake. The day they showed that sex film, we said, 'Lord, please let us stay in our seats and [let] Chris know we are not ashamed of him.' "

There's little question that Ron and Connie possess positive qualities. Quite a few people say that they can be warm, gracious, and endearing. They showed glimpses of such throughout the course of the trial.

Most of the reporters covering the trial wanted to accord them the benefit of the doubt. They wanted to excuse their troubling behavior—their rudeness, their disregard for Sheri's family, their apparent aloofness to the horror reflected in those crime scene photographs. The reporters tried to imagine themselves in their shoes. Here was a middle-aged couple whose daughter-in-law and two young grandsons had just been brutally murdered. And their very own son—their firstborn—was on trial for having committed the murders. Imagine the terrible burden of this. Imagine the torment.

The reporters wanted to admire them for standing by Chris. Wasn't loyalty of this sort a good thing? They wanted to excuse them for not seeming distressed over the deaths of Sheri, Garett, and Gavin. Perhaps they'd not yet had a chance properly to mourn the loss of their daughter-in-law and grandsons. Perhaps the process of mourning had been cruelly complicated by the charges facing their son.

But should they still be given the benefit of the doubt? At this late stage, should their odd behavior still be excused?

Ron and Connie presume to lecture us about religion and righteousness. "Most people don't understand Christianity," Ron told journalist Jeannette Cooperman. "What would Christ have done?" Connie asked rhetorically. "Would He have made a scene?"

Their chutzpah is remarkable. It would be hard to imagine anyone less qualified than they to deliver such a lecture. Neither Ron nor Connie had the decency to contact Sheri's mom or brother after the murders. Neither had the decency to consult them about the funeral. For two full years afterward, Ron rarely mentioned Sheri and the boys from the pulpit. He was too busy casting Chris as a holy martyr and decrying the charges against him.

And now that Chris has been found guilty by a jury of his peers? Are Ron and Connie chastened? Are they remorseful? Apparently not. They accuse the police of lying. They accuse everyone but Chris of lying. They blame Sheri for Chris's affair with Tara Lintz.

Connie says that she couldn't bear to watch the videotaped interview of Chris at the Columbia Police Department. *He was just like a lamb led to slaughter.* No, he was actually a cold-blooded killer who'd just slaughtered his wife and two young children.

Ron and Connie certainly didn't commit the triple homicide. This was Chris's doing. But their authoritarian, self-righteous worldview and unflinching support of their son might have helped prepare the ground for it.

CHAPTER FORTY-SIX

Chris Coleman became infatuated with Tara Lintz in the fall of 2009. He decided that he wanted to divorce Sheri so that he could start a new life with Tara. Almost at once, however, he faced a dilemma. How could he divorce Sheri and marry Tara without putting his dream job with Joyce Meyer Ministries at risk? Would he get fired outright from the ministry for divorcing Sheri? Perhaps not, but he'd almost certainly suffer a significant demotion.

So he came up with a plan. He'd kill Sheri and perhaps also his two sons. He'd try to throw the police off track by making it look as if the killings were the handiwork of some rabid enemy of Joyce Meyer. He began to implement the plan in November 2009 when he wrote the threatening e-mails on his own laptop. For added spice, he subsequently also wrote the threatening letters that he claimed to retrieve from his mailbox.

The e-mails and the letters reveal Chris's homicidal intent. They also reveal his fundamental ambivalence toward Joyce Meyer. On the one hand, there would seem little question that Chris deeply admired Joyce. He'd practically been weaned on her prosperity Gospel. He regarded her as a great servant of God, and he was thrilled to be working side by side with her. He saw this as his divine destiny.

On the other hand, he deeply resented her. He'd complained to friends that she failed to accord him proper respect. That she treated him as a lackey, making him shovel her snow and so forth. He was unhappy that she'd forced him into marriage counseling, and that her policy on divorce was preventing him from simply discarding Sheri and starting afresh with Tara. He also seemed to have had serious reservations about her prosperity Gospel and heavy-handed fund-raising techniques. He seems at some level to have thought her a fraud.

"Tell Joyce to stop preaching the bullshit or Chris's family will die . . . I will kill them all as they sleep," Chris wrote in one e-mail. "I am so sick of bitches like her taking everyone's cash so she can fly her jet and pamper her white ass," he wrote in another. And in one of the letters he wrote: "I have warned you to stop traveling and to stop carrying on with this fake religious life of stealing people's money . . . She is a bitch and not worth you doing it."

Chris planned on murdering his family. He wanted to cast suspicion elsewhere, which was his principal reason for writing the threat emails and the threat letters. But the e-mails and the letters might also have served a secondary purpose. They might have afforded him an opportunity to vent his inner feelings about Joyce. While masquerading as an anonymous enemy of her ministry, he could have actually been expressing his own views. At some level, perhaps he really did regard Joyce as a bitch. Perhaps he really did believe that she was ripping people off under the guise of religion.

The irony here is that Joyce's head of security—the very person charged with ensuring her safety—was perhaps her greatest enemy. Chris loved and admired Joyce. But he also secretly despised her.

Chris plotted the murders without knowing precisely when he'd commit them. His hand was forced when Tara gave him a deadline for serving Sheri divorce papers. Then he was backed into a corner. He couldn't stand the prospect of losing Tara. He decided that the time had arrived.

On Monday evening, May 4, 2009, Chris text-messaged

back and forth with Tara while he was in the living room with Sheri. He helped Sheri put the boys to bed. He said prayers with them and kissed them good night. Then later that evening, or in the wee hours the following morning, he went into the master bedroom and strangled Sheri with a ligature. He went into Gavin's and Garett's rooms and strangled each of them in turn. He sprayed obscenities over the walls and on young Gavin's bedsheets.

The killing was hard work. It was intensely personal. Chris wrapped the ligature around Sheri's neck and then around the necks of his sons. He squeezed tightly—with all of his might—for four or five minutes in the process of killing each victim. He battered Sheri into submission. He subdued Gavin when the young boy awoke and resisted. The entire ordeal lasted an excruciating twelve to fifteen minutes.

Did he linger over his sleeping sons before murdering them? Did he think about how he'd once held them when they were babies? Or how he'd watched them open their presents on Christmas mornings? Or played catch with them in the backyard? Did he hesitate before wrapping the ligatures around their necks? Did he say a small prayer that they'd go to heaven?

And what about afterward, after he'd strangled the life out of Sheri and the boys? Did he experience a moment of regret? Did he shed tears of remorse? Or did he simply grab the can of spray paint and begin to spew his venom?

Chris wanted out of his marriage to Sheri. He couldn't divorce her without putting his precious job in jeopardy, and so he killed her instead. But why Garett and Gavin? Why did he feel the need to kill them too?

Perhaps he wanted to make a clean break. He wanted to start fresh with Tara, and he regarded the boys as encumbrances from his past. He identified them with Sheri and the old life from which he was seeking escape. He identified them with everything that was preventing him from realizing his true destiny.

Perhaps, too, he'd never really loved or cared for them.

Perhaps he was so narcissistic—so thoroughly self-absorbed—that he was incapable of anything other than a sham love. Which would mean that he didn't really love Tara, either. She was merely an appendage to his ego. She made him feel—for the moment, at least—that much better about himself.

But consider also another, related possibility. Chris killed the boys because he'd promised that he would in the threatening e-mails and letters. This was how he'd structured his plot, his narrative of death. He'd wanted the e-mails and letters to sound as menacing as possible. He'd wanted to give them a bite of authenticity. Why would the mysterious enemy of Joyce Meyer threaten to kill only Chris's wife? If he were truly hell-bent on mayhem—if he truly wanted to send Joyce Meyer Ministries a message—wouldn't his letters and e-mails threaten to kill the entire Coleman family?

"Fuck Chris's Family. They are Dead!!!" "Tell Joyce to stop preaching the bullshit or Chris's family will die . . . I will kill his wife and kids . . . I will kill them all as they sleep." "Tell Chris his family is dead. They don't deserve to live with someone that protects the SOB Joyce." "Until then everyone will die starting with Chris's wife and kids."

This was how Chris had structured his plot, and he might very well have thought that he had no choice but to follow through on it. He wanted the police to believe that the person responsible for the killings was the same person who'd sent the threatening e-mails and letters. He wanted them to draw the obvious connection: *Look. This mysterious enemy of Joyce Meyer said he'd kill the wife and kids—the entire family—and that's exactly what he's now done.*

This, arguably, is one of the reasons why Chris killed not just Sheri but also Garett and Gavin. He killed his sons for narrative consistency.

One thing we know for certain. The murders weren't the product of some sudden impulse or burst of passion. They weren't carried out on the spur of the moment. Chris planned them for almost six full months. Every single day that he saw Sheri and the boys during this span, he planned on killing them. And once the time arrived, he comported himself as dispassionately as if he were a trained assassin. He exchanged text messages with Tara. He helped put the boys to bed. He got the ligature ready. He got the can of spray paint ready. And then he went to work.

But how could Chris do this? How could he murder his own wife and children? Is it possible that he was insane? That he suffered from some sort of psychosis?

This would seem highly doubtful. A forensic psychiatrist from Harvard evaluated Chris on behalf of the defense team well in advance of the trial. The results of this are not yet a matter of public record. Nevertheless, we might reasonably surmise that the psychiatrist found Chris to be narcissistic. And that he also found him to have delusions of grandeur, viewing himself as an exalted being especially favored by God. But he almost certainly didn't find evidence of severe mental illness. Otherwise O'Gara and company could have mounted a psychiatric or diminished-capacity defense and tried to persuade the court that Chris shouldn't be held criminally responsible for his actions.

So again: How in the world could Chris do what he did? Plenty of men feel trapped in marriage. Plenty of men take on mistresses. But they certainly don't murder their wife and kids, even if they're as narcissistic and innately selfish as Chris was.

The question of how Chris managed to kill his family can't easily be answered. Evil always contains a core of mystery. It can never be explained entirely.

In Chris's case, however, we can suggest a partial answer. We can piece together the rudiments of an explanation.

Chris was raised in an intensely religious household. His father, the Reverend Ron, preached a dogmatic, dualistic version of Christianity. In Ron's world, there was a strict division between the forces of righteousness on the one hand, and the forces of iniquity on the other. There was good and evil, black and white—and nothing in between.

And what was Chris's place in this dualistic schema? He

counted himself among the righteous, the elect. He was one of God's holy anointed. His parents likely would have assured him of this from an early age. They'd have assured him that his was a position of spiritual privilege. That he enjoyed God's special favor, that his salvation was certain and irrevocable. That there was perhaps nothing whatsoever that could cause him to forfeit it.

This sense of belonging to the elect, of enjoying divine favor, must have been greatly amplified with his rapid ascension at Joyce Meyer Ministries. Here was a small-town preacher's son who in no time at all became head of security for one of the world's most successful evangelists. Such good fortune surely didn't befall anyone. It only befell those of special spiritual privilege.

Add to this the influence of the prosperity Gospel, which played so critical a role in Chris's life. His parents preached it at Grace Church. Joyce Meyer was one of its foremost exponents. The prosperity Gospel can easily foster a mentality of entitlement. If you have faith enough, it might be interpreted to mean, you're entitled to material riches and creaturely comforts. In Chris's warped mind, it might also have meant something more than this. It might have meant that he was entitled to untrammeled happiness, to the fulfillment of his every desire. And why not? Wasn't he, after all, head of security for the great Joyce Meyer? Wasn't he one of God's chosen elite? Why, then, shouldn't he be entitled to sexual bliss with Tara Lintz? Wasn't this his right as a child of destiny? And wasn't this precisely what he'd tell Sheri when she refused to divorce him? That she was interfering with his *destiny*?

Chris was deeply narcissistic. He was innately selfish. And he also saw himself as divinely anointed, as one of the righteous few. All of which resulted in a remarkable capacity for rationalization and self-justification. Ordinary rules of morality—ordinary restrictions—simply didn't apply to him. He was above it all. He was an exalted being who was guaranteed God's eternal favor. Why shouldn't he kill Sheri and the boys? They were standing in the way of his job. They were standing in the way of his happiness with Tara. They were standing in the way of God's plan for his life.

"God is good," he wrote his parents from prison shortly after the trial. "And though the changes have been huge, His grace, peace and favor have been obvious."

The passage speaks volumes about Chris's mind-set. Here's a guy who's just been convicted of murdering his wife and young sons, and yet, he still imagines that he basks in the glow of God's favor. He still fancies himself a member of the holy elect. Insofar as he's concerned, he's done nothing terribly wrong.

This same mind-set helps to explain Chris's strategic blunders in the months leading up to the murders. Why, for example, purchase the spray paint with a credit card rather than cash? Why hang on to the BlackBerry and the laptop, both of which were loaded with incriminating evidence? Why not simply get rid of them instead?

Chris was hardly an intellectual, but neither was he dumb. He built up the security system for a major corporation practically from scratch. In the process, he demonstrated an impressive capacity for learning on the fly. He committed these blunders not out of stupidity but rather out of sheer arrogance. Believing as he did that he counted among the spiritual elect, he thought himself invulnerable. He never expected that the police would see through the ruse involving the threatening e-mails and letters. He never seriously considered that he might get caught.

Ron and Connie's treatment of Chris over the years would only have fueled his arrogance, his sense of spiritual elitism. By most accounts, he was always their favorite son. He was the one in whom they invested the greatest hope. He was their golden boy. And he remains so even today. They certainly didn't stalk out of the courtroom when their youngest son, Keith, was mentioned as a possible suspect. It's Chris they primarily care about. He's their poor little lamb being led to slaughter.

So how was Chris able to commit the murders? He believed that he was divinely privileged, that he was entitled to the fulfillment of his every dream. He believed that God's destiny for him was to continue working for Joyce Meyer after marrying Tara Lintz. And heaven help anyone who dared to stand in his way. He believed that he occupied a special spiritual class. That what counted as sin for other people didn't count as such for him. And far from disabusing him of these delusions over the years, his parents likely only would have strengthened them.

But this, again, is only a partial answer. For a fuller explanation, we'd have to turn to theology and philosophy. We'd have to come to grips with the mystery of evil. At his heart, quite simply, there is something inextricably evil about Chris Coleman. Only someone stamped with the darkest moral depravity could've done what he did.*

During the months leading up to the murders, Sheri knew that something was terribly wrong. She was frantic with worry. She was afraid. She wanted to save her marriage but she didn't quite know how to go about doing so.

So she reached out for help. She reached out to her friends. The problem here was that she wasn't entirely forthcoming. She'd give each friend scraps of information about Chris and her marital problems. She wouldn't give any of them the whole story. Meegan, Kathy, and Vanessa cared deeply about

---

* A rather more personal note might be warranted at this point. During research for various books over the past decade or so, I have attended dozens of exorcisms throughout the United States. I have sat down for lengthy interviews with prisoners convicted of horrible crimes. I have explored the subterranean depths of America while riding freight trains across the country. Not once during this research did I feel that I was in the presence of pure evil. I did, however, feel the chill of evil while undertaking research for this particular book. I felt it whenever Chris Coleman entered the courtroom and took his place at the defense table. I felt it while observing his bland reactions to the prosecution's evidence. It was ineffable but also unmistakable. It was the chill of a vacant soul.

Sheri. They'd have done anything in their power to help her. But their hands were tied. Each of them only knew so much. Each of them wanted to respect her privacy.

She also reached out to various ministers at Destiny Church. There would seem little question that each of these ministers likewise cared about Sheri. As a group, however, they seem not to have taken her seriously enough. They thought her prone to exaggeration. They thought that she tended to overdramatize. They offered her prayer when perhaps something more immediate and concrete was also called for.*

Sheri needed to go beyond Destiny Church. She needed to break out of her limited circle and reach out to family members. But she didn't do so. No one in her family had so much as an inkling that she was experiencing marital troubles. We know that she was estranged from her father. But it's rather a mystery why she didn't reach out to Mario. Perhaps she wasn't feeling especially close to him at the time. Perhaps she worried that he'd take matters into his own hands and confront Chris. With the benefit of hindsight, of course, this could only have been a good thing.

During the eligibility hearing, special prosecutor Ed Parkinson characterized Chris as a "weakling." No truer word was spoken throughout the entire trial. Chris was indeed a weakling. He was an ultimate coward. He'd have wilted upon being confronted by Mario. He'd have wilted upon being confronted by Joe Miglio or Don Weiss. It Sheri had reached

---

* As an aside, it's perhaps worth mentioning that in the course of my research I spoke over the phone with Pastor Phil Stern of Destiny Church. I asked him if I might meet personally with the individual ministers whom Sheri had contacted about her marital problems. Pastor Stern said that he'd have "to seek wisdom on this" before giving me the go-ahead. He said that he'd have "to consult with the church's lawyers" for such wisdom. There seems something sad about this. Preachers talk endlessly about spiritual discernment. They talk about trusting in the wisdom of the Lord. When push comes to shove, however, they themselves all too often seem content to place their trust in high-tech security systems and legal professionals.

out to any one of them, it might very well have altered the tragic course of events.

It's no less a shame that Sheri didn't contact the Columbia Police Department about Chris beating her. Chief Joe Edwards likely would've assigned Justin Barlow or Karla Heine to the case.

Good luck to Chris in that event.

Sheri weighed all of ninety-five pounds when Chris battered her into submission and strangled her to death. Garett and Gavin were skinny little kids.

After murdering them all, Chris scrawled FUCK YOU in red spray paint on nine-year-old Gavin's bedsheets. He likely would've scrawled something similarly lurid on eleven-year-old Garett's sheets had he not run out of paint.

In the end, this is all that we really need to know about Chris Coleman.

This tells the whole story.

AFTERWORD

October 2011

Since the murders, Mario and other DeCicco family members, along with the indefatigable Meegan Turnbeaugh, have been raising funds for the construction of some sort of a memorial to Sheri, Garett, and Gavin in the city of Columbia. They initially hoped to have a monument put up in one of the city parks, but plans for this have recently fallen through. Now they're working with the Columbia Blue Jay Football Association to build a new football field in Garett and Gavin's honor. (Donations toward the project can be made at SheriAnnHerBoys.com.)

Jenna and Joseph Miglio have raised funds for the memorial project at Eastern Illinois University, where they're both still enrolled as students, and the entire family has made contributions to the Violence Prevention Center of Southwestern Illinois.

The family has also been working at having Sheri, Garett, and Gavin's remains transferred from the cemetery in Chester to one in the Chicago area. "We don't think the person who murdered [Sheri and the boys] should decide where they are buried," Enrico Mirabelli told the *St. Louis Post-Dispatch*.

Of course, efforts of this sort scarcely make up for the

family's loss. They're still grief-stricken and still in a state of disbelief that anyone could've done what Chris did. Perhaps there are some wounds that time simply won't heal.

All of Sheri's family members are grateful for the conviction, and also for the terrific investigative work that went into securing it. No one is more grateful in this regard than Don Weiss. Don's greatest concern during the excruciatingly long jury deliberations was that if Chris somehow went free, Mario might feel compelled to take justice into his own hands. Don would then have faced the prospect of losing not only his daughter but also his son.

The tragedy has had repercussions beyond Sheri's family and friends. In its immediate aftermath, young boys in the area fell prey to terrible fears that their own fathers were also intent on murdering them. Some of these boys have required intensive counseling.

The criminal investigators were exultant when the verdict came down. Major Connor, Chief Edwards, Justin Barlow, Karla Heine, Kelly Cullen, Ken Wojtowicz, and James Newcombe—to name only a prominent few—had strongly suspected Chris from the outset. The guilty verdict was sweet music to their ears. Since then they've been preoccupied with new cases, though none quite as harrowing as this one.

The Columbia Police Department lost a fine detective when Justin Barlow answered the call from the U.S. Marshals Service. Jason Donjon has since replaced him, however, and there seems little question that he'll prove a worthy successor.

Reports suggest that Tara Lintz hasn't bothered to communicate with Chris in prison and that she no longer wears his promise ring. Perhaps she now realizes that marrying him might've been the worst of all possible moves. How long would it have taken before she, too, became an obstacle to his *destiny*? How long before she and baby Zoe Lynn were likewise seen as only so much excess baggage?

Ron Coleman seems to have remained true to form in recent months. He still apparently can't accept that his oldest son is a monster. This may be why he continues to snipe at the defense attorneys, the police, and everyone else involved with the trial. He insists that there was "deceit and twisting of the truth throughout the whole thing."

Journalist Jeannette Cooperman asked Ron how he'd respond if Chris were ever to admit to committing the murders. "Oh, I've been there," Ron said. "What would I do? Just what I'm doing. He's the Lord's anyway, and that's between him and the Lord. I've got a whole different look at anybody that's done that kind of stuff now . . . It is between the person that did it and God."

But this, of course, is perverse. Sheri's family obviously didn't think that the murders were simply a private matter between Chris and God. Neither did the Major Case Squad of Greater St. Louis and the Columbia Police Department or prosecutors Kris Reitz and Ed Parkinson. We can be grateful that they didn't.

Chris Coleman is hardly doing his own extended family a favor in refusing to admit to the murders. He's holding them hostage to his persistent denials. There are many fine people in the Coleman clan, some of whom attended the trial on a regular basis. The ordeal has been brutally hard on them too. Chris's brother Brad is a case in point. Despite his behavioral lapse in the courtroom, Brad seems a decent and likable guy. How can he hope to restore his life to any sort of normalcy while clinging to the false belief that his older brother is innocent?

In late June 2011, Judge Milton Wharton denied the defense's motion for a new trial. This was hardly surprising. It seems likely that any future appeals will also come to naught. The police work in the case was impeccable. So was the performance of prosecutors Kris Reitz and Ed Parkinson in the courtroom. There would seem no compelling grounds for challenging the conviction. Chris Coleman's fate seems sealed. He will indeed die an old man in prison.

More recently, Chris was transferred from Pontiac Correctional Center in Illinois to a maximum-security facility in Wisconsin. The move was presumably made in the interests of safety and security. Family members visiting him from Chester now face a much longer trip.

Sheri, Garett, and Gavin are buried alongside one another at Evergreen Cemetery on the northern outskirts of Chester. The simple stone at the foot of their graves is inscribed with their names, their birth dates, and the date of their deaths.

Sheri Ann was born on July 3, 1977.

Garett Dominick Eugene was born on April 30, 1998. *Dominick* is for Sheri's maternal grandfather. (The name is misspelled on the tombstone as *Dominic*.)

Gavin Christopher was born on January 25, 2000. *Christopher*, of course, is for the boys' father and Sheri's husband.

The inscriptions indicate that they all died on May 5, 2009.

The tombstone is adorned with a photograph of Sheri and the boys. Garett is nestled up against his mom, and Gavin is leaning across her left leg. They seem happy together, full of love and trust.

The graves are located on a gentle knoll at the edge of the cemetery, overlooking a copse of evergreens. It's a lonely spot, set apart from most of the other grave sites. It seems somehow temporary, transient. The visitor can't help but get the impression that Sheri and the boys aren't quite yet home.

Perhaps they're awaiting final burial in the Chicago area, where they're truly wanted. Where they'll always be cherished and never forgotten.

ACKNOWLEDGMENTS

I'm grateful to everyone who spoke with me during the research for this book, many of whom requested anonymity. Special thanks to Mario Dominick DeCicco, Joe Miglio, Jenna Miglio, Joseph Miglio, and Debra DeCicco-Rento. Special thanks also to Don Weiss, Ron Weiss, and Dortha Weiss.

For their rich insights and generous hospitality, I'm also grateful to Meegan Turnbeaugh, Lonnie Turnbeaugh, Vanessa Riegerix, Brandon Riegerix, Kathy LaPlante, Bob LaPlante, Audrey LaPlante, Austin LaPlante, and Alex LaPlante.

I owe a large debt of gratitude to Major Jeff Connor, Chief Joe Edwards, Captain Jerry Paul, U.S. Marshal Justin Barlow, Detective Karla Heine, Detective Kelly Cullen, Detective Jason Donjon, Officer Steve Patton, Sergeant Ken Wojtowicz, Detective James Newcombe, and Sheriff Daniel J. Kelley.

I'm indebted also to Sandra L. Sauget, Kim Kellerman, Aaron L. Reitz, Forrest Alex Bevineau, Mary Ann Brand, Kathleen Brunsmann, and Dana Hutchings for their generosity and professionalism.

I benefited from the excellent coverage of the case in the regional media. Special thanks in this regard to Beth Hundsdorfer of the *Belleville News-Democrat*; Nicholas Pistor,

Bill McClellan, and Dan Martin of the *St. Louis Post-Dispatch*; Jeannette Cooperman of *St. Louis Magazine*; Ed Wienhoff, John Conrad, and Joe Leicht of the *Monroe County Independent*; Mary Koester of the *North County News*; Ryan Dean and Casey Nolen of KSDK-TV in St. Louis; Marc Cox of KMOV-TV in St. Louis; and Brian Kelly of KMOX NewsRadio in St. Louis.

I'm especially grateful to Carrie Myers of the *Randolph County Herald Tribune*; Corey Saathoff, Kermit Constantine, Alan Dooley, and Andrea Degenhart of the *Monroe County Republic-Times*; and Jerry Willis, Larry Willis, and Greg Myers of the *County Journal*.

Carrie Myers proved to be a wealth of insight and information at almost every turn. Corey Saathoff and his superb country-rock band, the Trophy Mules, afforded me much-needed musical inspiration during the early stages of research. The *County Journal*, which is based out of Percy, Illinois, seemed generally sympathetic to Ron Coleman in its coverage of the case. Despite my contrasting views, editors Jerry and Larry Willis afforded me the benefit of their considerable insight.

Though understandably restricted in what they could say, defense attorneys John O'Gara, William Margulis, and James Stern were gracious and accommodating with the news media throughout both jury selection and the trial.

A special acknowledgment is due prosecutor Edwin R. Parkinson, whose keen wit and legal acumen were a delight to behold at every stage of the proceedings.

And also investigative reporter Chris Hayes and cameraman Dave Sharp of Fox 2 in St. Louis, with whom I filed reports from the Monroe County Courthouse throughout the course of the trial. It was a rare treat having the opportunity to work alongside such consummately skilled professionals.

Thanks as always to Margaret Cuneo, Rebecca Cuneo Keenan, Brenda Cuneo, and Ed Keenan. And also to Shane Cuneo and Ryan Cuneo, both of whom gave me valuable advice at every stage of the research and writing.

Thanks, finally, to Charles E. Spicer Jr., April Osborn, and Allison Strobel of St. Martin's Paperbacks, to David Chesanow for his superb copyediting, and also to Claudia Cross.